Annual Giving Strategies

A Comprehensive Guide to Better Results

Ann D. Gee, Editor

Council for Advancement and Support of Education

ISBN 0-89964-277-2

Printed in the United States of America.

In 1974, the American Alumni Council (founded in 1913) and the American College Public Relations Association (founded in 1917) merged to become the Council for Advancement and Support of Education (CASE).

Today, more than 2,900 colleges, universities, and independent elementary and secondary schools in the U.S. and 20 other countries belong to CASE. This makes CASE the largest nonprofit 501(c)(3) education association in terms of institutional membership. Representing the member institutions in CASE are more than 14,000 individual professionals in institutional advancement.

Nonprofit education-related organizations such as hospitals, museums, libraries, cultural or performing arts groups, public radio and television stations, or foundations established for public elementary and secondary schools may affiliate with CASE as Educational Associates. Commercial firms that serve the education field may affiliate as Subscribers.

CASE's mission is to advance understanding and support of education for the benefit of society. Central to its mission are its member colleges, universities, and independent schools. CASE fulfills this mission by providing services to beginning, mid-level, and senior advancement professionals; direct services to member institutions; and public affairs programs that bond higher education to the public interest.

CASE offers books, videotapes, and focus issues of the award-winning monthly magazine, CURRENTS, to professionals in institutional advancement. The books cover topics in alumni administration, communications and marketing, fund raising, management, and student recruitment. For a copy of the catalog, write to CASE RESOURCES, Suite 400, 11 Dupont Circle, Washington, DC 20036. For more information about CASE programs and services, call (202) 328-5900.

Cover illustration by Michael David Brown.
Copyediting by Susan Hunt.

Council for Advancement and Support of Education
Suite 400, 11 Dupont Circle, Washington, DC 20036

Contents

Figures

Foreword

CASE is pleased to present *Annual Giving Strategies: A Comprehensive Guide to Better Results,* its first book to focus exclusively on the annual fund—"the bread and butter of the development program," as chapter author Elizabeth MacIntosh calls it.

The annual fund is such a basic and central element of development programs at schools, colleges, and universities that we may be tempted to take it for granted. A capital campaign has more pizazz, major gifts are more impressive, and corporate and foundation support brings the institution more media attention. But the annual fund is with us year after year, and it's always more or less the same—or so you might think. Yet the annual fund is central to the development program:

> An annual fund may not generate the most money. It may not be the most cost-efficient form of fund raising. It will probably not provide the resources needed to build the newest campus cathedral. But it is the foundation on which the development program is built (Gary Evans, Chapter 1).

The annual fund provides a steady source of unrestricted income to the institution; it introduces the institution to new friends in all of its constituencies; it helps create a relationship between the institution and its supporters, teaches them the habit of regular giving, and, in many cases, serves as the first step toward a major gift.

Annual Giving Strategies describes the fundamental elements of the annual fund from planning to evaluation, and it treats in detail many variations of the three methods of solicitation that keep the annual fund going—solicitation by mail, by telephone, and person-to-person. The annual fund reaches all of the constituencies of the institution—students, alumni, parents, trustees, faculty and staff, and the community—and this book sets forth methods of dealing with each of these groups. A final section provides ideas on recognition and its importance to the continuing success of the annual fund from year to year.

Our thanks to Ann Gee of Texas Christian University who planned and developed this book for us, and to the 35 chapter authors who share with us their considerable wisdom and experience with the "bedrock of individual fund raising"—the annual fund.

Virginia Carter Smith
CASE President
December 1990

Introduction

The project of putting this book together began over a year and a half ago. Thirty-five authors and 32 chapters later, I am delighted with the results. As editor, my objective was twofold:

• to identify those topics that are most pertinent to the successful execution of annual fund fund raising, and

• to present those subjects to you, the reader, in the most concise and well-written form possible.

You will be the ultimate judge of the success of our joint venture. As you read the book, keep these key items in mind:

Sequential order. The sections and chapters are arranged in a specific order to permit you to build on your knowledge as you read from front to back. In other words, if you have never conducted an annual fund before, it will make more sense to you to read the book from cover to cover. If, however, you are more experienced and are searching for specific answers to specific questions, this book can also serve as a reference guide.

Size of institution. Each annual fund program has basic components whether it is run in a public or private, small or large, independent or university setting. To be sure, each type shop has different resources in personnel, budget, volunteer support, administrative direction, and so on. It is important for you as the reader to translate terminology and specifics to fit your own work situation.

The impact of capital campaigning. With the emphasis on capital campaigns in today's fund-raising environment, the temptation is to focus less on the annual fund or to at least cut corners to save time and money for major gift fund raising. If anything, the techniques of raising dollars for the annual fund are *more* important during the capital campaign, not less. So this book should be especially vital to you if you are in or planning to be in a capital campaign in the near future.

Making the case for support of *your* program. Often it takes an outside consultant or adviser to bring home the message that your program needs "extras" in resources, people, or new ideas. If you can't afford to hire such an outside expert, you can use this book as your means of support. Therefore, read it with that in mind. When you have concluded, you will be able to cite the philosophy and advice offered in these pages. Those statistics and examples can give you the documentation you need to make needed changes on your campus.

The annual fund is the foundation for all other development efforts. Without the annual fund, there is no mechanism to adequately build the base for capital or planned gifts, to cultivate volunteer interest and leadership, to orient staff to our programs, or to create a case for support.

The annual fund is also the first and most important way that our closest friends demonstrate commitment to our institutions. Therefore, it becomes a measuring stick for the success of all other development programs.

Institutions with the strongest annual fund support also have the strongest *total* support. Keep that in mind as you reflect on the importance of the annual fund to you and your institution.

Happy reading!

Ann D. Gee
Associate Vice Chancellor for Development
Texas Christian University
December 1990

Section 1

Overview of the Annual Fund

Chapter 1

The Annual Fund: The Foundation of the Development Program

Gary A. Evans
Senior Vice President
Barnes & Roche, Inc.
Chapel Hill, North Carolina
(Formerly Vice Chancellor for Development and University Relations
The University of North Carolina at Chapel Hill)

A ssume for a moment you have been named director of development at Hypothetical University. For some strange reason, HU has never had a development program, although the institution has a respectable academic program and knows the names and addresses of its alumni. The president asks you, "Where do you plan to begin?" With no more information available than offered here, most experienced development officers would respond, "I plan to begin by developing an annual giving program." That answer speaks volumes about what an annual fund is.

What *is* an annual fund?

An annual fund may not generate the most money. It may not be the most cost-efficient form of fund raising. It will probably not provide the resources needed to build the newest campus cathedral. But it is the foundation on which the development program is built. By making the annual fund the starting point of the development program at Hypothetical University, you are making clear the mul-

1

tiple purposes it serves.

Gift income. First and foremost, the annual fund generates needed gift income. To be sure, individual gifts to the annual fund will probably not be as large as bequests or capital gifts, and they will certainly not have the elegance of charitable remainder trusts, but more people will support the annual fund, perhaps modestly, than will support any other fund-raising program implemented by the development office.

In an institution with a mature annual giving program, there may be a number of staff with sizable budgets generating significant income. But even in an institution with a fledgling program, a part-time staff member, and a very small budget, the annual fund still generates gift income on a recurring basis in excess of the cost invested. And the gift income is usually available for one of the most pressing needs of any school, college, or university—its operating budget.

The habit of giving. It is the annual fund, more than any other development program, that introduces people to giving and helps develop the habit of philanthropy. Although there are exceptions, a donor's first gift to a college or university is usually made through the annual fund. Likewise the second. And the third. And then those who give habitually will begin to give more over time. As their interest in the institution grows, as they become personally involved with its mission and purpose, and as their resources increase, their giving also increases.

Because it is repeated each year, the annual fund can become habit forming. As a result, it not only produces needed gift income, but it also serves as the basis on which other development efforts are built.

Building relationships. Development is more than the implementation of fund-raising programs to generate cash receipts. Development is relationship building, and the annual fund helps to build those relationships. We all know it is important to involve potential donors with our institutions. Too often we think of involvement as a commitment of time: working on a committee, participating on a panel, serving on a board.

We should also remember that the act of giving is an act of involvement. Each person who gives to the annual fund becomes involved, to a greater or lesser degree, with the institution. And through involvement, relationships are developed.

Once we recognize giving as a form of involvement, as an expression of a relationship, we realize that no other activity sponsored by the development office brings more people into a relationship with the institution than does the annual fund. And those who help solicit annual gifts—volunteer class agents, reunion solicitors, matching gift coordinators—are even more involved and hence more closely tied. A comprehensive annual giving program offers more avenues for building bonds than anything else we do.

A prelude to major gifts. "All of that is fine," says the president of Hypothetical University. "I understand that the annual fund provides us with operating income, it creates in people the habit of giving, and it involves alumni and friends in the life of our university. But we need big gifts. Let's launch a major gifts program."

As the bright new director of development at Hypothetical University, you reply confidently, "Fear not. There is no better prelude to a major gifts program than a good annual fund."

Because the best prospect for a big gift is one who has given before, there may be no better means for identifying potential major donors than a careful analysis of past annual giving results. Those who give to the annual fund, who develop the habit of philanthropy and become involved by their giving and their labors, are those who, if they are able, will make the major gifts when called upon to do so.

We have all heard those wonderful stories of the unknown alumnus who, without any previous giving record, emerges from obscurity to make a major gift to alma mater. But these stories are repeated because they are so rare. Far more common is the donor who began with a modest annual gift, increased it gradually over time, grew in involvement and relationship with the institution, and eventually made a significant gift to a capital campaign. For most, progress toward a major gift begins with a gift to the annual fund.

Planning the annual fund

Once you have been at Hypothetical University for a few years and have gotten the annual fund beyond the survival stage, you will want to plan your program for maximum success. To do this, you must first answer the question, "What do we want to accomplish with our annual fund program?" There are usually two answers: maximum dollar support and maximum participation by alumni and friends.

Unfortunately, many institutions focus on the latter objective—maximum participation—and hope to achieve the former in the process. They begin their annual fund with direct mail to all alumni and friends, donors and nondonors alike. This brings early euphoria to the annual fund staff because all the loyal contributors respond to the first mail piece, and the rush of gifts arriving in the fall suggests that the annual fund is on its way to another good year.

But before you send out that September direct mail package with its artfully crafted letter and multi-colored brochure, ask yourself, "What is the best method of solicitation to obtain a generous response to any cause?" You will probably conclude that personal solicitation is best, telephone solicitation next, and then direct mail.

If your first obligation is to maximize dollar support, then plan your annual giving program to begin with personal solicitation of your best prospects. If you can organize staff and volunteers to solicit 10 to 15 percent of your potential donors, that is great. If not, try for 5 percent. Or 100 people. Or 50 people.

In any case, develop plans for the personal solicitation of your governing board and key volunteer committees. They are your most committed and most involved supporters. They will respond best to a well-presented personal appeal. Do not dilute their willingness to give with a generic direct mail solicitation.

After you have planned for personal solicitation, then consider the role of phonathons. Many institutions use the telephone to call the people who did not respond to the direct mail campaign. This means they are using a more expensive—and more personal—form of solicitation for those prospects who are probably least likely to respond.

But if you change the sequence and do the phonathon prior to direct mail, you could use it to solicit previous donors (LYBUNTs and SYBUNTs), and you would get better results for your money. Then you could use direct mail at the end of the annual fund calendar for those who have not yet given. This sequence is more likely to help you achieve your two goals—dollars and participation—and the planning, organizing, and implementing required may be no greater than doing it in reverse.

Now that you have planned the sequence of your annual fund program, you are in a position to set your goals. Once again, some institutions set goals by adding a percentage to the previous year's results. While that is better than having no goal at all, this procedure ensures that the goal has virtually no relationship to the strategy of solicitation developed for that year's annual fund.

I suggest you analyze the potential for each element of your annual fund program, set a goal for each, and then establish your total goal as the sum of its parts. For example, begin with the top 10 percent of your annual fund donor pool. How much could be raised from these donors if they were solicited personally? How many new people can you attract to your top-level giving club? How many more people could be called if you extended your phonathon by three weeks, and what would be the probable results from these increased contacts? Can you expand your annual giving program to include parents, friends, reunion classes, or other constituents not previously segmented for solicitation? What will be the results? Can you put together a challenge gift? How will it affect giving?

Once you have set a target for each part of your annual giving program, add these targets to obtain your overall goal. The resulting goal will be far more credible than merely picking some arbitrary increase over the previous year, and it will have an important advantage: Each person working on the annual fund will be able to see how his or her efforts are essential to the success of the whole.

Organizing to accomplish your plans

You must now organize for success. Much goes into organizing: scheduling, writing, printing, mailing, data processing, and logistical matters of all shapes and sizes. But perhaps the two major considerations in organizing are volunteers and staff.

Volunteers. Is there a role for volunteers in your annual fund program? Often, volunteers are more time-consuming and less efficient than staff. This seems to suggest that we build our annual fund program on staff rather than volunteers. Or does it?

Logic tells us that 50 people can get more done than five, even with some of the inefficiencies that come with size. Therefore, the key decision is not *whether* you use volunteers, but *where* you use them. Volunteers can be used as personal solicitors, telephone callers, or signers of direct mail pieces. The first takes more staff time, more hand-holding, more patience, and more staff support than does the second, and the second more than the third. Before you begin enlisting volunteers, you must decide where you can use them effectively by giving them the right jobs to do and the necessary staff support to do them.

Volunteers can be good solicitors, but only a few are so self-sufficient that they make personal calls willingly and effectively without prodding or guidance. Most require training, and many need to be accompanied by staff.

Volunteers also make good telephone callers, and they can write solicitation letters or sign letters you prepare. But don't forget that the more work volunteers are asked to do, the more staff time is required in support *and* the greater the gift results are likely to be. Conversely, if you can afford little time to support volunteers, they will probably do a minimal amount of solicitation, which will be reflected in lower gift results. You rarely find an institution that enjoys maximum volunteer effort with minimal staff support to produce significant results.

Staff. The plans you have developed will determine how big a staff you will need. An annual fund program based solely on direct mail with little or no donor segmentation can probably be handled by a development officer on a part-time basis. An annual fund program based primarily on a campus-centered telephone campaign will require more staff. Plans that call for extensive use of volunteers in personal solicitation, regional phonathons with volunteer callers, direct mail based on class agents with refinements for reunion campaigns, and corporate-based matching gift programs will require a number of professional and support staff to achieve them.

How many staff do you need? Unfortunately, there is no ideal answer, but asking yourself these two key questions should help:

• "On what level of programmatic activity is my annual fund goal based, and do I have sufficient staff to achieve that program?"

• "If I were to add one more person to the annual fund staff, what programmatic improvement would I make and what bottom-line effect would this have on our annual fund results?"

The answers to these questions will tell you whether you have a big enough staff to accomplish your plans and where you would make progress if additional staff were provided.

Budgeting to do the job

Budgeting, like staffing, must be based on your plans. Too often, the annual fund budget, like the annual fund goal, is simply based on an inflationary increase over the year before. "We need a 10 percent increase in budget to obtain a 10 percent increase in results."

Budgeting is an iterative process. If you have planned carefully, it is not hard to calculate your budget. How many professional and support staff will you need to achieve your plans? What will they cost? How many nights of telephoning will you do? How many telephones per night will be used? How many calls will be made per phone? What is the average cost of each call? How much direct mail will you send? What is the cost of reproduction and postage? The questions and answers derive from the plan.

The iterative process begins when you find that the institution cannot afford to increase your budget to the level you have requested. Your first response should not be to cut your program, but to take another look at your cost estimates to see where you may have overestimated so that you can trim your budget without trimming your program. If you still project a budget greater than your resources, you'll have to reduce your budget by reducing those elements that are least likely to have an adverse impact on your dollar results.

Can you do a little less donor recognition without breaking faith with your supporters? Can you maintain the frequency of your direct mail program if you use black and white brochures instead of multi-color? Can you convene your volunteers for breakfast rather than dinner? Back and forth you go until your program, your budget, and your resources come together.

While you are going through this process, continually ask yourself whether you can shift resources from one form of solicitation to another to increase results without increasing costs. You can put more and more money into bigger and fancier brochures that may have only a marginal effect on gift results. However, if some of your resources were shifted from printed material to phonathons, gift results would probably increase. You can reach a point where you can shift budget dollars from more and more phonathons into personal solicitation with greater results to the annual fund.

Never stop asking where you can get greater bang for your buck.

"How much will this annual fund program cost?" asks the president of Hypothetical University. There are no simple answers, but a first-time direct mail program aimed at donor acquisition could cost as much (or more) than it produces. A good annual fund program might cost 30 to 35 percent of the funds raised. Costs below 25 percent indicate a *very* efficient annual fund. But don't get so carried away on being cost-efficient that you fail to invest adequately in your program and sacrifice results-effectiveness.

Evaluating your program

Evaluating your annual fund is easy. If you meet or exceed your goal, it is a success; if you do not, it is not. Right? Not necessarily so.

To be sure, it is very important to your institution, to the program growth you are seeking, to your volunteers, and to you personally that you meet your annual goal. However, the dollar goal is not the only criterion for measuring success. Indeed, it would be possible for you to reach your goal and still have a successful failure—that is, your annual fund was a success because your goal was obtained, but it was also a failure because your program was not planned and implemented to maximize the support available to your institution.

In order to make a professionally sound evaluation of your annual fund, you should establish goals for each component of your program. Establish dollar goals for your personal solicitation, phonathon, and direct mail efforts. Set goals for the number of volunteers you want involved. Set budgetary goals, keeping your costs as low as possible.

If you have reunion campaigns, set goals for each class. Set goals for the number of donors you want in your various giving clubs. Have dollar goals for your governing board and percent participation goals for your alumni, with goals by decade or even by class.

Why is it important to establish goals for each component part of your program? There are several reasons. The first and most obvious derives from the adage, "What gets measured gets done." You are more likely to enlist the requisite volunteers, solicit for your top-level giving clubs, and work hard for successful reunion campaigns if you are measuring the results in each case. You are less likely to work conscientiously toward vague objectives (such as "This year I am planning to improve our use of volunteers") because you do not know what you are measuring and you do not know what you have achieved.

A second and equally important reason is that planning for next year's program begins with the evaluation of this year's results. If your only goal for the annual fund was to obtain a 10 percent increase in gift results over the previous year and you reach that goal, you may be inclined simply to do more of the same for next year to reach your new and higher goal. However, if each component part has a goal, you can then evaluate which parts of your program succeeded and which did not. This puts you in a position to make the strategic changes needed, based on your evaluation, to continue improving your annual fund in subsequent years.

If your reunion campaigns and phonathons succeeded, you should determine what special efforts made them successful and how those efforts can be repeated in the future. If their success was due largely to the quality of volunteer leadership (a factor you have less ability to control), you can begin planning the staff support necessary next year to help assure comparable volunteer participation.

On the other hand, if you did not reach the goal for your top-level giving club or your direct mail campaign, you can find out what went wrong and take corrective action for the future. Perhaps you lost a staff member during the year and thus sent out fewer direct mail pieces. Or your volunteers may not have done the personal solicitation for your gift club that you had hoped would be done. Why did this occur? Can the problem be corrected?

Examine each part of your program against its goal and ask the appropriate follow-up questions. You will then be able to make the adjustments necessary for continued improvement and set an overall goal for your annual fund that reflects those adjustments and is not merely an arbitrary increase over last year.

Conclusion

"Well," says the president of Hypothetical University, "you've convinced me that the annual fund is the place to start and with proper planning at the outset and solid evaluation at the conclusion, we can make this program grow every year. So when do you think we can get 70 percent participation with an average gift of $500 per donor?"

Oh, well, every job should have its challenges.

Chapter 2

Why an Annual Fund?

David M. Roberts
Senior Associate Vice President for Alumni Affairs and Annual Giving
The University of Tennessee
Knoxville, Tennessee

W hy an annual fund? The question isn't meant to be rhetorical. The immediate short-range benefit of an annual fund is obvious: It provides a quick source of cash to meet institutional needs. But more important are its long-range effects: An annual fund produces friends, advocates, workers, tradition—*and* a quick source of cash to meet current institutional needs.

Many institutions have established annual funds for the wrong reasons and with shortsighted goals. However, annual funds that have enjoyed immediate and long-term success have been built on basic principles especially applicable to these special fund-raising efforts.

Historically, annual funds have been largely molded by the society in which they took place, and it was not until the middle of the 20th century that the potential of the annual fund for support of American higher education was recognized.

The first recorded gift to an American college occurred in 1638 when John Harvard gave 800 pounds sterling and 300 books to the institution that would bear his name. Harvard College conducted America's first fund-raising endeavor in 1641 when it sent three men to England to "raise what funds they could without engaging in dishonorable begging." A member of the trio returned successfully a year later with several hundred pounds sterling, while his companions remained in Great Britain to continue their assignment. The three eventually fell into disagreement and abandoned the mission. Little professional fund-raising activity is recorded in America over the next 150 years.

Early American colleges, which today we call private, received support from both the municipal and state levels. And while their existence was tenuous, the communities in which they existed believed in the intrinsic worth of the institution and sold the idea that the community that invested in a college would ultimately profit from it. Early public support came in the form of income from such things as ferry tariffs and levies on skins, furs, and tobacco, as well as income from lotteries and local sewing circles.

However, by the mid-19th century, with the cessation of public support, the true private college emerged. Not only did public funding from all sources cease, but many state legislatures also limited the amount of property that these institutions could hold.

As a result, after the Civil War, educators began to look for major benefactors who could and would support their institutions or even—as in the case of Vassar, Smith, Johns Hopkins, Stanford, Chicago, and Wellesley—actually establish an institution. Institutions began to realize that alumni and friends could be their greatest assets.

Administrators gave attention to developing systematic, routine solicitation of these sources, as well as business and industry, to provide annual operating revenue. While Yale University is generally credited with having the oldest continuous annual giving program (1891), in 1869 Bowdoin College established the first alumni solicitation program. Bowdoin's program raised approximately $15,000, but was discontinued in the late 1870s.

The first decade of the 20th century marked the most dramatic changes in American philanthropy; these included the establishment of multimillion-dollar foundations, widespread philanthropy, and organized appeals from educational institutions seeking alumni support.

Meanwhile, alumni were beginning to organize; the first alumni association was founded at Williams College in 1821. Alumni groups became more prevalent following the Civil War, and administrators were at the same time hopeful about the potential these organizations held for progress and nervous about their becoming involved in "day-to-day" administrative matters.

In the late 19th century, college and university administrators came to understand the contributions that well-organized associations of former students were able to make to the infrastructure of a fund-raising effort. Alumni groups were recognized and eventually encouraged. As fund raising gained acceptability as a sound method of meeting legitimate needs, it became apparent that a system was needed to plan, implement, and conduct fund-raising drives. Accordingly, a whole new commercial enterprise—fund-raising and public relations counseling firms—came into being to assist colleges and universities and other nonprofit organizations that did not have the staff or the knowledge to undertake these activities.

At the same time, the inflation associated with World War I forced colleges into capital campaigns, and they began to utilize the services of such individuals and firms as the John Price Jones Company; Size, Seymour, Tamblin and Brown; and Ward and Hill. Largely through the efforts of these people and companies, fund-raising principles were standardized and practitioners became professionalized.

Aided by these efforts, alumni fund-raising campaigns were generally accepted by colleges and universities by the mid-20th century. Prior to that time, alumni had resisted the idea of recurring fund-raising appeals. As late as 1923, according to a CASE predecessor organization (the Association of Alumni Secretaries), data indicated that only six colleges had active annual giving programs, six had dormant ones, and nine were planning programs. Prior to 1939, not one state university systematically solicited alumni for annual gifts. By 1945 the picture had changed: There were 121 public and private institutions with annual giving programs, and half of these had been established in the previous 10 years.

By the latter part of the 20th century, American fund-raising efforts—especially annual giving programs at secondary schools and colleges and universities—had proliferated. Both institutions and their individual constituents had recognized and accepted their roles in society: Educational institutions would provide quality instruction, and alumni and friends would assist these institutions in achieving their academic mission.

Today, the institution/alumni relationship has evolved into a beneficial partnership. It not only strengthens the American way of life but adds quality and meaning to the lives (and families) of those who participate in this uniquely American pattern of support.

Benefits to givers

Those who participate in annual funds benefit as much as the institutions that receive their gifts of time and money. In fact, over the long term, the nonmonetary benefits to both the institutions and the donors tend to overshadow the immediate financial gains.

Philanthropy is a uniquely American phenomenon that has existed since the founding of the colonies. And since reports on philanthropy tend to emphasize the numbers of dollars given, the psychological benefits to the contributor are frequently overlooked. And yet these psychological benefits are a prime factor in the success of annual funds and other philanthropic causes.

Among the benefits that accrue to alumni and friends who contribute to an annual fund are the following:

1. *involvement with the institution:* Among other reasons, contributors get involved because they wish to be identified with a worthwhile cause. Their student experiences at an institution cause many alumni to identify with their alma mater for the rest of their lives. Through their gifts, they choose to become involved and associated with it. By their involvement, they endorse the mission and accomplishments of the institution, or, alternatively, they seize the opportunity to work for "change from the inside."

2. *confidence in and appreciation for the institution:* Alumni participants in annual giving programs recognize the benefits they have received from the institution—the intrinsic value of the institution in their lives and its contribution to the quality of life they enjoy. Therefore, their desire to help the institution to continue to flourish is natural and demonstrates an enlightened self-interest.

3. *a sense of ownership and partnership with the institution:* Many institutions promote participation in their annual giving program as an investment in the school's future. Alumni who consider themselves to be investors or stockholders

in the institution feel a greater sense of responsibility for it. Givers feel that they are to some extent owners of the institution in partnership with the administration and the trustees. Annual fund participants help the institution secure and ensure its future.

4. *a channel for volunteer service to the institution:* Recent studies on volunteerism demonstrate that the foremost reason people tend to become involved in causes is because they are asked. Participation in an annual fund results when people who feel strongly enough to give ask others to join them in volunteering their time and talents.

5. *a rallying point for expressing interest and concern:* When prospects become donors to the annual fund, they are recognizing the institution's value to society and demonstrating their desire to see its mission, aims, and objectives achieved. The best way for an individual to go on record as being interested in an institution is to give time, talents, and resources to it.

6. *an avenue for interacting with faculty, staff, and students:* An intangible benefit of active annual fund participation is that contributors become a part of the life of the institution, whether vicariously or directly. They may attend campus functions and meet and interact with faculty, staff, and students, or they may receive correspondence and recognition designed especially for them. In these and other ways, donors get to know the institution's people and to understand their hopes and aspirations. Contributors become insiders and develop a sense of belonging to the institution.

7. *creation of an individual record of support:* Many who support causes do so out of pride of association. It's human nature to desire to be recognized and appreciated. People like to hear their names spoken and see them written. Through donor recognition programs, colleges and universities have a wonderful opportunity to extend a meaningful thank-you to their "investors." In fact, good stewardship requires it. The institution that insists on accurate recordkeeping keeps track of years and amounts of gifts; these can then be "played back" in a variety of ways to the donors in each succeeding campaign. Such recognition instills in contributors a desire to continue their record of giving and often to increase their support.

8. *an opportunity to influence others to support the institution:* When Ben Franklin was helping to build a Presbyterian church in Philadelphia, he urged givers and solicitors to first "apply to all those whom you know who will give something." Through its annual fund donor base, a college or university can geometrically increase its potential audience by asking contributors to seek gifts from their friends. A third-party endorsement of the validity of an institution's cause can be a compelling reason for others to give. People who have been sold on a cause have a natural desire to influence others to join them in supporting it. Annual giving participation is important, but enlisting current contributors to influence others is the key to the future.

Benefits to the institution

Until recent decades, many institutions were wary of alumni involvement, fearing that it might lead to control or takeover by these "outside" groups.

However, it could be argued that alumni have an even deeper interest in and concern for their alma mater than the administration, which, along with the student body and the faculty, is largely transitional. The permanency of alumni interest, involvement, and support is vital to the long-term development of institutions of higher education. These institutions benefit greatly from having active alumni organizations and well-run annual funds.

In addition to the dollars collected, an institution benefits in many ways from an annual fund.

1. *The institution must define needs and priorities and draft a case for support:* People tend not to give to causes unless there is a documented reason for doing so. In order to generate support from alumni and friends, an institution must develop a written statement of institutional mission, needs, and priorities. From the mission statement must come a defense of the institution's existence and a description of why private support is necessary for it to continue to provide the services described in its charter and mission statement. The case for support becomes the cornerstone for explaining and seeking private gifts. Without such a document, no fund-raising effort can proceed or succeed.

2. *The institution identifies fund raising as a viable option for meeting documented needs:* Institutions that seek support for support's sake enjoy little success. As well as identifying needs that private gifts can help meet, the institution must also justify fund raising as a legitimate means of reaching objectives. In other words, fund raising must become "fashionable" within the institution's alumni and annual fund constituency and culture. It must become the accepted vehicle through which gifts are sought and directed to the institution.

3. *An annual fund effort facilitates the recruitment and training of volunteer workers:* Once an institution and its alumni body have decided that an annual fund is needed, an organization must be put into place to carry out the fund-raising function. Therefore, an institution has the right and responsibility to ask alumni to serve as volunteer workers. Further, it must train these volunteers by giving them institutional rationale and skills for seeking private support.

4. *An annual fund facilitates the building of a constituency interested in advancing a common cause:* People tend to give only to institutions and causes in which they believe. Consequently among its annual fund contributors, an institution has a broad base of alumni and friends who share a common interest in seeing the institution achieve its destiny. The annual fund program and its cadre of volunteer leaders become a key constituency in interpreting and explaining the institution's mission. Annual fund contributors are among an institution's best informed and most devoted friends and strongest advocates.

5. *An annual fund creates a prospective pool of givers for upgrading and for influencing gifts from corporations, foundations, and other individuals:* An institution can seek increasing levels of support from its closest friends—its annual

fund contributors. By carefully screening and researching its annual fund donors, an institution can discover key alumni and other friends who are in positions to influence additional gifts from corporations, foundations, and others. An institution that fails to take this additional step with its volunteer leaders is missing the greatest potential that the annual fund contributor base represents.

6. *Annual fund results serve as a barometer of the degree of institutional acceptance among alumni and other friends:* If an institution wishes to know how it's viewed in its marketplace (i.e., its own community, its peer institutions, and its alumni), it should carefully analyze its annual fund results. If an institution has no annual fund program, it will find it very difficult to get a solid fix on community and alumni opinion.

In order to fully comprehend the "message" an annual fund brings to an institution, the institution should carefully analyze the results each year, paying particular attention to the comparative number of contributors, amount of dollars received, number of volunteer workers, and so on. Increases in giving can be sustained over the short term by a strong, motivated volunteer organization. However, the institution will increase support over the long term only if its programs are meeting the needs of society, if it is communicating that information to its several audiences, and if it continues to account for and manage wisely the gifts it receives from private sources.

7. *The institution can use annual fund results to evaluate effectiveness of external relations activities:* There are many elements within an institution that impact directly and indirectly on the success of all of its fund-raising programs, especially annual giving. Because of the breadth and depth of an alumni giving program, annual fund results can be used informally to measure the effectiveness of the institution's alumni association, news bureau, public relations office, athletics programs, academic programs, and administration. The institution's external relations activities must be coordinated with the institutional mission statement and administrative leadership. All those connected with the institution must deliver a uniform message. Mixed messages produce confusion and mixed results.

Conclusion

In recent years, inflation and rising costs have posed interesting challenges to higher education administrators. The future should be no different. Statistics demonstrate that funding needs for higher education will continue to be great. But statistics also demonstrate that not all institutions have yet established functional, productive annual fund programs.

It is doubtful that an institution can succeed in the 21st century if it does not have the moral and financial support that comes from an annual fund donor base. And even if such an institution should survive, it will find it difficult to provide a quality academic program that will justify volunteer involvement.

The fundamental question, then, isn't *why* an annual fund but *when*.

Chapter 3

Goals and Strategies

Mitchell L. Moore
Director of Major Gifts
University of Richmond
Richmond, Virginia

W *ebster's New Collegiate Dictionary* defines "goal" as "the ends toward which effort is directed" and "strategy" as "a careful plan or method." Strategies are "efforts" toward an end. In other words, goals are global, while strategies can be measured.

For example, your goal may be to increase alumni participation in the annual fund. Strategies to reach that goal might include increasing the number of student phonathons, developing a reunion gift program, adding more direct mail pieces, or implementing a more effective class agent system. You can usually choose among several strategies to meet your goal. Those that you choose will depend on your institution's specific circumstances.

We all know that goals and strategies are essential to a successful annual fund. This chapter is not about how to set specific goals or implement detailed strategies. (Other sections of this book cover these topics.) Rather, it focuses on the five questions every journalist is taught to ask: who, what, when, where, and why.

Goals

Answering the following "w" questions will give you a deeper understanding of your annual fund goals.

What? What determines annual fund goals? Needs, both long- and short-term, determine annual fund goals. Annual fund goals are traditionally set to meet short-term needs that are budget relieving. However, the annual fund also has an impact on long-term needs.

Many institutions identify needs through a long-range or strategic plan that is reviewed annually. While long-term needs are often marketed as capital or endowment fund-raising projects, the annual fund also helps undergird these needs by presenting a convincing case for current unrestricted dollars. Unrestricted gifts help relieve the strain on the operating budget in the short term so that other resources may be directed toward long-term needs.

In a way, the annual fund provides the foundation for the planning process. We couldn't plan properly for long-term needs if funds were unavailable to meet short-term needs. Many institutions now incorporate the annual fund into comprehensive campaigns instead of segmenting it from the capital campaign. These campaigns recognize the important role of the annual fund in the development program.

Likewise, annual fund goals help an institution satisfy the long-term needs identified in the planning process as well as providing the unrestricted funds to meet its short-term needs.

Who? Who sets annual fund goals? At institutions that rely heavily on unrestricted dollars to meet their operating budgets, the governing board may set annual fund goals when the annual budget is approved. At other institutions, goals are set after discussions between the president, the chief financial officer, and the chief development officer. In some cases, the development staff sets the yearly goals.

Ideally, annual fund goals should be approved by the governing board, the president, and the chief financial officer after consultation with the chief development officer and the annual fund staff. Unfortunately, this does not always happen.

Staff and volunteers who do not know who sets annual fund goals will have a harder time understanding the urgency and importance of meeting the needs of the institution. They will question the fund's credibility. This questioning, in turn, may affect volunteers' commitment of time and resources. It is important to know who sets annual fund goals if the annual fund is to provide a sense of urgency for action.

Why? Why set annual fund goals? Goals are normally set during the budgetary process. Many institutions rely on unrestricted gifts to bridge the gap between operating expenses and tuition. While this situation alone is a compelling case for setting goals, there are other important, but perhaps not so obvious, reasons to consider.

1. Goals provide something with which to measure objectively the progress of your program. If your program is meeting its annual goals, then you know that you are progressing in the right direction. Similarly, goals to be achieved over a multi-year period become benchmarks to measure success.

2. Goals give direction to the annual fund and provide a starting point for staff and volunteers to plan the annual fund calendar. Such direction sets the pace for the year's activities.

3. Goals help create a sense of immediacy for annual fund staff and volunteers. Immediacy helps them more fully understand and appreciate the role of the annual fund in meeting institutional needs. No longer are "why" questions answered with vague statements: "We need more money," or "Our president wants a higher percentage of participation." Instead, the answers are substantive and, therefore,

more convincing: "Tuition covers 80 percent of annual operating expenses; your annual gift helps provide the difference," or "Our president is concerned about our corporate support and knows that alumni participation is important to the business community."

4. Finally, goals provide objective criteria for evaluating staff, especially when staff participates in setting those goals and has a clear understanding of what is expected. While goals should not be the only standard used in the evaluation process, they should be an important consideration.

When? When are annual fund goals set? The time to think about annual fund goals is when the budget process begins. Your financial officer can help project the amount of unrestricted dollars needed for the new year. While this amount will certainly change between the beginning of the budget process and its final approval, the earlier you hear how much in unrestricted funds will be needed, the sooner you can begin to plan annual fund strategies.

Goals are usually set several months prior to the beginning of the new fiscal year. While most goals will address short-term needs of the current operating budget, long-range or strategic planning will include long-term goals as well. Such goals are usually viewed as benchmarks for an annual fund program. Strategies may change to reach these goals, but the goals themselves will most likely remain unchanged until the plan is updated or a new plan is in place. For example, the institution will continue to have as a goal achieving a targeted alumni participation rate over five years or increasing restricted giving to a certain level over time; it may change or adjust its strategies, but it will still continue to work toward the goal.

Strategies

We can answer the five "w" questions for strategies.

What? What annual fund strategies will you use to reach your goals? The priorities assigned to annual fund goals and the resources available to reach those goals will determine annual fund strategies.

Consider priorities among annual fund goals first. For example, if alumni participation is your top priority, then strategies to meet this goal may be to add more class agents, hire a phone/mail vendor, or institute a reunion gift program. On the other hand, if your first priority is to increase unrestricted dollars, then an aggressive leadership gift approach, more direct mail, or different market segmentation may be more appropriate. Certain strategies work better to address certain priorities. Knowing your objectives is the first step in determining what strategies you will use.

Annual fund strategies are also contingent upon staff and program resources. For example, contracting with an outside phone/mail vendor will certainly raise alumni participation, but the cost of such a venture may be prohibitive for this year's budget. On the other hand, bringing participation up to an acceptable level by using class agents may require more staff than is available.

In summary, you must establish priorities and evaluate your resources before deciding on strategy. Doing so creatively and efficiently enables you to provide a convincing case for asking for additional resources or further clarification of institutional priorities.

Why? Once you have selected the strategies you will use, think about why these particular strategies are better than other possibilities. Do they use budget and staff efficiently and effectively? How will you capitalize on the strengths of the strategies while limiting their weaknesses?

For example, a class agent system for reunion classes may increase participation to the desired level and make the best use of your time and money. The results may produce compelling evidence to support a request to fund this strategy with additional program and staff resources.

Annual fund strategies also establish the annual fund niche within the development program. Without the annual fund, the success of other fund-raising programs would be limited. The corporate and foundation officer will have greater success in achieving his or her goals if alumni participation is increased. The major gifts officer will have more calls to make when the annual fund discovers new major gift prospects. Alumni will be more involved if they participated in phonathons as students.

Strategies also provide for a more comprehensive evaluation of staff. While staff should be held accountable for "bottom-line" goals, this should not be the only criterion for evaluation. Strategies that demonstrate creativity, fiscal responsibility, and time management show an understanding of institutional needs, annual fund priorities, and budget limitations.

Who? Who sets annual fund strategy? While annual fund goals are sometimes set by others, annual fund strategies are the responsibility of the development office and, specifically, the annual fund staff. Paid staff, who understand annual fund priorities and resource limitations, are most able to develop effective strategies to achieve annual fund goals.

It is important to provide staff with the training and encouragement they need to be creative. Many good ideas come from visiting other development offices, attending professional conferences, and soliciting the advice of volunteers. Training reinforces staff belief in professional growth and enhances staff commitment. Regardless of the methods you use, remember that strategies should complement your institutional culture. Enlist the advice of those who understand this culture well to plan those strategies that will best work for you.

When? When are annual fund strategies set? Although strategies are usually set prior to the beginning of a fiscal year, the process is ongoing. If you do your planning at the beginning of the year, avoid the temptation to "file" the plan. It should not be a historical document but a working paper that you regularly review in order to assess performance. Without this review, you cannot evaluate your strategies properly and make modifications as needed. Keep a notebook or file handy for ideas about techniques that may work for your annual fund. And review that file frequently throughout the year.

At the University of Richmond, we try to review new ideas for strategy four times a year. These review sessions begin in May when plans are finalized for the upcoming fiscal year. We review again after the rush of phonathons in October, at the close of the calendar year in January, and in April when most of the year's mailings have been completed and we can analyze our results. The timing for you may be different. The point is to review your current plan often, be willing to modify it when necessary, and never forget that next year is just over the horizon.

Where? Where are annual fund strategies set? Planning is a detailed and exhausting process. To do planning properly requires a review of last year's successes and failures, an evaluation of staff, and an analysis of the budget. It is better to do this away from the office in a relaxed atmosphere.

At the University of Richmond, we schedule half-day or full-day retreats with the annual fund staff. Our proximity to the mountains and the ocean provides several opportunities for the right escape. The right setting helps us bring our challenges and opportunities into focus, renews staff commitment, and provides a sense of direction for the months ahead.

Conclusion

Asking these five "w" questions helps focus on the importance of annual fund goals and strategies. Even though we all work for different institutions and therefore do not have the same goals or strategies, we know that every institution has specific short- and long-term needs that annual fund goals should reflect. The immediacy of these needs is better understood when we know who sets these goals. Setting goals should be a dynamic process that keeps the current year's objectives in focus while looking ahead for next year's opportunities.

Strategies measure how well goals are being met, and they demonstrate an understanding of institutional priorities. Annual fund staff who are responsible for these strategies should show efficient and effective use of resources while being willing to modify strategies when necessary. They should be given the time, training, and encouragement to do this properly.

While goals and strategies are essential to a successful annual fund, perhaps even more important is an understanding of the origins of these goals and strategies. Answering these five questions—who, what, when, where, and why—will help provide that understanding.

Chapter 4

Implementing Strategies Through the Planning Calendar

Daniel G. Reagan
Director, Notre Dame Annual Fund
University of Notre Dame
Notre Dame, Indiana

You are responsible for your institution's annual fund, and you know what you have to accomplish, but you aren't quite sure how to get there. Where do you begin? What's realistic, what's not? How do you coordinate this monster within the framework of your entire development operation? What are the priorities this year? Where will this program be five years from now?

Creating a planning calendar will *not* answer all of these questions. However, you must try to answer these questions before you can have a good calendar, a workable action plan. With a little logic, you can develop a simple plan that will help get you on track in no time.

Determining goals and developing strategies

Before you begin the process of creating a planning calendar, you should have done the following:

1. *determined your goals for the next 12 months* (your annual fund calendar) and broken these goals into:

• financial goals—your dollar target for the upcoming year's annual fund.

• awareness goals—the ongoing process of educating your constituency about the purpose and value of annual fund raising. If your program is relatively new, you will need to send your constituency frequent messages explaining why it was created; if you have a traditional program, you must make donors aware of the good they are doing. Never assume that your prospects fully understand your program; revise and repeat your message; make them aware.

• innovation goals—because annual fund raising can easily become "assembly line" fund raising, it is important to keep pushing your program for unique ways of making an approach. Repeated success within an annual fund program can sometimes lead to complacency and a desire not to try new and different solicitation ideas. The better established your annual fund is, the harder it is to do anything new. An innovation can be something as simple as using a new color scheme in your mailings or as complex as creating a corporate agent program to promote matching gifts. Each year should include an effort of some sort to be innovative. A repetitious year exactly identical to the previous year may produce good results, but your donors will eventually begin to lose interest if you don't vary your efforts.

2. *determined goals for the next three to five years* in each of your annual fund program categories for the three areas (financial goals, awareness, and innovation) and for market analysis as well. That is, you want to analyze those activities within the annual fund that seek a result (e.g., a direct mail solicitation, phone solicitation, volunteer efforts, and so on). Look at each of these activities and determine which are working and which are not and, more important, why. Since analysis can go beyond the 12-month period, we categorize it under long-term goals.

3. *prioritized your short-term (one to 12 months) and long-term (three to five years) goals.* You have fully notified your superiors and volunteers of your plans and, what's more, all are in agreement.

4. *created a strategy or set of strategies for each of your goals.* These strategies are the linchpin in the creation of your planning calendar, so be certain this area is discussed among the annual fund staff to distill the best set of strategies. The following examples show how goals are translated into strategies:

• You have set a financial goal of $1 million for your direct mail results for this year. This goal was based on previous years' results and the fact that you are stepping up your direct mail activities. Your strategies include: increasing the number of mailings; completely revamping your color scheme and logo; and personalizing one of the mailings and sending it out as a first-class appeal.

There could be more, but the bottom line is that you will never reach your goal unless you create specific strategies that lead you to a set of planned activities. One caution: If you have exhausted your strategies, and you still do not think you can reach the goal, be smart—lower the goal.

• You have set a goal of expanding your membership in the XYZ Giving Club by 500 this coming year. Your strategies include holding a series of events throughout the country to promote the program and attract new members; segmenting a portion of the phone center's prospects for direct calling concerning the club; and utilizing your volunteer chair's good name through various specialized and personal mailings.

• You want your alumni classes to become aware of how the other classes rate in terms of giving participation. You hope that this awareness will lead to a healthy competition and ultimately more contributions for your institution. Your awareness goal strategy finds you looking for ways to publish class giving results. The class section in alumni publications is one way; the top 20 list (the best classes) in annual fund publications is another. Your long-term goal within market analysis will eventually cause you to try to measure the awareness of class competition and how it affects donor giving patterns.

For the Notre Dame Annual Fund, we set a financial goal for each of our annual fund components and then develop a series of strategies for each of those goals. Some of the strategies stay the same each year; others change from year to year. The sum total of all of the component goals gives us that year's overall annual fund financial goal.

The awareness and innovation goals are specific but less quantifiable until you have done market analysis. And remember that market analysis can be as simple as a 10-question survey. We recently mailed a survey to a random sample of Notre Dame constituents to find out if they were reading our relatively new annual fund newsletter, *Communique,* and to learn the areas of greatest interest to them. The results of this survey helped us establish our communication priorities for *Communique* for the next couple of years. We learned that our constituents are reading the newsletter and that they want to know more about how their contributions are being spent by the university.

The 12-month calendar

Your short-term goals are set. Your strategies for those goals are complete. Now you're ready to set up a 12-month planning calendar.

All you need to do to create a planning calendar is list all of the activities that are spawned by the strategies. You put the activities in chronological order, month by month, watching carefully for conflicts both within the annual fund and with other development activities. You should assign specific dates to the more important activities.

Let's take a typical month on the Notre Dame Annual Fund planning calendar. You will see that we usually list deadlines ("Nostalgia mailing dropped, 6th"); initial activities on a project ("Mailing materials gathered for first, third, and fifth rounds of corporate agent"); and events ("Sorin Society function, 9th"). (The Sorin Society is our gift club for donors of unrestricted gifts of $1,000 and over.) In addition, we keep an eye on major, ongoing projects ("Continue national gift phase calling"). We expect that each item will be completed or initiated during the month assigned, and each staff member knows who is responsible for each entry in the calendar.

Figure 4-1: Planning Calendar for October 1989

- Sorin Society reminder mailing
- Sorin Society network recruitment/meeting set-up
- Drop chairman's request for Sorin nominations with annual report
- Sorin acquisition mailing to parents
- Complete articles for *Communiqué*
- Nostalgia mailing dropped (6th)
- Sorin Society function (9th)
- Mailing materials gathered for first, third, and fifth rounds of corporate agent
- Caller evaluations
- Continue national gift phase calling
- Reunion giving calling, '40 and '65
- Corporate agent reception

The long-term planning calendar

The purpose of the long-term calendar is to help you get organized and stay that way, to keep you focused, and to eliminate conflicts before they happen. For example, you are sending a specialized mailing to a select group of prospects at the same time that your phone center is calling that group on a different matter. This is a major conflict that good planning would have prevented. Planning forces you to look to the future as well. It makes you think not only about this year, but next year and the one after—this is why you need a long-term calendar.

The long-term calendar, which usually covers five years, is neither as involved as a long-range plan nor as detailed as a short-term calendar. But it is necessary if you are to keep sight of the total program. The long-term calendar should list, by components within your program, those strategies and/or activities that will emerge in the future. It should also indicate when you will stop an activity.

A good example of a long-term calendar component is the one we developed for the Sorin Society. Five years ago, we laid down a general but useful five-year projection of activities. (See Figure 4-2 at the end of this chapter.) You can see that in 1987-88 we stopped having functions—events held to promote the society. This was because our capital campaign had a multitude of events during this period. So we put society functions on hold rather than have them conflict with campaign events. Knowing that we would not need to hold events during this period was important. It eliminated an activity and altered our strategy which ultimately changed our goal.

We did a five-year calendar for each of our annual fund components—direct mail, the Sorin Society, Phone Center, and matching gifts.

In order to do a long-term calendar, you will have to plan for future activities by means of short-term organization. A program you plan to begin in the future will require specific planning in advance. As a result, your short-term calendar should reflect planning for a future, long-term calendar item. For example, we wanted a fully operational corporate agent program to help promote matching gifts by 1987-88. We knew that this needed to be planned in advance, and in 1985-86 we began listing this item throughout the short-term 12-month calendar, gradually moving toward the full program in time for the 1987-88 target date.

Conclusion

Follow these tips when you are creating your own short- and long-term planning calendars. ,

1. Hold an annual meeting to build the short-term calendar and invite everyone who is involved in executing the annual fund. This will be an arduous task, but if everyone comes prepared with their strategies and activities, it won't be as painful as it sounds. Go through the entire year, month by month, mapping out your annual fund activities.

2. Keep the monthly portion of the short-term calendar in front of you. We have a large marker board in our office that lists the most important activities for the two upcoming months. Without that daily reminder, it might be "out of sight, out of mind."

3. Make sure your annual fund plan takes into consideration activities of other offices so you can avoid conflicts. Communication is the key.

4. Update your long-term plan annually, so that you are always ahead of the game.

To summarize, following these six steps will help you implement strategies through the planning calendar:

- Create your goals.
- Map out your strategies for each goal.
- Plan your activities for each strategy.
- Develop the timetable of activities.
- Superimpose the timetable over the calendar.
- Assess the entire process.

Remember, attention to detail at the start of your planning can eliminate a lot of glitches as the year wears on. Good planning helps everything fall into place. All it takes is a little logic.

Figure 4-2: Five-year Calendar for Sorin Society Activities

1985-86

- functions (fund-raising events, usually luncheons to promote the society)
- networks (volunteer solicitation efforts in specific cities to secure new membership)
- reminders (monthly notes to members asking them to renew their memberships)
- upgrades (letters sent quarterly asking those giving $500 annually to move up to the $1,000 Sorin Society level)

1986-87

- functions—spring '87 and before May 9 (kickoff date for $300 million Strategic Moment Campaign)
- chairman's letter (explaining how the society will be affected by the campaign)
- networks
- reminders
- upgrades
- Recognition Weekend

1987-88

- no functions
- limited networks
- reminders okay (reminders can still be sent after the campaign has been announced)
- upgrades okay if not on pledge (upgrade letters can be sent if prospect has not already made a pledge to the campaign)
- acquisition mailings okay on non-flagged (those being solicited for the campaign were coded by the computer; those without the code were available for a direct mail solicitation)
- new chairman

1988-89

- no functions
- limited networks
- reminders
- upgrades
- acquisition mailings
- Recognition Weekend

1989-90

- no functions
- networks
- reminders
- acquisition mailings

Chapter 5

Linking the Annual Fund To Other Programs

Shawn J. Lyons
Director of Development
Centre College
Danville, Kentucky

One of the biggest challenges a development professional faces daily is knowing when *not* to think like a development professional. Although *we* may understand the relationships between capital gifts and endowment funds, between planned giving and annual giving, or between unrestricted and restricted gifts, the majority of our constituents don't know a LYBUNT from a sacrifice bunt. If we are to communicate effectively with our volunteers and prospective donors, we must do so on their terms rather than our own. Otherwise, we may find ourselves repeating that old phrase, "I know you think you know what I said, but what I meant is not what I actually said, which you misunderstood."

Annual giving—a central position

Because annual giving requires, by its very nature, ongoing communication between the institution and the donor, it provides an opportunity to introduce other development programs and institutional needs. If we think of the institutional advancement program as a building in which each room represents a different program, annual giving would be the central hallway connecting all of the rooms. At least three characteristics give annual giving its central position in the institution's development program:

• *constant need:* All institutions, regardless of size or mission, require operating funds every year. Other priorities, such as building new facilities or renovating existing ones, are likely to shift in importance from time to time.

• *universal appeal:* Almost everybody is a prospect for annual giving—alumni, parents, faculty and staff, friends, churches, corporations, and so on. Giving potential need not be a barrier in annual giving. The struggling young graduate student with $25 to spare may feel her gift would be an insignificant drop in the multimillion-dollar bucket of a major endowment or building campaign, but she can easily understand that her gift will purchase a book for the library—if only a small one.

• *comprehensive use:* Annual giving dollars flow into virtually every phase of the operation of most institutions—salaries, financial aid, building maintenance, student activities, library acquisitions, and so on. As a result, the annual giving program provides a kind of training ground for donors and volunteers who may later be asked to support a campaign to provide endowment funds for financial aid, as well as for the individual who may be asked to establish a unitrust that will eventually endow a chair.

As a result of these factors, a well-executed annual giving program will build a base that can strengthen capital campaigns and planned giving as well as other development or institutional programs that may utilize volunteers, such as student recruitment and career counseling. In turn, those programs can enhance the annual giving program.

Coordinated implementation

As you proceed from the theoretical relationship between annual giving and other programs to the coordinated implementation of those programs "where the rubber meets the road," consider these three factors:

1. *institutional objectives:* Before you attempt to link annual giving to other programs and to market those programs to volunteers and donors, you must understand how your efforts will help accomplish broad institutional objectives.

For example, you are forming a new $1,000 donor society and must decide whether to include all $1,000 donors or only those making unrestricted gifts. You know that your institution plans to construct several buildings in the near future. For this reason, you may wish to include all donors in the society in order to reduce the likelihood that membership will drop and momentum will suffer when members are solicited for the construction projects.

2. *institutional traditions:* As in any profession, it is wise to periodically review policies and practices in the light of a changing environment. Yet if you think like a prospective donor rather than a development professional, you will see that it's sometimes a good idea—although not always—to do things "the way we've always done them."

For example, if your institution has a tradition of capital campaigns that run independently of the annual giving program, you may decide *not* to include $1,000 donors to the building project in your $1,000 annual giving society unless they also make a $1,000 unrestricted contribution. That would be consistent with your contributors' past experience and might very well motivate them to make gifts for both of these purposes.

On the other hand, if your institution has a history of comprehensive capital campaigns, you may choose to include those donors whose only gift is $1,000 for the building project. To exclude those individuals may alienate them. From their perspective, the only thing they changed was designating their contribution for a purpose determined to be a high priority by the institution.

3. *institutional resources:* As a wise person once said, "Don't bite off more than you can chew." Any decisions about how to integrate annual giving with other elements of the advancement program must be guided by such harsh realities as budgets, staff size and experience, and office technology. These factors generally impose limitations that place a premium on managerial creativity.

The rest of this chapter describes ways to integrate annual giving with programs in three areas: capital campaigns, planned giving, and nondevelopment volunteer programs such as student recruitment.

Capital campaigns

Whether annual giving is included as part of a capital campaign or run separately during the campaign, the two efforts have as much potential to enhance one another as they do to detract from one another. A strong annual giving program can prepare donors for the case statement to be presented in the capital campaign.

A university that was a year away from publicly announcing a campaign for faculty salaries and development highlighted the importance of annual giving in this area by determining the percentage of the average faculty salary that was derived from annual gifts. Training materials communicated that message to class agents and gift club chairs who in turn communicated it to their prospects. A year later, when the university announced the campaign and included figures showing faculty salaries lagging behind those at peer institutions, volunteers and prospects already understood the importance of faculty compensation and knew that tuition income alone could not produce the necessary increases.

Campaigns can serve to strengthen annual giving as well. A college that had just concluded a successful endowment campaign wanted to maintain that momentum in an annual giving program that had previously been only moderately successful. By explaining that the institution budgeted 6 percent of the endowment for annual expenses, the college demonstrated that $600,000 in annual gifts (the goal for that year) would be equivalent to an endowment of $10 million.

Both of these institutions used strong programs to bolster others. These strategies were successful because volunteers and donors were already committed to the existing program that was used to introduce or promote the new program.

Planned giving

While the importance of a good planned giving program may be self-evident to institutional advancement professionals, many loyal supporters are mystified and even frightened by the subject. In many cases, relating planned giving to annual giving can open a dialogue.

An independent school with a very high percentage of alumni contributing to the annual fund adopted such an approach to initiate a planned giving program. The school asked alumni to consider endowing their annual gifts. For example, a regular annual fund contributor of $1,000 could endow that level of giving with a bequest of approximately $20,000. The program demonstrated that planned giving was a possibility even for people of fairly modest resources, and once again, it communicated a new institutional priority through a program the alumni were already supporting.

Prospect identification is another important link between annual giving and planned giving. Because the annual giving program generally touches every individual in the prospect pool, it should help generate prospects for planned giving. For example, annual giving business-reply envelopes can include a box that donors can check to request information on "wills and bequests." (Remember to think like a prospect—the average prospect may not know what planned giving is.)

But prospect identification is not a one-way street. A donor who has been cultivated and solicited for a planned gift may well emerge with a renewed sense of interest in supporting the institution annually.

Nondevelopment volunteer programs

Most universities, colleges, and independent schools rely on volunteers for programs in addition to development and alumni programs. The linkage between annual giving and some of these programs can produce stronger volunteers and better donors for the institution.

For example, a college was expanding its cadre of admissions volunteers to help achieve the objective of enrolling more out-of-state students. Because the college was less expensive than many of its peer institutions, the admissions volunteers were able to make a case for their alma mater on a cost-benefit basis. The cost differential was due, in part, to a very strong annual giving program. The development office was able to demonstrate the importance of annual gifts in attracting new students. And because the students knew that annual gifts helped to reduce their tuition, they were more likely to become donors after graduation.

Conclusion

These examples demonstrate the importance of integrating programs to enhance communication with volunteers and prospective donors. It is not enough to give compelling reasons to support the institution. The case for support, whether in annual giving, capital campaigns, or planned giving, must be presented in a manner that is clear to your constituents and consistent with the other messages they receive from your institution.

Chapter 6

The Annual Fund In a Capital Campaign

Joseph S. Collins
Managing Director, Alumni Activities, and Director, Alumni Fund
Massachusetts Institute of Technology
Cambridge, Massachusetts

Annual giving is the bedrock of individual fund raising at most educational institutions. Year after year, annual giving provides a substantial portion of unrestricted income, which is counted upon to help balance the budget. As development officers, we must educate our faculty and staff colleagues about the importance of annual giving as the basis for successful alumni support for the future of our institutions.

Annual giving does much more than provide money to the institution. Its benefits include the following:

• Annual giving develops the habit of financial support.

• Annual giving provides volunteer opportunities for alumni to identify their interests in student recruitment, affiliative activities, fund raising, and so on.

• Annual giving recruits committed alumni as volunteer leaders.

• Annual giving seeks upgraded gifts from regular donors.

• Annual giving involves the best volunteers on national committees.

• Annual giving educates young alumni about institutional needs and their responsibilities to future generations of students.

Periodically, most institutions undertake capital campaigns, short-term efforts to raise a maximum amount of dollars. This chapter shows how an institution can use a capital campaign to enhance appreciation of the annual fund; it identifies ways to link more closely the efforts of campaign and annual fund staffs.

Annual giving and capital campaigns: What's the difference?

Because many educational institutions are so decentralized, faculty and staff often do not understand the differences between the annual fund and the capital campaign. It's human nature to assume that people who raise "big bucks" are more important than seekers of smaller gifts. Among our many challenges is the ongoing responsibility to explain to our colleagues the ways in which these two fund-raising efforts differ:

Annual Fund	**Capital Campaign**
Annual/fiscal year cycle	Multi-year effort
Broad-based participation	"BIG" gifts
Credits only cash-in-hand	Credits multi-year pledges
Mail/phone/face-to-face	Personal contact including cultivation and a tailored ask
Focuses on groups (e.g., "Class of X")	Focuses on individual donors
Needs lots of volunteers	Uses selected volunteers
Unrestricted current-use money	Unrestricted gifts with naming opportunities

The key element here is that both the campaign and the annual fund are important. The annual fund is a long-term proposition, the base builder, the future. The capital campaign is a short-term undertaking to raise a maximum amount of dollars. Each effort benefits from the success of the other.

The challenges of concurrent annual fund and campaigning efforts

The first and primary challenge to staff throughout a capital campaign is to adopt and follow the principle, "We are one team with different functions and objectives." The next priority is to create a climate of mutual support between campaign and annual fund staffs. These four critical elements can help accomplish this:

- *Wall-to-wall counting.* Make it as easy as you can for the prospects: Count annual gifts, reunion gifts, class gifts, and so on in the campaign.
- *One big team.* Encourage cooperation and information sharing by minimizing rivalry over which staff takes credit for any specific gift.
- *Establish a prospect control system.* Prevent embarrassment over different "asks" to the same individual at the same time.
- *Establish a volunteer control system.* Prevent overuse of key volunteer leaders. Campaign staff should be free to engage proven volunteers as long as they intend to use them as solicitors. The annual fund should use the capital campaign as an opportunity to identify and recruit new fund-raising volunteers—that is, individuals who have no or very limited prior experience in fund raising.

It is important to promote a high level of interaction between the annual giving and campaign staffs. Because institutions frequently hire additional staff for the capital campaign, a high percentage of both staffs are new to the institution as well as to their assignments. Joint staff meetings, periodic full-day gatherings, a circulating "reading/correspondence" folder—all these things help the staffs to get to know and appreciate each other. Beyond that, every staff member should be provided the opportunity to acquire a sense of institutional mission, history, and culture. For example, organize meetings with academic deans, the director of admissions, institutional "greybeards" with wisdom and memory, and so on.

The key participants in a school, college, or university campaign—both as prospects and as solicitors—are the alumni. An open atmosphere between staffs will encourage them to share information about alumni. Often, due to a tradition of five-year reunions and reunion giving, the annual fund staff knows the under-graduate alumni better than the campaign staff. In order for both fund-raising efforts to be successful, there must be a willing and complete transfer of information about alumni. Helping new staff members meet and get to know alumni is essential.

Other members of the institutional community must also understand the importance of annual giving, especially the senior officers, the president, chancellor, and provost, who often come from faculty ranks. While they are likely to know some of the big donors and may be aware of solicitations to major prospects, they may have little appreciation for the broad-based efforts of the annual fund.

Volunteers

One key to a successful capital campaign is the work performed by enthusiastic volunteers, who contribute time and energy as well as financial support to the endeavor. Volunteers are the lifeblood of the annual fund; only if they are fully engaged will the capital campaign be successful. These steps can help ensure willing and enthusiastic volunteers:
- "Promote" all current annual fund volunteers to capital campaign status.
- Recruit a new cadre of annual fund volunteers for the next campaign.
- Ensure that the capital campaign staff has the opportunity to decide on the prospects it will solicit.

How we did it at MIT

MIT is now in the midst of its "Campaign for the Future," a five-year effort that originally had a $550 million goal. This is MIT's fourth campaign since World War II, and its specific objective is to increase the endowment. MIT President Paul E. Gray asked the leadership of the alumni association and the annual fund to participate fully in the undertaking.

Fulfilling this mandate required a clear division of responsibility between the annual fund and campaign staffs. The prospect/program "tree" on the next page shows how we divided the tasks:
- The campaign staff is responsible for major gifts ($500K +) and leadership gifts ($50K to $500K).

rev. 1/22/90

Figure 6-1: MIT Prospect/Program Tree

(71,000 Active Alumni)

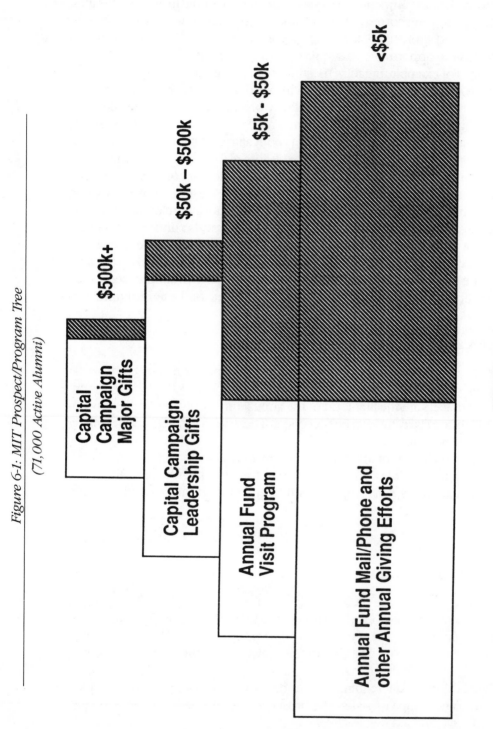

$500k+

$50k – $500k

$5k - $50k

<$5k

Capital
Campaign
Major Gifts

Capital Campaign
Leadership Gifts

Annual Fund
Visit Program

Annual Fund Mail/Phone and
other Annual Giving Efforts

Annual Fund Major
Reunion Gifts Program

• The annual fund is responsible for a geographic visit program ($5K to $50K) and gifts under $5K that are solicited through phone and direct mail;

• In a coordinated program, major reunion giving at the 25th, 40th, and 50th reunions falls within the staff responsibility of the annual fund, with major and leadership gifts support provided by the campaign staff.

The annual fund took responsibility for raising $100 million of the campaign goal of $550 million (recently revised from $550 to $700 million) and also set these key, end-of-campaign objectives:

• increase the number of annual fund donors to 30,000;

• double the median gift to $100; and

• achieve a $20 million annual fund.

In order to reach these objectives, we are asking all alumni to make a "stretch" gift. We have also arranged a one-year $1 million challenge from an alumnus who said, "If you will make a gift of $100 or more to MIT, which is an increase over your gift last year, I will give MIT an amount equal to 50 percent of your increase."

The major reunion gift and annual fund visit programs will recruit volunteers on a selective basis to seek quality gifts from individual alumni who make significant contributions to the annual fund ($250 or greater), but who are not considered capable of making a $50,000 campaign gift. We are recruiting volunteer telephone solicitors on a mass basis in an effort to involve as many people as possible in the campaign. We've increased our staff and our budget to meet the fund's campaign objectives.

Once we have established the campaign and annual fund goals and defined the lines of responsibility between the two organizations, we should pause and consider the pressure and problems of our colleagues on the campaign staff, such as the following:

• the premium on reaping dollars during the campaign "window": Once the goal is set and the campaign launched, there is pressure on everyone—the president, campaign chair, senior development officer—to meet or exceed the goal within the campaign period;

• lack of familiarity with volunteer management: During noncampaign periods, development staff tend to work alone on potential prospects; usually the annual giving staff provides support to organized groups of volunteers;

• limited recognition of their efforts: Unlike the annual fund with its fixed "clock" providing annual measurement and accountability, a five-year campaign does not lend itself to periodic assessment and renewal; once begun, the "race" is long with little opportunity to stop on the way for congratulatory messages.

So you ask, "How is MIT doing?" Quite well, I respond. Overall with two years left in the campaign, results have been exemplary—$490 million received in gifts and pledges. Moreover, the fund and campaign staffs have strong rapport. It is my belief that the decision to create a climate of mutual support with regard to prospects and volunteers is the primary reason for the strong working relationship between the two groups. I trust this spirit will continue throughout the campaign and beyond.

Section 2

Techniques

Chapter 7

Printed Materials

John F. Gallagher
Assistant Vice President of University Relations/Director of Development
Seattle University
Seattle, Washington

An annual fund is a program of fund raising for a specific purpose, most commonly to support the institution's general operating needs. An annual fund is not a technique or a group of techniques although some institutions seem to confuse the annual fund with the fund-raising techniques it uses. Virtually any technique can be used in support of the annual fund.

Just as there is no predetermined list of techniques that you *must* use for your annual fund, there is no mandatory set of printed materials to support the annual fund. Rather, you should first determine the best ways to approach your supporters and then choose the techniques and accompanying printed materials that will best accomplish this.

Certain fund-raising methods are regularly used in annual fund programs because they produce consistent results. Among the most commonly used techniques are direct mail, phonathons, special events, giving clubs, constituency agent programs (such as a class agent program or a geographic agent program), and corporate associate programs. This chapter discusses the printed materials most commonly used to support the annual fund.

The purpose of printed materials

The selection and design of annual fund printed materials are tasks that are usually completed relatively late in the annual fund planning process. Because materials should reflect the specific purposes they will serve in the annual fund, they cannot be developed until you have fully understood their purposes.

The following are some of the common purposes that annual fund materials may serve:

- *to carry a request for a gift:* One of the most common uses for printed materials is to carry a request to the institution's prospects as in a direct mail program, a brochure, phonathon support materials, or follow-up to a special event.

- *to acknowledge a pledge or to remind a donor of a pledge:* Following a successful phonathon contact or personal call, many institutions mail a pledge acknowledgment and subsequent reminders. Pledge reminders may be sent once or periodically—on a quarterly basis, for instance. Your reminders may be simple or complex, depending in large part on the sophistication of the computing resources at your institution.

- *to formally acknowledge receipt of a gift:* Many institutions mail a formal gift receipt to donors indicating the date, designation, and amount of a gift.

- *to thank a donor or volunteer:* You can thank donors in many ways, but one of the most common is a letter or card that conveys the institution's appreciation. Materials are sometimes developed specifically for this purpose (especially if cards are used), or you can use the annual fund stationery and envelopes.

- *to provide detail about the purposes of the annual fund campaign:* Printed materials often provide background information to help donors understand the purposes of the annual fund. Many institutions use brochures or newsletters, but you can also include this information as a part of other materials.

- *to reaffirm (or create) an image:* The visual impression made by printed materials—and the quality of writing they display—helps to create or confirm an image of the institution. You should consider your institution's supporters and what is likely to appeal to them as you choose color, paper, print style, type and placement of photographs, writing style, and so on.

- *to update donors and prospects about the institution:* Alumni often hear from the development office more regularly than from any other part of the institution. You can use annual fund printed materials, particularly brochures and newsletters, to provide alumni with timely updates on campus changes and progress. In turn, such messages lead naturally to requests for support.

- *to acquire information about donors:* An annual fund program may seek to gather better information about prospects and supporters. You can modify your materials—or design new ones—to accomplish this. For instance, you might design a questionnaire to mail to your constituency or use a return mail device, such as a pledge card or a business-reply envelope, to gather information about your institution's supporters.

You can develop printed materials to serve each of these purposes, or, with a little forethought and creativity, you can design materials that will accomplish several goals at once. It is very important that you understand what you wish to accomplish during the annual fund year and that you think through the ways printed materials can contribute to these goals.

In order to do this, you need to know as much as possible about your audience. Are all the people who will receive the materials substantially alike? Or are there some important differences that should be reflected in the materials? Similarly, think through the purposes of each item. Are the purposes the same for all supporters?

Will all supporters receive the same materials?

Review the materials used in previous years to spot ideas or themes that might be successful again this year. Many institutions routinely enlist the help of their volunteers to assess the appropriateness of their annual fund materials. Feedback from supporters, through formal focus groups or in some other way, provides insights that often escape development staff members. Consistent use of outside help like this can often lead to more effective printed materials.

Selection and design of materials also depend on the type and capability of the computer support available for the annual fund program. For example, the size and weight of your annual fund business paper (stationery, envelopes, and business-reply envelopes) should be appropriate for the printers you will use.

While the following discussion covers the most commonly used annual fund printed materials, each institution should choose the type of materials best suited to its own particular needs.

Direct mail

Many institutions prepare their basic printed materials primarily for use in the direct mail portion of the annual fund program. They design stationery, envelopes, and return devices with this in mind and then use them for other purposes as well.

The direct mail package usually includes business paper (letterhead stationery, second sheet, conveyance envelope, return envelope) and a brochure.

Some institutions use institutional letterhead for annual fund contacts, but most develop a special annual fund logo that can be redesigned regularly without concern for the basic institutional identity. Using a logo or other design element from year to year helps develop a visual identity for the annual fund.

Business paper comes in several standard sizes. Is 8½ by 11 stationery the most appropriate for all of your uses, or would another size—such as monarch—be better? As in all direct mail programs, the rate of success of your annual fund mailings depends on getting the letter opened, and unusual-sized materials are opened more often than "regular" envelopes.

A personalized look to the envelope will also increase the likelihood that it will be opened. Hand-addressed envelopes, which are the most personal, are usually impractical. Direct printing on the envelope—the "typed" address look—is becoming common. A label is the least personal, but if computer limitations make labels necessary, consider using a window envelope and applying the label to a card inserted in the envelope behind the window. Research suggests a higher rate of opening with windows than with plain labels.

In any event, the envelope should carry some sort of message or device that encourages the recipient to open it. Any method that increases the likelihood that the letter will be opened will have a positive impact on the program. Be sure to consider any design or size problems that such messages create when you are selecting envelopes; if your message or device will be oversize or of an unusual size, make sure that the envelopes are big enough.

In fact, before you purchase any paper or envelopes, you should test samples with all printers or feeders that you plan to use with the finished business paper. Computer printers, paper feeders, and envelope feeders sometimes have difficulty with certain weights and sizes of paper and envelopes.

Return envelopes can be full flap or regular flap. Regular-flap return envelopes provide a convenient way for the donor to return a gift or a comment, but serve no other purpose. They are often used to send a pledge or information card.

Because full-flap return envelopes have flaps large enough for you to print questions for the donor to answer, they are more commonly used for basic direct mail contacts. These envelopes provide excellent ways to update information. The donor can write in name and address corrections, gift designations, special messages or directions about the gift, and planned giving information or requests.

Many organizations provide postage on the return envelopes to make the task of sending a contribution as simple as possible for the donor. The argument in favor of this practice is that even the absence of a stamp might cause the donor to defer the decision to contribute. However, recent research suggests that the presence or absence of a return stamp has no discernible impact on giving rates. As in all direct mail activities, you should consider testing to determine the best course for your institution.

Annual fund brochures are widely used to provide supporters with detail about the annual fund campaign. They may be complex (employing multi-color design and intriguing layouts) or extremely simple. As with all printed materials, cost is an important factor in the ultimate selection of a design.

Because most direct mail programs contact prospective donors several times during the annual fund year, you will have to decide how many times you will send a brochure and whether you will send the same brochure each time or develop different versions. If you use several versions, you can achieve considerable savings by designing and printing all of the brochures at the same time.

Some people, however, argue against the use of brochures in direct mail fund raising; they suggest at least three reasons against using brochures:

• Because brochures usually invite reflection, they are inappropriate when the desired outcome is a decision.

• A brochure usually does not express urgency, an important element in successful direct mail pieces, and may, in fact, actually interfere with the sense of urgency you wish to convey.

• It is usually difficult to sustain a single, simple message theme when both a letter and a brochure are included, especially when a brochure is written and designed for several audiences or purposes. The result may be a mixed message for the reader, which interferes with the decision to make a gift.

People who use brochures like them, but others think they are a waste of money. Test them with your constituencies to see if they work for you.

Many annual fund campaigns use pledge cards to elicit donor intent, even if the actual gift is not possible until later in the year. You can design a pledge card to fit in the return envelope or print a shortened version on the flap of the return envelope. (The appendix at the end of this chapter contains an example of typical pledge card language.)

The materials described above make up the traditional direct mail package, but many other types of direct mail materials are possible and may be more appropriate for certain programs. For example, some institutions use self-mailers, newsletters, or even catalogs in their annual fund programs.

Various types of materials hold people's attention differently. Figure 7-1 shows the relative response on a few key variables to several kinds of direct mail materials used by for-profit organizations. The trade-off is in cost. The types of materials that draw the greatest interest and sustain the highest rates of opening and retention are the most expensive.

Figure 7-1: Typical Response Factors in For-profit Direct Mail Programs

Type of mailing	Cost	Percent opening	Percent reading	Retention	Depth of review (min.)	Purpose	Pass to others
Self-mailer	Lowest	85	75	3-4 days	1-2	Quick message	High
Junk mail	Low	40	30	Hours	2-7	Educate, solicit	Lowest
Letter-invoice	Low	100	70	Hours	2-5	Educate, solicit	Medium
Newsletter	Medium	100	80	2-3 weeks	10-30	Educate, entertain	High
Catalog	High	100	90	3-6 months	10-30	Educate, entertain	High

Donor acknowledgment materials

Donor acknowledgment materials are used to thank donors or to remind them of outstanding pledges. These materials are among the most important in the annual fund because they acknowledge the commitment the donor has made and help ensure that current donors will remain as supporters in the years to come.

Many institutions prepare and mail a donor receipt for each gift. Although not really necessary for tax reasons, the receipt confirms that the gift arrived, thanks the donor, and affirms any special purposes for the gift. Receipts, which are often enclosed in a thank-you letter or card, usually have the same visual identity as other annual fund materials. They may be hand- or computer-generated. Thank-you cards may be developed to carry receipts or to provide a convenient form for personal messages to donors or prospects.

Pledge reminders can have a dramatic impact on the rate at which donors honor their pledges. If possible, these reminders should indicate the amount and date of the original pledge, the purpose or designation of the pledge, the amount paid to date, the amount remaining, and the amount due during the current period. If you have the computer software to generate the information, you can easily develop a pledge reminder form.

Decide how often you will mail pledge reminders before you order the forms to assure an appropriate supply.

You should design both donor acknowledgment forms (reminders and receipts) to include a name and address field so that you can mail them in window envelopes. This simplifies production by eliminating envelope addressing.

Phonathon materials

Phonathon materials include those for callers and those for prospects and donors. You should review the needs of your phonathon program to see what materials are required.

Institutions often announce an upcoming phonathon. This announcement may be made in a variety of ways, so the selection of a printed device to accomplish this depends on the goals of the piece and the available budget. A post card announcing the purposes of the event and the calling period is probably the least expensive method. When the goals for the contact are more substantial, institutions use brochures or newsletters to alert those who will receive calls. Announcements about an upcoming phonathon can also be placed in publications—such as quarterly magazines or newsletters—that are mailed regularly to supporters.

Whether your phonathon uses paid callers or volunteers, you may need recruiting announcements and materials to enlist callers. Recruiting materials often include items such as post cards that are mailed to previous volunteers, table-tents for use on cafeteria or student union tables, posters on campus bulletin boards, and similar public devices.

During the phonathon, callers benefit from printed instructions and sample scripts. While you can do this in a variety of ways, one good method is to create placemats with instructions printed on them. Callers like placemats because all of the information they need is right in front of them.

You will also need computer cards (or some other device) with phone numbers and other information about prospects, unless callers will work directly from computer terminals.

You should make sure pledges received during the phonathon are acknowledged as soon as possible, preferably within 24 hours. Many institutions use a special thank-you card; as soon as the call is finished, the caller fills in the amount of the pledge and the date when the first installment is due and adds a short personal thank-you message. Phonathon staff mail the card the next day. These thank-yous can be designed as post cards or as inserts to be mailed in envelopes. If you use an envelope, you can also enclose an annual fund brochure and a return envelope. Most experienced annual fund officers believe in including a return envelope in every written contact with a donor.

Other annual fund materials

Annual fund programs often include special events either to raise funds or to offer appreciation to donors. The printed materials needed depend on the nature of the event. Special events often require invitations and envelopes, announcements, thank-you cards and envelopes, nametags, menus, souvenir brochures, tickets, folders, and virtually any other item you can imagine. Preparation of these materials should take place after an event plan has been developed, but remember that invitations must be ready well before the event in order to ensure timely delivery.

You may also need materials for giving programs within the annual fund, such as gift clubs or other targeted efforts. The requirements for these programs are usually similar to those for the general program, including stationery, brochures, newsletters, folders, and other supporting materials. If you design and print these materials at the same time as the other annual fund materials, you can ensure graphic similarity and also take advantage of cost savings.

Working with printers and graphic artists

Graphic artists and printers are primary partners in the design and preparation of printed materials. They not only provide ideas, they can help development staff avoid countless—and expensive—mistakes as materials are produced. It is imperative that you consult graphic artists and printers as early as possible in the design cycle for annual fund materials.

Usually, an in-house graphic artist or outside artist or art firm works closely with you and your staff to produce the design and mechanical layouts necessary for the printer. While graphic artists have ideas of their own, they will usually work hard to create the kind of product you want. But artists are not development officers. Even in-house artists work with a variety of clients for a variety of purposes. You can't expect them to understand all of the needs of development work and to design materials that reflect those needs without guidance from you.

You must know what you want to accomplish and provide the artist with clear and consistent information about your needs and wishes. Plan on staying in constant touch with him or her, reviewing work in progress, and providing frequent feedback. When you develop a production schedule, with the artist's assistance, provide regular points to check and recheck design progress as well as firm completion dates for all pieces. Be sure that the artist understands the production timetable and any other timing issues that might be involved. And discuss budget limitations candidly; a graphic artist can be a wonderful source of money-saving ideas for materials of all sorts.

You might also consult the graphic artist on the selection of a printer and then use the artist to work directly with the printer as the materials are prepared. Working with the printer takes considerable time and at least a minimum knowledge of printing operations, so it is a task that you may wish to delegate. The artist will understand any multi-color requirements and any problems created by odd sizes; he or she can ensure that the printer has access to the proper paper styles and weights. Most graphic art firms and in-house shops provide this service routinely.

Talk with your artist about the size of brochures, announcements, newsletters, and other items to minimize paper wastage during the printing process. You can realize substantial savings in larger press runs that use all (or nearly all) of the paper you purchased. Ask your artist to work with the printer to take advantage of any unused parts of the paper sheets.

Ultimately, however, the responsibility for printed materials rests with you and the rest of the development staff, not with the graphic artist and the printer. Spend the time to clarify your wishes and needs before you begin to talk to the artist. It is a good investment.

Be sure that you have a place to store materials as soon as they are printed, and that you have arranged for delivery. Some printers charge for storage beyond a predetermined minimum. Don't underestimate the amount of space you will need—a year's worth of annual fund materials can take up a lot of room. And the storage space must be dry; even a small amount of dampness can ruin the glue on the envelope flaps or cause problems with printers and sheet feeders.

Conclusion

Although you may not actually begin the design of the materials until relatively late in the annual fund planning cycle, it is a good practice to think through your needs as you plan. As you consider a program, think about the supporting materials. Can you afford them? The saying, "Plan your work, then work your plan," is appropriate here. Know what you want to do, design the materials to do it, and then use them in the times and ways originally planned.

Even if you know that the look of the materials will change during the year, try to plan and execute all of your design and printing work at one time. Printing a larger volume will result in considerable savings, and designing and reviewing the materials all at one time will help you to assess the overall impact, Seeing everything at once gives you a much better sense of how the pieces fit together. Inevitably, you will add items during the year to take advantage of special opportunities, but try to keep these to a minimum, and, as you develop them, consider how they will fit into your total annual fund "look."

Finally, always assume that problems will emerge during the design and printing of materials. Graphic artists and printers are deadline oriented, but mistakes inevitably happen, people get sick, and communication may sometimes be poor. Expect this, and build a timeline that provides the flexibility that will enable you to meet these challenges.

Special thanks to Forrest Wilcox, director of development at the Charles Wright Academy, and Madonna Dunn, director of the Seattle University Fund, who read and commented on versions of this chapter.

Appendix: Sample Pledge Form Language

To the Board of Trustees of [institution name]:

In recognition of the distinctive and important role of the annual fund, in support of the objectives of the Board of Trustees of [the institution,] and in consideration of the commitments of others:

I (we) pledge the total of $ _____ for the purposes of the annual fund.

I (we) intend to make my (our) commitment in the form(s) of (cash, securities, trust, life insurance, real estate, etc.)

_____

I (we) intend to honor this pledge in __ monthly __ quarterly __ semiannual _____ annual installments of $ _____ beginning on _____ and/or as follows:

_____

Note: [Institution name] requests that all pledges be honored by the end of the fiscal year on (last day of month, 19xx).

Enclosed is the amount of $ _____.

[Institution name] _____ may _____ may not publish my (our) names among those of other annual fund donors. I (we) wish to appear on the Honor Role of Donors as follows (please print):

_____

_____

PLEASE SEND PLEDGE PAYMENT REMINDERS TO:

Name _____
Address _____
City _____ State _____ ZIP _____

I understand that this pledge is not binding on my estate unless I establish specific provisions to that effect.

Signature(s) _____   _____
Date _____   _____

Chapter 8

Direct Mail: The Basic Ingredient of the Annual Fund

Elizabeth D. MacIntosh
Director of Annual Funds
Swarthmore College
Swarthmore, Pennsylvania

The annual fund is the bread and butter of the development program, and the basic ingredient of any annual fund is its direct mail program. The goal of direct mail solicitation is to send a compelling, cost-efficient communication that is so personally convincing that it evokes the desired responses from your constituents:

- an initial gift;
- an increased gift;
- an increased percentage of participation; and/or
- a sustained habit of giving.

Competition is fierce in mailboxes today. If your direct mail program doesn't stand out from the rest, it won't be read.

Although yours is not the only appeal in the mail, it may be the only written contact from your institution, the only "warm voice" your constituents hear. Your obligation, then, is to be an effective ambassador for your cause. This may be your only chance to motivate your constituents.

People like to be remembered; they like to be identified and recognized as part of a special group. They respond best to things that stir their pride and build their confidence. People like to "go with a winning horse." They support leaders or causes that have gained their confidence. They like to identify with other successful alumni and with the successful institution that produced the successful alumni.[1]

So remind your constituency that they are part of your special group. Try to establish—or reestablish—the contact and continuity that are increasingly harder to maintain in this world of increased mobility. Remember the lengthening generation gap: Alumni contributors may span eight decades, representing all ages from the teens to the 90s. What appeals to the class of 1991 may bitterly offend the 50th-reunion class—and vice versa.

Your appeal must speak for your institution. This makes you responsible for educating prospects about current needs. You are also accountable to these donors: Tell them how their dollars will be spent and what their current gifts will provide.

As Harold J. Seymour said in *Designs for Fund-Raising,* "Giving is prompted emotionally and then rationalized."[2] Once rationalization sets in, however, prospective donors respond to clear, direct needs. Giving prospers with challenge. But regular donors will follow their old gift habits unless you jolt them into refocusing their attention. They also respond to creativity and humor, so tickle their funny bones whenever you can.

To make your mailing piece stand apart from the competition today, you must plan a direct marketing approach. But first begin with these basic principles:

1. People don't read their mail; you must *force* them to. Make it hard for them to throw away your piece. Repeat the message clearly, again and again.

2. Once you have captured your readers' attention, remember that they will take what lands in their mailboxes seriously. If challenged, they will respond, particularly if your message seems to be written personally to them.

3. You have to *ask* donors to give and tell them what they are giving to. Your direct mail should contain a mini-case statement that tells the readers:

- why to give;
- when to give;
- what to give; and
- how and where to give.

Now it's time to plan your direct mail program. It will probably include five pieces: a brochure, an envelope, a covering letter, a reply mechanism, and an acknowledgment.

The direct mail brochure

The brochure is the best vehicle to capture attention as well as to state your goals. Start with the bottom line of your department budget: What can you afford? Design the piece yourself if necessary. Better yet, build a relationship with several designers and printers, choosing one or two who really know your institution. Work closely with them to help foster an understanding of your mission and build rapport for a long-term association.

Entertain competitive bids that are made *in writing.* Include costs not only of design and exact number of brochures and envelopes, but also of paper, printing, colored ink, color separations, screening, photographs, trimming, folding, and author's corrections.

Scheduling your mailing. Start with a "backwards calendar." When do you want this appeal to be mailed? A good appeal can take from three to six months to complete. Allow spare time at each step for unforeseen yet unavoidable delays; then plot a timeline that covers the whole process from mailing to the original creation of the idea:

- the actual mailing date;
- delivery date;
- time on press;
- final proof;
- corrected proof;
- first galleys;
- delivery of copy to typesetter;
- designer's presentation;
- initial meeting with designer;
- approval of final copy;
- writing the initial copy; and
- brainstorming the original idea.

Be sure to give these dates and the number of brochures and envelopes needed, *in writing,* to both the designer and the printer you finally choose.

Writing the copy. Like the chicken and the egg, the size of your brochure and your budget determine length of copy; yet you can't design a brochure without the copy. The message is key. It must be both creative and catchy.

Turn to advertisements for inspiration. The cleverest creative writing today exists in the advertising field. Look at the ads in newspapers and magazines. Can you adapt an idea for your appeal?

Develop an identity for your cause in the reader's mind. Create a logo or theme that you can use through a year-long set of appeals. It will help readers remember and will help you state your case over and over again.

Before you start to write, put yourself in the prospective donor's shoes and look at your institution from his or her perspective. As the "Music Man" said, "You gotta know the territory." Learn how donors see your "territory" by studying your institution's marketing image, how it is perceived, and the results of any awareness studies that have been done.

What is your institution's mission? What fond associations do prospective donors have? They like to identify with a successful cause or with other distinguished alumni. Donors may treasure the time spent at your institution. Help them rekindle personal memories.

Be sure to include the reasons *why* your readers should contribute. Explain what their contributions will be used for and how individual gifts will help. Describe the personal satisfaction or benefits they will gain from their gift (donor recognition, membership in a gift club, tax deduction, and so on).

Consider using questions and answers to inform yet maintain copy flow. Using the second person "you" makes busy readers feel personally involved. Succinct, easy-to-scan segments move them forward. Examples of real situations or people grab the readers' attention.

Tell the readers *when* to give. Do you have a fiscal year-end or internal timetable? Donors not only respond better to deadlines, they respond emotionally to a sense of urgency. A mini-crisis or impending emergency spurs action. But be careful: Always include a potential solution to the crisis (through the receipt of the donor's gift), and never try to fund raise for a deficit budget balance, projects already completed, or mini-campaigns that have already failed.

Donors need to be told *what* to give. Avoid the phrase "whatever you can give" and emphasize instead, "It is important to us that you *do* give." If you can do it, segment your readership by the size of previous gifts, and write a covering letter with an "ask" appropriate to that segment. Don't ask for the exact amount you'd like them to give, but suggest a range: "Please consider a gift in the range of $ __ to $ __." The smaller figure is the gift you hope to receive, the larger a "stretch amount." The reader will usually opt for the lower figure, which may be higher than he or she would otherwise have given.

Once convinced and ready to give, the donor looks for *how* and *where*. Make it easy; never assume he or she has kept the reply envelope or memorized your ZIP code. Repeat your institution's name and address and how the check should be made out.

Finally, before giving the okay to print your direct mail brochure, proofread, proofread, and proofread again. Every annual fund office has a horror story of how seven sets of eyes failed to spot the wrong date or the misspelling of the institution's name or the president's. Read every word; sound out each syllable; check and re-check the envelope, the figures, and any other place a gremlin may have been busy.

Designing the brochure. The most cost-effective brochure fits into a standard number 10 envelope and is printed on either 8½ by 11 or 8½ by 14 paper. For variation, only the sky and your budget are the limit. Most expensive of all is the odd-size brochure that must be cut from larger sheets of paper (wastage), from two-sided colored stock (expensive grade), printed in full color (runs through presses more than once), with special folds, cut-outs, or inserts, necessitating custom-size rather than standard envelopes.

A creative designer with a liberal sprinkling of imagination can come up with something unusual such as printing your appeal on a brown lunch bag full of hay or making a puzzle with movable parts. Or you might prefer something less exotic, such as incorporating a decal of your institution or reprinting newspaper publicity or magazine articles extolling your programs. Including a premium (a photograph of a nostalgic campus site, a bookmark, poster, stamps, post card, or calendar) increases the chances that recipients will save or remember your mailing and respond appropriately.

The size and shape of your piece depend upon what you want to say, so create your copy first. Have the "powers that be" approve it for accuracy of content and consistency of institutional message. Then trust your designer to fit it into a compelling graphic setting.

Remember, chances are that, *if* it's opened, your piece will be skimmed or only partially read, probably by someone near a waiting wastebasket. Make the copy flow, make it eye-catching and easy to read even though it will most likely be read on the run. Don't use a typeface smaller than 10 point. As people age, the size of the type they are able to read may be in direct proportion to the amount of their discretionary funds you receive.

The easiest to read typefaces are classic serif faces like Times Roman. You can add some bold Gothic headings, like Helvetica, for variety, but avoid using more than two styles and stay away from the many ornate or novelty faces that are available. Be sure to keep copy brief enough to allow plenty of white space on the page.

The use of some color is probably a necessity today if you want to be competitive. As with type, keep it simple. Addition of one or two harmonious colors can give your piece a more emotional appeal, but too many colors or colors that are too strong will only confuse the reader and may make your message look like a supermarket ad.

Some marketing experts suggest that warm colors evoke a better response and that red and orange denote a sense of urgency. In fund raising, yellow is thought to produce the best response of all, and blue and green are often used to convey a dignified, more sedate message. On the other hand, analysis has also shown that black ink on white stock increases retention value of the message and that, in fact, readers may prefer it.

Are you on a limited budget? Instead of using prohibitively expensive paper, try for a creative design. But keep in mind that this brochure speaks for your institution. Poor, shoddy quality translates into shoddy services. Yet the type of brochure must be appropriate. Consider using handsome, very expensive paper only for major donors. Others may resent having dollars spent unnecessarily.

Graphics can help you lead the reader along. Vary copy, if possible, with different type sizes or with drawings or photos. But photos or artwork must be good, repeating the message you want to convey (men *and* women students, minority representation, well-known buildings, good sportsmanship, helpful faculty, student camaraderie). People rather than places sell, and the best shots are those of subjects looking the reader directly in the eye. Are photographs clean and clear; will they reproduce well?

Production of your brochure. Maintaining good relationships with three or four printing establishments is as important as getting to know your designer. Before undertaking an actual contract, entertain several bids in writing. Paper can be your most expensive item. Choose paper quality, weight, and quantity with your budget in mind.

Don't forget the postage. Before signing the final contract, ask for three samples of your preferred stock, cut to size. Make up three dummy mailings with brochure, outer envelope, business-reply envelope, letter, and so on. Weigh all three mailings together at the post office and divide by three. Only then can you be positive that each average envelope with enclosures will be within your postal limit.

Remember there are several ways to cut costs. The sophistication of desktop publishing may allow you to provide camera-ready copy. Although you will need to plan typeface, spacing, and design, you save costs (and potential errors) over having typesetting and layout done commercially.

For small orders, ask your friend, the printer, about end-of-run leftover paper from someone else's order. If you're carrying out an annual theme, print your year's supply all at once. Substitute colored ink or creative design for costly stock. Gear the size of the brochure to standard paper size; plan to use only standard, not custom-designed, envelope sizes.

And never get caught in the embarrassing "numbers game." Each printing order can legally have as much as 10 percent over- or underrun; be sure to allow for this. Contract for 10 percent more than you actually need and be prepared to pay for it. (Of course if the printer doesn't print the 10 percent extra, you don't have to pay for it.)

Finally, always indicate in writing the type, color, and weight of stock; the quantity needed; the date and place of delivery; and the individual to contact. Ask for printer's proofs when the type has been set; when you have corrected the proofs, photocopy and date them and keep these copies on file with a copy of the contract letter. If discrepancies arise over when corrections were made, you can back up your argument. Remember, you pay for each author's alteration made and most dearly of all in the blue-line stage of production.

By creating a backwards calendar in collaboration with your staff, the designer, and the printer, you will have the time to produce a handsome brochure, one that is ready well in advance of the projected due date without trying the patience of the publisher or your staff.

Mailing the direct mail piece: The envelope

Go home this evening and count the number of personal letters you receive. Then plan your next direct mail package accordingly. Do you want your envelope to stand out, to be noticed, opened, read, acknowledged? Then approximate, as nearly as possible, a personally addressed envelope. Your in-house computing system may be able to generate addresses directly onto your envelopes, either in alphabetical, graduating class, or ZIP code order.

Key your envelope stock and color to your entire mailing package. Keep it dignified for serious mailings. But colored ink for the return address helps it stand out. New postal regulations for scanning/sorting machines limit available space, but there is still room for a logo or "teaser" on the front (e.g., "Open quickly" or "Time is running out").

The size of the envelope must conform to postal regulations, but you may want to put an eye-catching design on the front. Be sure to leave enough blank space to accommodate the largest label (the longest mailing address) and postal metering or a stamp. If you use a window envelope, consider incorporating the window into a catchy design (ring it with leaves; place a zoo animal across the window, peering inside; and so on).

The return address can be in the upper left-hand front or on the back of the envelope. The name of the person signing the letter, a distinguished alumnus or patron, lends immediate impact. (Temple University had a very successful appeal that was "sent" from Bill Cosby.)

To clean up your mailing lists, include the words "Return Requested" on the envelope twice a year. You'll pay a postal fee to receive the new address, but this will enable you to keep track of constituents when their mail forwarding orders eventually expire.

If you must use address labels, use a typeface size that allows the greatest number of letters per inch. Colored labels that exactly match your colored envelopes may minimize the depersonalization of address labels. But above all, make sure the labels are put on right. Nothing turns off a prospective donor faster than a crooked label and printed bulk indicia.

Why not meter your bulk mail? Print appropriate nonprofit clarification on the envelope; then set the meter for the proper cents and fractions. You can add a message to the postal meter to commemorate an institutional anniversary, announce an event, or promote the annual fund. This will dress up your envelope and raise it a step above general bulk mailing.

Colorful postal commemorative stamps abound. The most successful mailings today use "live" stamps, commemorating an event appropriate to the institution and/or color-coded to the color of the envelope. (One class agent we know prides himself on the fact that his letters are always opened. He uses a combination of stamps—two two-cent stamps, a three-cent, an eight-cent, and a 10-cent stamp—strung across the top of the envelope. It looks like he ran out of stamps, but it's so distinctive the recipients open it every time, and many save the stamps for their grandchildren's stamp collections.)

Many annual fund offices have budget restrictions that force them to stuff and stamp in-house, but if it is at all possible, have an outside mailing house handle your large projects. Once again, contract with the mailing house in writing. Specify the number of pieces to be mailed, number of enclosures, rate per thousand, and exact date the piece should be in the donors' mailboxes. Consult with the mailing house in the design phase. Unusually shaped enclosures require hand-stuffing at a significantly higher price per piece. Envelopes can open on the side or along the top. Be sure that the kind you order from the printer will fit the automated equipment the mailer uses.

Just before delivery of all the enclosures, give the mailing house a sample envelope, stuffed exactly the way you want it. But bear in mind that the mailing house may not be able to do it the way you would do it by hand. For example, automated equipment may preclude folding a "hanger" over one part. Try to make sure that the contents will appear in the order you want them when the recipient opens the envelope.

Be sure to give the mailing house an ample supply of your mailing, and allow for some spoilage. Ask that everything not used be returned to you. Otherwise, a zealous helper may trash your entire file supply.

Letters that work

You've designed a catchy brochure that is a mini-case statement. Those alumni who often won't read their mail have opened the envelope. They're paying attention. What happens next?

The best annual fund appeals have covering letters. You can repeat your case statement in the letter, spelling out the why, when, what, where, and how, and tailoring these in specifically personal ways.

The salutation is important. It lets the donor know the constituency in which you're placing him or her. If this is the wrong group, the recipient will be likely to write back and tell you so. Be sure to greet the reader in the singular—"Dear Alumnus...Classmate...Colleague." After all, you don't really expect two or more alumni to assemble to read the letter together.

Better yet is the personalized salutation, which has been generated by computer or mail/merge typewriter. It indicates that this isn't just another piece of junk mail. Here, too, a word of caution is in order: Proofread *every* name and triple-check for accuracy; you'll quickly destroy credibility if there's a wrong nickname or, heaven forbid, a computer blurb ("Dear The Honorable," "Dear Retired Air Force General Smith"). Always send these in "typed" envelopes with live stamps.

If you can't address each letter personally, at least try to segment them to include appropriate recognition of donors' gift history (regular contributors, members of special gift clubs, lapsed donors, "never-evers").

The most important section in each letter may well be the last. Prospective donors read in a variety of ways: They skim, read back to front, or read only the first few words of each paragraph. They almost certainly look ahead to see who is writing to them. The choice of signer is always important. Donors want to identify with an important colleague; they are flattered to have an association, however tenuous, with someone famous.

Curiosity about the signator lends preeminence to the postscript: It's graphically visible and physically set apart. Use the "P.S." for your most important emphases; summarize the purpose and urgency of the entire letter. This may be the only part that the prospect actually reads.

The letter must be written from the signator's point of view; it must sound like him or her but relate personally to the recipient. If you're drafting the letter for someone else to sign, be sure that this person approves what you have written.

The first or lead sentence is critical. Create immediate interest. Keep it short. Capture the reader's attention. Identify your theme or purpose.

Next, state the need: Educate, tell why you are writing. Again, include an "emergency"—a sense of urgency to evoke a quick response (*when*). If none exists, use a special event, anniversary, reunion, or inauguration of a new president.

Include the promise of success: State the problem, but offer a solution by means of the donor's gift (*how*); make the donor feel personally important, confident that his or her dollars will be well spent. Encourage the donor's confidence and trust, and ask for his or her help.

Put yourself and the signator in the donor's shoes: "We thought you would be interested to know...," "All of us who are graduates..." (*why*). Use "you" rather than "I" and ask only questions that can be answered by "yes." Give a choice, both options of which are positive. Never apologize or scold, but urge the prospect to jump on the bandwagon. In fund raising, redundancy is a virtue. You're not the only thing on your prospect's mind that day or the only cause he or she supports. So repeat your message several times.

Ask for money. Do it early. Do it often. Include your overall goal, but ask for an amount in a specific range (*what*). Encourage the prospect to join a donor gift club or to increase his or her gift to a new level. Tell nondonors that their gifts do matter. Tell lapsed donors that their gifts have been missed.

Consider the style and format of your letter. It should be friendly, easy to read, and enjoyable. Include enough white space to avoid claustrophobia, and always be sure that thoughts and sentences flow. Lead the reader cleverly toward the end. Keep it simple, clear, and easy to scan so that he or she will want to read more carefully. Is it typed cleanly; is it elegant-looking, worthy of your institution?

How long should it be? As long as it takes. Long letters do work, but they push postage costs higher. Be sure to break pages in the middle of a sentence or thought; this will force the reader to turn to the next page.

For the final test, put your letter aside for a while. Then produce it as it will appear and mail it to yourself. Pretend to be an innocent prospect. As you sort your mail, does the envelope get past the first cut? After you have scanned the letter, do the contents survive the wastebasket?

If so and if you've personalized each letter, consider making photocopies of each finished one. In two months, repeat the mailing to the people who haven't responded. A short message printed across the top corner or a covering note reminds them: "Perhaps you haven't had an opportunity to respond yet, but...."

The reply mechanism

Whether a business-reply envelope, simple card, or sheet of paper, the reply mechanism is the key to getting a response to your direct mail. It must be compatible with the rest of the package, and the size and color of ink are important. Colored paper or ink helps it stand out in a group of bills to be paid. To lend greater importance, have it return-addressed to an individual—the chair of the board or of the annual fund, for example.

Keep the request for information simple; if it's too complicated or detailed, donors won't want to respond. Yet be sure to ask for what you need:
- the name by which the donor prefers to be listed;
- the name used in college, class, or year as it appears on your records;
- affiliation (alumnus, parent, friend);
- anonymity or permission to print ("We will plan to list your name...unless you so indicate here");
- matching gift eligibility ("My employer has a matching gift program. Enclosed is my signed matching gift form"); and

• planned giving inquiry ("I would like to discuss the advantages of a life income gift").

Do you use this envelope to gather news for the alumni magazine? If so, allow enough space to ensure that the glue on the reply envelope won't obscure any handwritten return.

Finally, be sure to include, in smaller print, reminders of when your fiscal year ends and the extent of income tax deductibility.

Debate continues over the advantages of using postage-paid business-reply envelopes. One option is to omit the postal permit and let the donor pay the postage. Or you could use a business-reply envelope, but include the statement, "Your stamp on this envelope saves us money." (However, you must save these envelopes and take them to the local postmaster for refunds.)

You may want to test this for yourself, but "live" stamps affixed to reply envelopes do outdraw business-reply mail.

Acknowledgments

The dollars are flowing in. Congratulations on a successful direct mail presentation. But don't forget the importance of your acknowledgment; it should also be part of your package or theme. We sometimes feel that donors hold their breath to see how quickly and enthusiastically we respond. Ideal turnaround time between receipt of a check and mailing of the acknowledgment is 48 hours. That's the ideal, but it's not so easy to accomplish.

Modern technology makes it possible to computer-generate distinguished looking receipts with gracious messages. If the donor's gift history accompanies this (for in-house use only), annual giving officers can immediately assess results and also send personal thank-yous, when appropriate.

For donors of smaller gifts, print a standard acknowledgment letter or card, preferably over the signature of the person who signed the original letter. The standard acknowledgment could continue the year-long theme or logo. For more generous gifts, the development staff could draft personal letters to recognize special results. For example, you could use letters to:
• welcome donors into a gift club;
• thank donors for a first or an increased gift;
• thank donors whose gifts have triggered corporate matches or remind eligible donors to send in their matching gift forms.

An additional handwritten note or letter from the president bodes well for future major gifts from your supporters. Everyone wants to be appreciated; you can never say thanks too often.

Evaluating success

Remember to record the number of appeals you actually mail. For multi-appeals, code business-reply envelopes (colored mark, difference in printed typeface, or a code number printed on the back). Keep computer records of the appeal that generated each gift. Then compile statistics on the percentage of return from each appeal. Which were the most effective?

Test two meaningful samples and compare results. Consult colleagues in peer institutions whose appeals you've admired. Which really worked? Which seemed clever professionally, but failed to get results?

Use your results to implement change. You can then become more cost-effective. You'll plan direct mail appeals that draw best with your various constituencies.

And finally you'll know you've stretched to reach those goals by which each annual fund is ultimately measured: greater numbers of initial gifts, increased percentage of participation, increased average size of gifts, and a constituency with a long and loyal habit of contributing to your institution every year.

Notes

[1] Harold J. Seymour, *Designs for Fund-Raising* (New York: McGraw-Hill, 1966), p. 14 and chapter 3, pp. 25-33.

[2] Ibid., p. 29.

Chapter 9

Direct Mail for Special Constituencies

Susan B. Green
Director of Development
Emory University
School of Medicine
Atlanta, Georgia

D irect mail for annual giving may seem to be a panacea that can replace face-to-face fund raising with several letters each year. If only it were so easy. But direct mail can be effective when you use it to reach special groups within your institution that have identified interests in particular areas such as athletics, health care, fine arts, a school or department, or even class reunions. These prospective donors have interests that link them to the institution in a different way, and possibly a stronger way, than the general alumni population.

Once you have defined your institution's special constituencies, you can begin to build on past relationships and giving patterns to increase their annual giving. When prospects have strong interests in specific areas, their special constituency status may overshadow their more basic relationship, such as being alumni of the college or university. Sometimes a special constituency relationship is the primary continuous exposure an individual has with an institution, so it is important to build upon that particular interest rather than being more general.

While special constituency direct mail should not necessarily supersede other forms of institutional direct mail, it may be the most attractive to certain prospective donors. By capitalizing on that basic attraction, you can increase annual gifts in specific areas.

As you begin your direct mail program, it may help to break the process down into several major steps:

- research and planning;
- designing the mailing;
- follow-up; and
- evaluation.

Research and planning

You may be tempted to start your direct mail program by writing a bang-up solicitation letter. Resist this temptation. The first thing you need to do is to design an overall program based on the broad giving patterns of the donors within your special constituency. For that you need to analyze the gifts made by the constituency in the last several years. Do donors make several small gifts a year or one large gift? Do they make pledges or send gifts outright? Are pledges paid in several payments? Is there an infusion of new constituency members whose giving patterns are not yet known? Are there never-yet donors among the constituency?

When you are able to see the patterns in the giving history of your donors, you may develop several individual categories within the special constituency. You can then design specific mailings or follow-up for these different categories.

Begin with large donor prospects. You'll need to identify these people and to treat them differently. Although statistics show that direct mail is least effective in securing large gifts, it can be an important source of renewal and acquisition of gifts of as much as $1,000 or more, particularly when the constituency lives in a widespread geographic area. At the Emory Eye Center, any $500 donor whom we cannot solicit in person is put into our top direct mail category.

Emory University's Lamplighter Society is a gift club recognizing donors of $1,000 or more. For our Eye Center constituency, we adapted that club to create the Lamplighter Society of the Emory Eye Center, and we prepared a special mailing for prospects and former donors rated at that level. Our first year's appeal at that level quadrupled the number of direct mail gifts of $1,000 or more. Many of these gifts were from people who had never responded to mailings requesting gifts at lower levels.

A word of caution about gift clubs, however. If you have so many clubs or levels that it's hard even for you to keep them straight, give them up. Simplify. Most donors will be totally bamboozled by such abundance, and confusion is rarely an impetus for gift giving. Also, as development programs mature, many institutions find themselves tied historically to a gift club that recognizes a gift amount that no longer stretches the donor. A typical "Century Club" gift of $100 seldom represents a gift level that should receive the significant recognition it deserved some 15 to 20 years ago.

A number of our former patients make small gifts in response to every mailing they receive. Individually the gifts are not particularly significant, but when we looked at the total giving from these individuals each year, we determined that they were worth special appeals. For this group, we have increased the number of mailings while attempting to hold down costs. Because we can expect these people to give, we don't need to invest in special brochures or inserts that might be necessary to gain the attention of a once-a-year donor.

Good timing is essential to the success of direct mail, so plan your calendar early. When you schedule the critical dates, be sure to allow enough time to prepare special materials and have them approved, as well as time for mail to be delivered and responses received. Most fund-raising programs are designed to include two gift "deadlines"—the end of the calendar year and the end of the giving or fiscal year. If you time mailings to take advantage of these deadlines, you can add a sense of urgency to your appeals.

Consider also how your mailings fit into the overall institutional calendar and how they relate to direct mail from other parts of your institution. Be a team player. Don't insist on your mailing being the first fall appeal to alumni if it's actually targeted to a special constituency within the alumni population. But expect a little consideration in return. You can't be successful in raising funds for athletics if you miss the football season because other mail is timed first.

Because most institutions can spare neither the time nor the funds for full-scale direct mail research, we must become our own researchers. "Junk mail" is never junk to me. I read every appeal letter I can get my hands on, whether its message is to save Native American sites in New Mexico, subscribe to *Fortune* magazine, or raise research funds for the American Cancer Society. Large concerns invest in the research and staff necessary to develop direct mail that works, and you can learn a great deal from their materials.

Evaluate what these large organizations do—the look and length of their letters, postage choices, varieties and styles of inserts. Compare successive mailings, and note whether changes were made or the package stayed the same. You can bet that changes aren't the result of someone getting bored with the original package. As long as an appeal continues to draw significant responses, its use will continue.

One of the best examples of a mailing that obviously worked is a *Wall Street Journal* subscription appeal that told the story of the careers of two high school graduates—one ended up a financial success and one didn't. The story caught my imagination the first time I read it, and it has been interesting to note that, with very few changes, the same letter has been used for more than three years. How often would our institutions be willing to stick to the same appeal letter for four years, even if it were wildly successful?

Designing the mailing

Now you can write that letter.

The basic element of any direct mail program is the solicitation letter. A good letter should tell a story, and that story is infinitely easier to write if you know the interests of the recipients. Rather than sending a broad, general appeal that might be addressed to anybody, you can hone in on personal concerns and values with a letter that speaks specifically to the reader. Letters for special constituencies allow you to use more drama, stronger images, and deeper emotion than general direct mail programs usually permit.

In any direct mail pitch, the least effective motivator is "because we need the money." Citing budget deficits, referring to unrenewed research grants, or attempting to make alumni feel that they "owe" the institution—these tactics have little drawing power. In medicine, cures and progress are the strongest motivators for giving, but keep in mind the vulnerability of patients. Don't promise too much too quickly. It's important to be principled as well as effective.

Inherent in every good story is conflict. Will Scarlett lose Tara? Will Indiana Jones recover the Lost Ark? Will Dorothy get back to Kansas? Whatever conflict is described in the fund-raising letter's story should be able to be resolved, or at least helped, by the donor making a gift. "Your $500 contribution will help Miss Scarlett and her sisters turn Tara into a conference center for the university."

Several years ago, personalization of fund-raising letters seemed an absolute must. Direct mail vendors will tell you it still is, but I like to experiment with test groups in our constituency. With the advent of Publisher's Clearinghouse and *Reader's Digest* sweepstakes mailings, personalization has become so commonplace that it has lost much of its impact and credibility.

In dealing with small-gift donors, if I were faced with the choice of personalizing, sending more mailings, or adding an interesting insert, personalization would be the first to go. But when I write to our Lamplighter Society donors of $1,000 or more, I feel that personalization is a necessity. Besides, we have far fewer prospects on that list, which means the cost is not prohibitive.

As you begin to prepare your direct mail package, remember that you don't need to use everyday institutional letterhead for your letter. Although you'll want a tone and look that match the institutional image, the field is wide open when it comes to selecting papers, type styles, and sizes. What's needed are good solid design that is free of trendiness and an attractive paper/type/color combination.

Certain elements of good direct mail design apply whether your audience is a special constituency or not. Be sure to use the best quality you can buy, keeping in mind that larger type is important if your population is aging or visually impaired.

A two-page letter will almost always outpull a one-page letter, but it must be interesting. I've had great response from a three-page letter, but production costs may rise significantly. If you are printing front and back, the letterhead must be of sufficient weight so that the quality remains high and the print doesn't show through the paper.

The response device is usually the trickiest part of the mailing. Often this piece will cost far more than other inserts since you may need to have special envelopes constructed or intricate cards designed. The most important point is that the response device includes a method for tracking responses so that you can determine how the mailing succeeded in relationship to others. This can be done by printing a donor code during addressing, using different colors for the return envelopes for each mailing, or any other appropriate mechanism.

Unless you track responses, you won't learn from your mistakes. You may even repeat them. A certain type of mailing that garnered strong responses at one point may lose its effectiveness, and you may be continuing to send this type of mailing year after year, to diminishing returns, just because you don't analyze the response it actually did receive.

The response card should also tell the donor how to make out a check and where to send it. If there is no institutional rule against it, designate that the check can be written directly to your part of the institution. A far more personal link is forged when the donor writes a check to the Emory Eye Center than if he or she writes it to Emory University. And the special designation on the check will reassure those skeptical donors who might otherwise wonder if their gifts actually go where they intended them to go.

The type of postage—both on the carrier envelope and on the return envelope—is another hot topic. A carrier envelope with commemorative stamps pulls best, but if you are mailing to 50,000 people, the cost of applying commemoratives is prohibitive. Metering can be quite acceptable, especially when the carrier envelope is interesting enough in itself to get the package opened.

Likewise, as postage costs rise for BREs (business-reply envelopes), consider including a box in the upper right-hand corner of the return envelope with the statement, "Your stamp adds to your gift." It's a lot friendlier than a blank envelope, and it gently nudges the donor to give a bit more. Those small gifts add up when you consider the enormous expense of paying postage on BREs.

Brochures make great additions to a direct mail package when the budget allows, but a strong letter can produce the same results. A brochure is especially effective, however, when your subject has strong visual appeal—children, animals, athletics, or fine arts. But if the topic of your letter is one in which imagination plays a larger role—scientific research or medical treatment, for example—a good letter can create more powerful images in the mind of the reader than a brochure can show.

Although the primary purpose of direct mail is to raise funds, at the Eye Center we also use our mailings to provide former patients with continuing education on health issues. We have recently begun to include in our mailings a Briefing Letter that outlines current developments in research and clinical programs in four specific clinical areas, along with the importance of gift support. By focusing on topics of mutual concern, we develop rapport and set the stage for giving. For those patients who are unable or unwilling to make a donation after paying a fee for services at the Eye Center, we consider the newsletter to be a communication rather than a solicitation. We produce these patient Briefing Letters on our office computers and mail them in conjunction with an appeal letter, response envelope, and gift information form.

We have gotten strong responses from our former patients to these newsletters and find that the number of complaints from people who had been receiving our appeal letters has dropped to virtually zero.

Follow-up

Don't begin your mailing program without designing a specific procedure for follow-up. You may think you can deal with acknowledgment letters and the special materials they require after you have begun to receive responses, but by then it's too late. Consider the acknowledgments as part of the total project so that you'll be ready when gifts do come in, and your materials will reflect the image you have set throughout your appeal package.

Many institutions are beginning to use an acknowledgment card for donors who make smaller gifts. This seems to make sense, but there may be specific cases when you want to communicate with all donors, no matter what their level of giving. For example, you may want to share specific information with these donors. A "P.S." at the bottom of an acknowledgment carries the same punch that it does in the basic appeal letter, so think about adding that special message.

Most institutions have a schedule of acknowledgment letters that designates who signs letters for gifts at various dollar levels. Often these "canned" letters are computer-generated and include different messages for friends, businesses, foundations, alumni, and special constituency categories.

At Emory University all donors of $1,000 or more get a personalized acknowledgment letter (not merely a personally typed letter with the donor's name in the salutation). These acknowledgment letters include a sentence or two that is personal and meant just for them.

A former colleague of mine was a real stickler for personalization of letters. He believed that just one personal sentence could make the whole letter sound as if it were written for that particular person. Although I initially questioned why I should spend so much time digging through files to find something that would help me write that one personal sentence, I soon learned the value of my efforts. Now it's second nature for me to personalize acknowledgment letters, and that practice has resulted in some wonderful responses from donors.

Some easy personalizations might include an acknowledgment of an upcoming class reunion (if the class year indicates it would be appropriate) or even an invitation to a special out-of-town activity for a donor living in that city. For former patients, we often describe new treatments or clinical advances for the patient's area of interest or special news of his or her physician. If you have a personal relationship with a donor, the acknowledgment letter is a way to build on information you already have and say the kinds of things you know that particular donor will find interesting.

The envelope for the acknowledgment letter can also serve as a convenient carrier for other information. It's the perfect opportunity to send your most committed special constituency members an informal calender of upcoming events or a notice about an important happening.

You might also enclose special information about the program you represent—a brag sheet or facts brochure designed to fit into the envelope with your letter. Printing it to correspond with your acknowledgment stationery or cards can make a most attractive package.

Acknowledgment is just the beginning of your follow-up process. It's also important to stay in contact with donors. If you're dealing with huge numbers, you may have to whittle this group down to top givers. At the Eye Center, we try to stay in touch with all donors of $1,000 or more a year. Periodically, when an important story about an Eye Center topic has been in the newspaper or in one of the university's prize-winning magazines, we send our Lamplighter donors a copy of the story accompanied by a note from our department chair stating, "As one of our valued Lamplighter donors, you may enjoy this story about the Emory Eye Center." It's a quick, easy, and inexpensive way to stay in touch.

Evaluation

In this age of cost-effectiveness, we tend to judge direct mail only by the dollars it raises. Ultimately, of course, that is the most important consideration. But other factors are also significant.

If a mailing was designed to be educational as well as gift-producing, did it work? Were there fewer complaints, fewer repeated calls for information? Were individual recipients pleased with the mailing? Did they understand it? Did they find it attractive? Was it in keeping with the constituency's image of the institution?

Talk to donors and find out what they like and what they don't like. Make individual telephone calls or, if you have the resources, do a full-blown survey. The more you learn, the more effective your program will be. When possible, use some of the survey results on a test group in your next cycle of direct mail. The timing should be convenient since you will be beginning to plan the next cycle of mailings at the time you are surveying the first.

The over-arching concern in evaluating direct mail for special constituencies is whether giving actually increases if you manage this segment differently from the way you manage the general population. If responses are positive, then you've probably defined your constituency accurately and the segmentation has been effective. If after two years or so of segmenting, you can't see any significant increase in giving from this group, you need to reconsider your approach.

My prediction is that if you have sufficient staff and funds and if you are careful to define the constituency well, overall fund raising should increase dramatically, providing important new funds to your annual giving program.

Chapter 10

Phonathons: Improving The Return on Your Investment

Mark H. O'Meara
Consultant
Fairfax, Virginia
(Formerly Director of Annual Giving, Alfred University, Alfred, New York)

L et's face it: Phonathons are an integral part of any advancement program. In effectiveness, phonathons are second only to face-to-face solicitation, and amounts raised constitute a large component of the annual fund. Phonathons can be small or large, broad based or project specific, on campus or regional; they can run all year or last only a few days, involve hundreds of people or just a few. The bottom line is that they work, and they won't be replaced any time soon.

Advantages of phonathons

The most common reasons for conducting phonathons are to raise money cost-effectively, solicit those prospects you cannot visit personally, and reach a large percentage of your constituencies with a format that you can control from start to finish. In addition, there is no better way to update records, get feedback ("How're we doing?"), raise the sights of your donors, pass on an important message from the president, conduct prospect research, survey reactions to new campus policies, do networking, find prospective students, or maintain a "surefire" alumni outreach program.

The solicitor need not be neat and tidy, young, handsome, or "dressed for success"; the only qualities desired are that he or she be sincere, energetic, and willing to ask for a donation. The involvement of any or all campus constituencies during a phonathon will improve the image of the annual fund office, help validate your existence on campus ("So *that's* what those people do"), and provide a proving ground for future volunteers.

Once you have made the commitment to initiate a phonathon or strengthen the one you have, the debate begins. Should you use volunteer callers (students and/or alumni), paid callers, a telemarketing firm, or any combination of the three?

All three methods have merit and should be used to best meet the needs of your annual fund. At Alfred University we incorporated all three methods to contact over 10,000 alumni in five weeks.

Advantages of volunteer callers

Using volunteer callers during a campus phonathon has a dramatic impact on how the campus perceives the annual fund. There is no better way to make the case that the annual fund is vitally important and really does help provide campus improvements.

Students learn that the funds raised help support their scholarships, that tuition doesn't cover all the expenses, and that many alumni are proud to give to their alma mater. When these students become alumni, they will better understand the importance of supporting the annual fund. Faculty and staff learn the value of the annual fund and get to renew old friendships. Fund-raising activities motivate them to sign up for payroll deduction.

Remember, volunteers can be quite effective if trained properly, encouraged a lot, and enabled to work in an atmosphere that is stimulating and positive. Their involvement translates into long-term loyalty for the annual fund.

The key factor is to make the campus phonathon "an event." Pizza, soda, balloons, bells to ring when a pledge is secured, door prizes, competition among residence halls and Greeks, free T-shirts, free phone calls home, and lots of energized coordinators in the room make for a successful volunteer calling session. By creating a campuswide program, you gain visibility for the annual fund, its location, and its purpose, and you establish the time of year everyone can expect the phonathon to take place.

During Alfred's parent telethon, the campus radio station broadcasts live at the phonathon house for four evenings. The callers make their pitch and then ask the parents (who have been forewarned) if they want to send a message to their son or daughter over the radio (whether or not they pledged). The results are fantastic. The radio station gets great campus exposure, and all the parents feel good about receiving the call.

All volunteers, including alumni at regional phonathons, become personally involved and have a sense of ownership in the annual fund. In addition, they get to see immediate results of their efforts in the evening's tally. As they secure pledges, alumni interest increases, and they develop a better understanding of institutional goals and greater support of all fund-raising efforts.

Advantages of paid callers

Another phonathon goal is to solicit as many people as possible. Here the paid caller can play an important role. Staff can screen and hire the best caller prospects and provide extensive training. All of this results in better job performance. Ultimately, the callers will make more contacts, be thorough in paperwork details, handle difficult calls with care, and be more persuasive with those who initially refuse to pledge. The more they call, the better they get. Staff do not have to worry about volunteer "no-shows." Another big advantage of paid callers is that you can fire those who don't work out. Staff also feel good about putting students to work and helping them through college with jobs.

Advantages of third-party callers

Since volunteers *and* paid callers resist calling never-givers, one option is to ship these prospects off to a telemarketing firm. If you have the budget, it is a reasonable alternative and allows the campus phonathon to focus on better prospects. (See the next chapter for more on this subject.)

In summary, any one of the three types of callers alone or combined may produce good results for the annual fund. Depending on your budget, calendar, and the amount of commitment of your staff, you can compose a phoning effort that fits the needs of your institution and has far-reaching effects on the campus perception of the annual fund program.

Preparation

An important part of any phonathon happens well before the first call is made. Your primary objective is to organize, by computer if possible, prospect cards that contain the following basic information:

• name (and maiden name if married), address, business title and address, spouse work information (for gift match), campus identification number, selection criteria identification number for tracking;

• year of graduation, major (or college), Greek affiliation;

• giving history for at least three years including date of gifts and in response to what appeal (annual fund, capital campaign, etc.) and which mailing; response to previous phonathons;

• tear-off pledge acknowledgment form (to be mailed next day) to include identification number and year of graduation, gift match appeal, and space for donor to write in alumni news and to fill in credit card information or other billing instructions if pledge will be paid in installments;

• space for caller actions—no answer, answering machine, no direct contact (got the babysitter, etc.), date of call, caller's name, space for comments on call and for messages to other alumni or campus friends; and

• tear-off section for data entry staff to record new information (for legibility it's best to have one person transcribe from all caller notes to this form).

The database should be set up so you can use several different criteria to select prospects to call. These include LYBUNTs (gave last year but unfortunately not this), SYBUNTs (gave some years but unfortunately not this), nondonors (however the institution defines this), lapsed (gave in one of the last five years but not last year), previous year donors (separate by giving club levels), and never-ever givers.

Any of these prospective donor groups can be segmented by era or class, graduate or nongraduate, major, giving history, occupation, ZIP code, and so on. The more you segment your prospects, the better you can prepare your callers and track results. For example, a consistent $25 donor living on Long Island, New York, with an impressive job title, who graduated with a business degree in the early '60s, played football, and was a Greek, ought to be moved up in giving club level with a more specialized ask.

Next, you should have a phonathon theme to rally the campus and alumni. Use special stationery, posters, and banners, and place ads in the alumni news and school paper. Your promotion should point out the benefits of participating (free calls home seem to be the most popular, with food and a T-shirt running a close second), which will also enhance your recruitment of callers.

Setting the stage

The pre-call letter is an important step in a phonathon. It can provide information that you cannot relate by phone, either because of the brevity of the conversation, the complexity of the material, or the need to offer visual descriptions. These pre-call letters have many purposes.

• They announce the phoning effort;
• They state your case;
• They describe the uses of the gift; and
• They ask for a specific amount and refer to the giving club levels.

The letter also eliminates the "cold call" aspect of the solicitation, since the prospect will know in advance about the phoning effort. Some institutions include a business-reply envelope with the pre-call letter; this enables donors to respond by giving via the mail. The prospective donor should receive the pre-call letter a few days before he or she is contacted by phone. The letter should be as long as it takes to accomplish the purposes mentioned above. Be sure the letter is written in a style that fits the institution and is familiar to the reader.

Caller selection and training

Whether you use volunteer or paid callers, caller selection and training are crucial to the phonathon's success. Surprisingly, there are more and more college students who have already had some sort of telemarketing experience. Students with a high energy level and engaging personality and who know what's happening on campus are usually excellent candidates to be callers. Still, they need the perspective that only the staff can give them in a thorough orientation.

For best results, you should hold the orientation over two or more evenings, since you will need to cover a lot of information. The introductory session should include discussion of development programs for higher education and of the shop at your institution. Focus on answering the following questions:

1. Why have a phonathon?
2. How does it work?
3. Why do people give?
4. What is the annual fund?
5. What are the goals for your annual fund, and how does the phonathon fit in?
6. What role does the caller play?

Ask the trainees to articulate the reasons they believe others should give. Then have them use those statements as testimonials during the call.

If you use alumni volunteers as callers, always ask them to make their pledges before they start phoning. Then they can tell those with whom they talk that they have already made their own commitment.

The second session can address the mechanics of the call. In addition, you can use role-playing methods to make sample calls.

Some of the mechanics of calling include:

• asking for the right person;

• using the first 10 seconds of the call to make a positive impression: This involves stating the purpose of the call and then listening to the prospect's response;

• establishing a rapport: Ask donors questions to clarify the information printed on their cards or to identify their interests, and the conversation will develop accordingly;

• asking for a specific amount: A high first ask leaves room to negotiate or "deflect" objections, with a chance to mention giving club levels, installment payments, and so on;

• listening to what the prospect is saying: Instruct callers on how to handle difficult calls and how to wait for a response before speaking;

• asking for messages to deliver to people on campus (faculty-grams are a good idea) and for news for the alumni magazine; reconfirming the pledge and the donor's address and work information (to determine if the donor's gift is eligible for a match); instructing donors that they'll receive a confirmation; and saying "thank you."

Support materials

All callers should have a script. The main function of the script is to help the caller get the prospect to the phone and establish rapport within the first 10 seconds. The script should include the annual fund goal, the ask, the negotiation, the close, and several thank-yous. While the script serves as a guide and helps provide focus, under no circumstances should the caller read it to the prospect.

Some institutions print the script on a placemat for each caller. The phone is placed on one side and around it blocks of copy describe the annual fund, uses of gifts, gift club levels and benefits, new programs on campus, the phonathon goal, and any special gift promotions. Other items unique to the institution may also be helpful.

The calling session

The atmosphere must be energized, positive, and upbeat for all callers. Don't forget that callers need incentives and variety to keep up the pace. Volunteer callers especially need pats on the back. They need constant encouragement including responses to all questions, even those already covered in training.

One effective way to lighten the callers' responsibilities (especially those of volunteers) is to employ several "roving supervisors" who move around the room from caller to caller. Supervisors can conduct training, handle emergencies, and verify pledges and addresses by finishing calls. This method assures donors that the institution takes their pledges seriously and has helped to increase pledge fulfillment. It also relieves the staff of routine duties with the callers.

Style of the call

Callers should use a style that allows them to be themselves while incorporating some or all of the following:

- The caller should be polite, considerate, and upbeat. He or she is the institution's representative and should act professionally. Alumni in particular respond well to students' honesty.
- The caller should not apologize. He or she is performing a noble service in raising money for the institution.
- The caller should encourage donors to give. It is not the caller's duty to judge the capacity of the donor to give to the institution, but only to encourage his or her willingness to give.
- The caller should treat the donor as a friend.
- The caller should leave the donor with a positive feeling and a sense of pride in the institution, regardless of the results.

Callers should be monitored for ineffective calling skills. Callers who are not good on the phone could be reassigned to research telephone numbers, stuff pledge cards, keep statistics, and so on.

Recordkeeping

Accurate and extensive recordkeeping is important in evaluating phonathons. Tracking the results of the various solicitations helps identify areas that need attention. New criteria for selection should be sought and tested. For example, if you monitor the contact rates for prospects over 65, you may learn that daytime calls are more effective than evening calls.

Phonathon tallies should include total number of prospects, total contacted, dollars pledged, average pledge per contact, pledge rate of contacts, number of pledges, refusals, and "will considers." You should keep these same statistics on a daily and weekly basis within donor, nondonor, lapsed, and LYBUNT and SYBUNT populations (and any other groups you choose, such as $25 or less donors, nongrads, Greeks, and professionals). Keep a separate record for the results of volunteer callers as a group and individual paid callers.

Budget

Costs may include caller salaries and bonuses, mailing costs, printed forms, promotional materials, equipment rental and toll calls, space rental, prizes for competitions, and food. Don't forget to consider staff salaries for time spent on the phonathon as well as travel to and from regional sites, volunteer recruitment efforts, and proportionate departmental overhead. The average cost per dollar raised is usually between 12-25 cents for solicitations by phonathon.

Goal setting

Two major aims of the phonathon solicitation are to move previous year donors up in average gift each year and to acquire new donors. You can monitor previous year donor behavior as a group by comparing their overall responses this year to their respective responses last year. Donor upgrade (for the previous year donor population) should not fall below "0" and ideally should show a 2-7 percent increase each year.

Bringing new donors on board helps strengthen and broaden your donor base as well as increase the participation rate of donors to the annual fund. The number of years you have been calling your constituents impacts on the number of nondonors who can be successfully solicited. Several years of asking without results may suggest that you consider "resting" those names for a year or two.

The size of the phonathon goal is different for every institution. New phonathons can expect relatively high pledge rates and rapid growth in the early years, while long-running phonathons can expect more modest growth.

When you are setting a goal, consider these factors: the number and type of prospects you wish to contact, their previous gift history, and your institution's previous success rate with such efforts. Another item to be considered is how long you plan to run the phoning program. Obviously, the longer the program lasts, the more dollars you will raise, but you have to have the resources to support such an effort. The staff commitment to the phonathon has an impact on the size of the goal as well as its success.

You will need to establish pledge rates or response goals before calling begins. As a general guide, 75-80 percent of previous year donors should make a pledge. On the other hand, 30-40 percent of the lapsed prospects and 12-20 percent of the nondonors should respond positively. Many factors will affect these rates, including the type, size, and history of your institution's constituency.

Pledge fulfillment

Ensuring that pledges are fulfilled takes a good deal of effort, but it has an impact on the success of the phonathon. Installment requests should be honored. Mail monthly reminders in the middle of the month preceding the due date so donors receive them in time to pay bills on the first of the month. Follow-up reminder calls can be most helpful at the 90-day past due mark. We've found it effective to send a letter asking if the donor had succumbed to the "cookie jar theory" (putting the reminder under the cookie jar and forgetting about it).

Depending on the type of caller base, length of time of the phonathon, and extent of the follow-up, your pledge fulfillment rate should be no lower than 70 percent. Interesting statistics to watch are the number of people who pay more or less than their original pledge and the number and average gift of those who did not originally make a firm commitment (the "will considers"). These numbers can help you plan your goal for next year.

Conclusion

Every year phonathons become more sophisticated in their approach. And every year there are more worthy groups and organizations conducting telephone solicitations, so the competition for "quality time" on the phone is fierce. What makes your annual fund phonathon successful is the way in which you notify your prospects, make your case, train and inspire your callers, record your results, and collect your pledges.

Whether you use paid or volunteer, student, alumni, or third-party callers, your program can be a success. Whatever your process, phonathons are an important means of securing gifts for the annual fund and carry a high return on investment. Focus on the strengths of your institution in planning your phonathon, and you will have a winner.

Chapter 11

Who's Calling My Alumni? Using Professional Telemarketing Consultants

Molly Mayo Tampke
Director of Development for Student Affairs
University of Illinois at Urbana-Champaign
Champaign, Illinois

For most institutions the question is not *whether* to call alumni for annual funds campaigns, but *who* will make the calls. Launching a telemarketing campaign to all your alumni, no matter what size your constituency, is a major undertaking. Many institutions today are deciding it is too big an undertaking to do on their own, and they're bringing in outside consultants for this purpose. In many cases, these companies can complete more calls, produce more and higher pledges, and provide more sophisticated analysis about alumni than in-house programs can.

Is a telemarketing firm the answer for your institution? This chapter will help you make that decision.

Why consider a telemarketing consultant?

Before you even catch the eye of a telemarketing representative at your next CASE district conference, you need to decide whether professional telemarketing fits into your overall development program and, more specifically, your annual giving program.

First, consider the attitude of your administration toward telemarketing. The deans and chancellor on your campus may be enthusiastic fans of telemarketing.

Or they may feel that direct mail is as aggressive as they want to get. The administration's attitude will help determine if and how you choose an outside consultant.

You should also examine your staff's philosophy about the use of paid versus volunteer callers and students versus professionals. Many development officers believe strongly in the practice of building future donors by recruiting student volunteers to call. Many also believe strongly in the good feelings engendered by student callers and are willing to sacrifice the potentially higher gifts obtained by professional firms for the interaction between alumni and students.

Staff and financial resources are vital factors in determining what your telemarketing program should be. If you already have a phonathon, how much staff time is devoted to it? What does the program cost per year? (Count everything from stamps to caller training materials; a professional firm will charge for these and similar items.)

If you do not already have a phonathon program, establishing one may require hiring new staff and buying new equipment. Can you afford it?

Finally, you need to look at the size of your constituency and your time constraints. Even an alumni base of 3,000 may require weeks of calling to reach just half your prospects.

Choosing a telemarketing firm: Off-site vs. on-site

Once you have determined that using a telemarketing firm is the route for you, you must decide whether to select on-site or off-site consultants.

On-site consultants. On-site telemarketing consultants call from your facility. They use your students as callers and tailor the program to fit your campus environment. An on-site telemarketer may appeal to you if you want to use your own students and be able to play an active role in the telemarketing program without running it completely.

The primary benefit of on-site firms is that they hire your students as callers. Thus, you retain that valuable student-to-alumni communication. Your callers are also the "product"; they know the institution and, to many alumni, they *are* the institution. The actual contract arrangement—are the students working for you or for the consultant?—will vary according to the telemarketer and the institution. What will be most valuable to you is the firm's role in hiring, training, and supervising the callers. Because of their experience, professional telemarketing firms can organize a program more efficiently than can a staff which also has myriad other responsibilities.

In particular, a telemarketing consultant knows:
• the number of callers needed for your constituency;
• the number of interviews and the amount of time required to hire that number of callers; and
• the anticipated turnover rate of the calling staff.

Finally, the professional telemarketer understands and is prepared for the complexities of caller supervision.

On-site telemarketing consultants offer other advantages. They have worked with many different kinds of databases and will be able to quickly understand and work with your system. Thus, the firm can help you anticipate and solve problems you may encounter in producing calling materials and reports.

Hiring a consultant to build a program on your campus may be exactly what you want to do. There are a few disadvantages to on-site consultants, however. For example, the primary benefit—using student callers—can also be your biggest limitation. Even with the best training, student callers are still just that: students who devote a few hours each week to calling alumni. While you will no doubt find some outstanding fund raisers among your students, they will have many competing and time-consuming priorities in their lives. In addition, their tenure in your program will almost always be shorter than that of a professional caller working for an off-site consultant. Shorter tenure means less experience, and in telemarketing that can translate into fewer dollars and lower participation rates.

Another disadvantage of on-site telemarketing is that your callers are limited by your phone equipment. For example, on-line automatic dialing greatly increases the number of calls that can be made in a night. Most development programs, however, are limited to push-button phones and thus must operate more slowly. This means your students can make fewer calls and obtain fewer pledges.

Depending on your database, the sophistication of your reports may also be limited. With off-site telemarketers, you will probably have access to state-of-the-art software and hardware that can provide you with more detailed and sophisticated reports. While an on-site telemarketing firm can help you use your present system more creatively, you may still be limited to the same basic kinds of information you have always had.

Finally, if your goal in hiring a professional firm is to reduce the staff time devoted to telemarketing, think twice about an on-site program. Having the firm on campus can take much more time than you anticipate. It will be hard to ignore the presence of "new" staff members, even if they are only temporary. You will want to visit the program frequently to make sure it is running smoothly and that the pledges are coming in.

Off-site consultants. Off-site consultants design a program to fit your specific needs, but the actual work of calling takes place at their facility. This aspect is both the best and the worst point of off-site telemarketing.

In most cases, callers for off-site consultants spend many more hours per week on the phone than student callers can. These hours translate into more experience and thus higher pledges for your program. The professional caller has encountered most objections or refusals before and knows how to address them.

This experience can also be helpful as you explore new aspects of your constituency. For example, professional callers are less intimidated by hard-core never-givers or by major prospects, so you may want to use a telemarketing firm to explore these opposite ends of your constituency. For the same reason, a telemarketing firm may be ideal to develop a new constituency such as parents. Most likely, the firm has solicited parents before and its callers know how best to approach this constituency.

Most professional telemarketing firms use sophisticated equipment that allows their callers to dial faster and make more calls per night. As a result, an off-site consultant may contact a greater proportion of your alumni in a much shorter period than an in-house program can. Thus, the campaign itself is shorter.

A major advantage of off-site telemarketing firms is their computer support systems. The best firms use advanced equipment that enables them to produce sophisticated reports more quickly than most campus programs can. In the short term, this advantage allows these firms to produce detailed reports nightly. These reports, combined with on-line equipment, can give you the information and ability to adjust your campaign immediately if necessary. In the long run, an off-site firm can provide you with more detailed information about your constituency. These statistics can enable you to set better and more exact strategies.

Using an off-site consultant can also require less staff time. You will, of course, spend much time creating the telemarketing program with the firm, and you will probably want to visit the site during the campaign. You may even be fortunate enough to work with a consultant whose equipment allows you to monitor calls from your office. But you will not spend as much time on the day-to-day details of telemarketing with an off-site consultant as you will with an in-house program.

Freeing up staff time is a primary benefit of going off-site. But it has its downside too. Because you will not be with the callers and supervisors on a regular basis, you will give up some control. Ideally, you will have built a good, open relationship with your consultants and can trust them. For many people, however, even the best relationship cannot substitute for day-to-day control.

Choosing a telemarketing consultant

The demand for professional telemarketing in the nonprofit sector is growing rapidly, and telemarketing firms are flourishing. There are more companies competing for your business than ever before. This competition places you in a wonderful position to find a firm that can meet your institution's specific needs.

But the fact that it's a buyer's market does not mean that you can sit back and wait for the perfect firm to offer you the perfect proposal. You also need to do your homework.

Once you have decided that consultant telemarketing fits into your program, look at both on- and off-site firms. Ask each prospect for a complete list of clients; if a firm hesitates or refuses to provide you with a list of referrals, cross that company off your list.

Call the clients and ask them about their experiences with the firm. Specifically, ask what the firm's projections were on contact rate, pledge rate, average pledge, cost, and so on. Did the firm meet those projections and, if not, why? As you talk to a firm's clients you may see patterns emerge that will give you good reasons either to accept or reject that company's proposal.

Ask the firm about its success rate in meeting its projections. Does its answer come close to those of its clients?

Request scripts and pre-call and acknowledgment letters from other campaigns the firm has done. The telemarketers will want to retain some confidentiality, so ask them to blank out the institutions' names. What you are looking for is general style: Are the scripts too aggressive for you? Do you like the tone of the pre-call letters? While you can work with the consultant on the details of your program, the tone of these different pieces will give you an idea of the firm's general philosophy and approach.

In addition to assessing the credibility and experience of the firm, evaluate the staff personally. In particular, get to know as well as you can the specific people with whom you will be working. Do they have a clear understanding of both fund raising *and* telemarketing? Can they explain clearly all the functions of their firm? Have they worked with a variety of institutions? Are you comfortable with the people with whom you will be dealing daily?

Finally, watch the firm in action. If it is an on-site telemarketer, arrange to visit a client institution with a program and constituency that closely resemble yours. If the consultant is off-site, visit the facility. Whatever you do, do not decide on a telemarketing consultant until you have seen the firm's callers at work. Glowing client recommendations and a firm's PR materials are no substitute for listening to callers during a real campaign.

Working with the telemarketing firm

During your search process, you made clear to the consultant your philosophy and goals for your telemarketing program. Now it is time to put those goals and philosophy into action.

As you plan your campaign, you must retain control of the program. You have hired a consultant to relieve you of many of the day-to-day details, but you cannot turn every decision over to the firm. You must make sure that you are intimately involved with the major aspects of the campaign. There are five key areas where your involvement is crucial:

1. *The pre-call letter.* The consultant may use a professional writer to compose the pre-call letter. Take full advantage of this wonderful service, but work closely with the writer to make sure that both the tone and the text of the letter are appropriate to your institution and the signer of the letter.

2. *The script.* The ability to create a successful script should be a primary criterion in selecting your consultant. Use this expertise and experience, but make sure you are comfortable with the language and the level of assertiveness in the script. The script should accurately reflect your philosophy and goals and be appropriate to any special needs of your constituency.

3. *Caller training.* Your consultant will probably want you to be intimately involved with this part of the program. It will be up to you to supply the facts and figures of your institution in order to educate the callers as thoroughly as possible. You will also want to attend as many of the training sessions as you can in order to meet the callers and answer their questions.

4. *Supervising the project.* No matter where the calling location is, you and your staff will want to visit the facility periodically. You will want to listen in on calls and talk to the callers so you can get a feel for the comments and questions they are hearing from your alumni.

5. *Follow-up.* As you plan with your consultant, consider the tasks that will be required after the campaign. After the telemarketing is over, your office will be responsible for follow-up support. Does your office have an efficient system for pledge reminders, acknowledgments, requests for information, and the multitude of other tasks that are part of successful telemarketing? You also want to think about the long-term results of your telemarketing project. What will the next campaign look like? How will you use the information the telemarketing firm gathers about your prospects?

As you plan your telemarketing campaign, you may feel that the firm is being inflexible at times. Remember that the company's suggestions are supported by a variety of experiences in telemarketing, and you are paying for that experience and expertise. But don't lose control. If, after listening to your consultant and giving an issue thorough consideration, you and your staff are still uncomfortable with the firm's recommendation, follow your instincts. It's your program, they're your alumni, and you have to live with the results.

Q&A

Here are some questions to consider as you decide who will call *your* alumni.

1. *How much does a consultant cost?* Telemarketing firms list charges in a variety of ways, most of which are described in ratios. Each ratio depends on what is being counted. Some of the ratios about which you will hear the most are:

• cost per complete: This is the cost per completed call, that is, the cost to have a phone number answered. This figure describes how much it costs to find out what phone numbers are good, who has died, and, of course, who has pledged. Basically, this ratio tells you how much it costs to clean up your records. In many programs, this is a much-needed service.

• cost per contact: The "contact" is the alumnus; thus, this ratio describes the cost of actually talking to an alumnus and receiving a pledge decision. This charge is higher than the cost per complete.

• cost per pledge: What are you paying for each pledge? This will be your highest cost. To increase your accuracy, ask your consultant to break this number down into cost per specified pledge, cost per unspecified pledge, cost per pledge from new donors, and cost per pledge from previous donors.

As you review the telemarketer's numbers, remember that cost ratios increase as the "universe" they include decreases. That is, the more specific the information you get, the more you pay for it. Remember, too, that you are not just paying for pledges; you are also paying for cleaned up records, new ideas for segmentation, and more.

2. *What will I be paying for?* Again, it depends. You may decide to have the con-

sultant do everything: produce the stationery, send your phone numbers to a matching service that can research and update them, send pledge reminders, and so on. Or you may decide that you can do some of these things yourself more economically. A good telemarketing firm will help you decide on the most cost-efficient way to distribute the work.

Because of the wide variation in types of programs and combinations of services offered by professional telemarketing firms, cost ratio estimates will differ for each firm and for each campaign.

3. *Won't it annoy or even anger my alumni to be called by "hired guns"?* Negative reaction to "outside" or paid callers is minimal. Few alumni ask exactly who is calling them. Fewer still care whether the caller is a paid student or not a student at all. You will get a few complaints—it happens with any telemarketing campaign—but the number of upgrades and new gifts easily outweighs the complaints.

Conclusion

For many programs, professional telemarketing consultants are the ideal way to temporarily expand a development staff. Before you hire an outside consultant, however, do your homework: Know who is out there and what they can offer you. The professional telemarketer's experience and expertise, combined with your knowledge of your constituency, can result in more and larger gifts now and a new understanding of your institution's alumni that can lead to continued growth well into the future.

Thanks to Charles W. Ashford, assistant vice president, Telecom ★USA Direct; Denise Jackson, director of annual giving and stewardship, Texas Tech University; Lynette L. Marshall, director of resource development, College of Agriculture, University of Illinois at Urbana-Champaign; Michael Satterfield, assistant director, Region 9, American Heart Association (former director of the Telefund, Indiana University); James C. Schroeder, associate dean, College of Liberal Arts and Sciences, University of Illinois at Urbana-Champaign; and Kit Trensch, development coordinator, University of Georgia.

Chapter 12

Making the Call

Richard B. Eason
Vice President for Development
Southwestern University
Georgetown, Texas

T*he future is purchased by the present*—Samuel Johnson.
Many people perceive fund-raising professionals as "seekers of money" rather than "agents for the empowerment of givers," and unfortunately many in our profession contribute to this misperception. In fact, ours is a service-oriented occupation. We are engaged in empowering people to give. We are facilitators of our prospects' charitable aspirations. If that sounds as if I believe we are professionals who do great favors for our donors, you're right: I do!

The keys to success

There are four keys to success in our profession: commitment, knowledge, skills, and practice. You must have **commitment** if you are to succeed in this profession—or in any other for that matter. The committed professional will seek the knowledge, sharpen the skills, and practice the tenets of our profession.

Knowledge is power. You must have knowledge to help those you serve make informed decisions. You wouldn't buy an automobile, life insurance, or a television from someone who did not have a thorough knowledge of the product's features and benefits. Yet there are thousands of fund raisers who ask for support for organizations of which they have little or no knowledge. Many advancement professionals in hospitals, colleges, art museums, and so on, can recite their organization's general mission statement but know little of its daily activities in service to its constituents.

To be effective, you need a thorough understanding of the aims and objectives, as well as the programs, of the institution you serve. You'll need this knowledge when you ask prospects to give of their resources to maintain or enrich your institution's programs. Comprehensive knowledge of the objectives and programs of your institution is your tool to inform (empower) your donors and affirm their decision to give.

For example, a college development officer who has not attended classes, used the library, listened to guest lectures, worked with faculty on special projects, and served on institutional committees with faculty, staff, and students, does not know the real work of the institution and is not prepared to do the best possible fund-raising job.

Not only should you know your institution, but you should know where it fits into the family of similar institutions. Successful college and university fund raisers are also lifelong students of higher education. They are familiar with various types of institutional organizations (from large major research universities to small liberal arts colleges and junior and community colleges), major foundation and commission reports on programmatic and demographic trends that will affect higher education, and, as important, the regional and national political agenda for higher education.

Each person you call on will have a unique perspective on what factors are most crucial to the success of your particular institution. The more you know, the more likely you are to be able to relate well to each unique perspective.

You will also need to know everything you can about each individual prospect. For example, you should know the following:
- history of previous giving to your institution and others;
- place of residence;
- place of business and length of present employment; past employment;
- dates of formal association with the institution (graduation year, years of trustee service, and so on);
- other family ties to the institution;
- investments;
- names and ages of spouse, children, and grandchildren;
- past and present directorships and civic commitments;
- professional associations;
- club affiliations;
- friends;
- birthday and wedding anniversary; and
- hobbies.

Anything else you can learn about your prospect will increase your chance of success.

The dictionary defines **skill** as "the ability to use one's knowledge effectively in doing something." When you make a successful call on a prospect, you effectively transfer your knowledge so that it causes the prospective donor to do something for the institution (become involved in some way, whether by making a gift or by serving as a volunteer). When you make a call, any time not focused on this objective is time lost and a poor use of your institution's resources. This is not to say that every moment you spend with a prospect must be spent talking about charitable giving. However, you should always be conscious of your objective.

Practice, according to the Merriam-Webster dictionary, is "to perform or work at repeatedly so as to become proficient." Another definition in the dictionary is "customary action: Habit."

In our case, both of these definitions apply. The *only* way to become a really good fund raiser is to make calls on prospective donors. In doing so, we sharpen our basic skills in responding to the behavior of our prospects, and we develop good habits through our tendency to repeat actions that produce positive results. It is no accident that the most effective fund raisers, whether professionals or volunteers, are those who have the most call experience. I know of no exceptions to this basic rule.

Even if your primary responsibility is managing direct mail and telephone solicitation programs, making personal calls will improve your effectiveness. Meeting your prospects will put you more in touch with their concerns and inform you as to the types of messages that are most likely to motivate them to give.

Practice, practice, practice in making calls will be the single most important factor in your continuing advancement as a development professional.

The anatomy of a fund-raising call

There are four basic parts of a fund-raising call or solicitation: presentation, query, overcoming objections, and closing. But before you make the call, you must set up the appointment. It is usually best to have someone else call to make the appointment. If you try to do it, you may end up asking for the gift over the phone, and telephone requests are never as effective as personal visits. The resulting gift or pledge is not likely to be as large or made with the same level of commitment as a response to a personal visit.

The person making the appointment should stress that the purpose of the visit is to provide information on the plans or activities of the institution. If Ms. Prospect's secretary asks whether this will be a fund-raising call, the caller could respond, "We certainly hope that Ms. Prospect will consider supporting our institution, but the purpose of this visit is to provide information to facilitate the partnership between our institution and Ms. Prospect."

Once the appointment is made, be sure to show up on time or, if possible, five minutes early. As one of my institution's most generous friends says, "The only reason for being late is that you didn't start on time, and that's no excuse."

Presentation. As defined by the dictionary, presentation means "to bring into the presence or acquaintance of." The presentation is your opportunity to inform your prospect about your institution or project. While it's true that "people give to people," this doesn't mean that people don't give to support projects or programs; rather it means that people decide to give because of information they receive from people they trust whose message is credible and clear.

Strunk and White emphasize the importance of being clear:

Muddiness is not merely a disturber of prose, it is a destroyer of life, of hope: death on the highway caused by a badly worded road sign, heart-break among lovers caused by a misplaced phrase in a well-intentioned letter, anguish of a traveler expecting to be met at a railroad station and not being met because of a slipshod telegram. Usually we think only of the ludicrous aspect of ambiguity....But think of the tragedies that are rooted in ambiguity; think of that side, and be clear! When you say something, make sure you have said it. The chances of your having said it are only fair.[1]

A presentation normally begins after some initial pleasantries or "small talk." Small talk may seem trivial, but if you're paying attention, it can put you in touch with the attitudes and interests of your prospect. No amount of research will tell you what the prospect is thinking about when you show up for your appointment. Listening carefully and gathering information about his or her attitudes and interests can make the difference between obtaining a major gift decision and receiving no decision or a polite but emphatic "no." I know of a case where a college fund raiser was invited to leave a prospect's office because the development officer was not listening to the prospect. The prospect actually said, "You are wasting my time!"

During a fund-raising call, listening effectively is at least as important as speaking effectively, because listening clues you in as to what is of interest to the prospect. As you listen, you can also pick up some visual clues. Take a discreet look for clues that may point to the prospect's interests in the following areas:

1. Places: Look for travel pictures or posters—you may be able to relate your institution's programs to the prospect's travel interest: "I see you have a poster of Greece. We have a summer institute in Athens...."

2. Activities: Almost anything your prospect does in the way of recreation or hobbies can somehow be related to your institution. Current issues of magazines may give clues to personal or business interests. (Older issues may mean the prospect is just a pass-along reader.)

You might want to visit the periodicals section of your library to familiarize yourself with various general circulation magazines. In one of my recent calls, a discussion of an article in *Ducks Unlimited* magazine (I am not a subscriber) revealed that the prospect owns a very large ranch, harboring a prime duck habitat on the central migration flyway of North America. Could this information have bearing on future discussions pertaining to charitable giving?

3. People: Draw on "field research"—conversations you have had with other prospects about your prospect. Relating yourself to your prospect's friends improves your credibility rating although, of course, you shouldn't share confidential or sensitive information and you shouldn't be too obvious (be careful about blatant name dropping).

Once you have discovered an interest, you need to listen for cues in order to make a smooth transition to the positioning statement. For example, a travel interest may relate to a foreign studies program that needs endowment support. Bingo! The small talk is over, and it's time to move on to business.

The positioning statement is the first critical component of a successful call. It is an essential part of the presentation. It defines the subject of discussion and *always* relates to your institution or project. At this point, the prospect's concentration is focused on your reason for making the call.

The positioning statement is the foundation on which the solicitation is built. For example, Ms. Prospect has a travel poster showing ancient Athenian architecture, and you have determined through small talk that she has been to Greece and is interested in Greek culture. Here's where your knowledge is important: The more you know about your institution's programs, the better equipped you are to make positioning statements that clearly pertain to your institution's needs as well as the prospect's interests.

Your positioning statement might be as follows:

> As you know, our institution has a summer institute for the study of Greek language and culture in Athens. It's directed by the chair of our department of foreign languages and is open to students, faculty, and alumni of our institution.

It is good practice to make a list of positioning statements that serve the various priorities of your institution. Although you won't be able to come up with a statement to meet every situation, practice will sharpen your skills and enable you to formulate an appropriate positioning statement almost automatically during the fund-raising call.

Follow the positioning statement with story/information—that is, describe the program or project in such a way that Ms. Prospect has enough information to envision herself involved in it. As you do this, be careful to convey not only the features of the program but the benefits to the participants as well. Features don't interest people in your program or project—benefits do.

Consider the chart below of features and benefits. You can make such a chart for capital and endowment needs as well as for current operating "annual fund" priorities. Study your list until it's second nature for you to communicate the benefit when you think of the feature.

Features

Participants explore architecture, geography, art, politics, transportation, trade, and literature of ancient Greece.

Benefits

Participants receive firsthand knowledge of geographic, climatic, political, language, transportation, and architectural conditions that shaped the lives of ancient Greeks, whose society is considered to be the foundation of western civilization.

Students may earn up to six hours credit in classical studies or political science.	Students are able to use this experience to assist them in meeting their degree requirements.
Needy students may receive financial aid in order to attend.	Students are not denied the opportunity for foreign study for financial reasons.

In the presentation, talk about programs, not money. It is amazing how many fund-raising calls begin and end with the development officer saying, for example, "We need $1,000 this year from folks like you in order to meet our annual fund goal of $1 million." If you bet that your prospect will be more interested in your program objectives than in your fund-raising goal, you'll be right at least 90 percent of the time. If you begin by talking money, the best prospect will ask, "What is all this money for?" The capable prospect, who needs convincing, will be likely to say, "I'm not looking for any new opportunities for charitable giving." This is an appropriate response if you haven't provided an information base to support an alternative decision.

Often annual fund programs are for unrestricted gifts only. This doesn't mean that you can't talk about specific programs. Every program is enriched by a gift for general purposes, but if your donor wishes to talk about scholarships, talk about scholarships. Know what portion and amount of the operating budget are allocated annually for scholarships, teacher salaries, equipment purchases, and so on.

As you present features and benefits, watch and listen for cues to make the transition to the query.

Query. Your prospect will likely give a signal when it's time for questions. It should happen naturally and flow out of a discussion of a topic of interest to the prospect. For example, when you are discussing the summer institute in Greece, it might be natural, at some point in the conversation, to ask Ms. Prospect, "What were your most memorable experiences during your visit to Greece?" Now you are ready for probing, which provides the transition to the prospect's agenda.

Never use closed questions, which the prospect can answer "yes" or "no." Your objective is to keep the conversation going and find out the prospect's priorities. In most cases, you should be able to match the prospect's agenda with that of your institution.

Make a list of open-ended questions. For example, if you ask, "What do you feel are the most important components of an international studies program?" Ms. Prospect might answer, "Scholarships to help needy students travel and have cross-cultural experiences."

You can then respond, "We currently allocate $250,000 of our operating budget for scholarships to support international study opportunities. Annual gift assistance is a vital resource that contributes to the enrichment of this important program." Get the picture?

Overcoming objections. Maybe this is your lucky day, and Ms. Prospect will take out her checkbook and ask you how much you need. It's more likely, however, that she will have objections that you must answer. First, restate the objection. Sometimes, this in itself will overcome the objection. If the objection is pointless or unfounded, Ms. Prospect may realize this as soon as she hears you repeat it. Sometimes, the objection is only a tactic to assess how serious you are about the cause. Restating the objection tells her that you are listening and that you are serious.

But many objections can't be dismissed in this way, and you will have to respond thoughtfully as in the following examples:

1. Objection: The prospect doesn't like something your institution is doing or has done. Possible response: "I see that you are upset that we have dropped the Bachelor of Business Administration degree. Perhaps you were not aware that this was voted by the faculty upon the recommendation of our Department of Business Administration. They felt that, given our mission as a selective liberal arts college, a move toward offering the Bachelor of Arts or Bachelor of Science degree in the business disciplines, accounting, economics, finance, etc., would better prepare our graduates, most of whom go on to graduate or professional programs in one of these disciplines. *What do you feel are the advantages or disadvantages of such a move?*"

2. Objection: The prospect's objectives don't match with the institution's. Possible response: "I understand that after graduation from our institution, you went on to obtain an engineering degree, which we do not offer, and that you feel your professional achievement is based on your engineering education. We have many graduates, like you, who have earned both a liberal arts degree from our institution and later a degree in engineering. Like you, most of these alumni have achieved positions of leadership in their profession, and many attribute this success, at least in part, to their liberal arts background. *What can we do to ensure that our institution's 3/2 program in engineering, leading to completion of two degrees, is recognized as a foundation for contributing to the success of persons like you?*"

3. Objection: The prospect has already committed his or her resources to other projects or priorities. Possible response: "We realize that, as generous persons, most of our donors and friends have other charitable commitments. In order to achieve the objectives we discussed, we must invite those who are able to place our institution among their charitable priorities at some appropriate level."

Whatever the objection, do not apologize for your institution's policies or programs—unless it's an institutional decision to do so.

Once you have dealt successfully with the prospect's objections, you can make your final query: "What else would you like to know about our institution and/or its programs?" In the ensuing conversation, watch for *buying signs*—signals that your prospect is ready to make a decision—such as the following:

- "How much will this project cost?"
- "What does the institution spend for teacher salaries?"
- "How does the institution rank among similar institutions with respect to teacher compensation, library resource allocation, per student scholarship expen-

ditures, and so on?"

- "The acquisition of those books will result in a major improvement of the library collection."
- "That's an ambitious project."
- "What would you like me to do?"

Your knowledge is particularly important here—you'd better know the answers.

Closing. Closing is the invitation to the prospect to act on a set of options that you have carefully identified and explained. Closing is a critical component of your solicitation. If you get this far and fail to ask for something, you've wasted your time and your institution's resources.

This is the only place in a solicitation to ask a closed question, but word it carefully to offer a range of possibilities. For example, while you could ask, "Will you give or pledge $1,000 in support of our annual fund?" this offers the prospect only two choices—a $1,000 gift or nothing. It's much better to say, "We invite you to consider pledging $1,000 to $1,500 to assist us in meeting the objectives supported through our annual fund."

In most cases, it's better to offer a range rather than an amount. Always put the minimum at a level you believe your prospect can afford and set a higher level that you think might be a reasonable stretch, based on the prospect's previous giving history and/or level of interest. This range can vary enormously and yet be appropriate to the individual prospect.

For example, you undoubtedly have prospects in your pool of previous donors who have given $100 per year for several years yet are actually capable of giving $5,000 or more per year. (Trust me, they are there!) These people probably do not see themselves as capable of giving that amount. Your job is to help them move into a different category. If your institution has a $5,000 gift club, there will be people in that club with whom your $100 donor/$5,000 prospects can identify. Match professions, types of club affiliations, and so on in order to provide the information your prospects need to make this identification.

Then, when you get to the closing in your call, you might talk about the folks in the $1,000 gift club and then say something like, "...but you know your classmate, Barbara Smith, is a member of our $5,000 club, and we consider you to be among those few whose financial assistance at the highest level possible can have the most impact on the quality of our program. We hope it might be possible for you to consider annual participation in our $5,000 club." In this way, you've opened the gate for the $1,000 gift, but you've also unlocked the door for the $5,000 gift.

Practice

Practice, practice, practice leads toward success. However, there is never a perfect call. Perfection is an ideal, not a reality. Strive for perfection, take pleasure in good results, and always evaluate each call based on your progress toward objectives. Reflect on every call by asking how it could have been improved.

The cultivation call

When you make a cultivation call that does not involve a gift request, you should still include the four basic parts of the call—presentation, query, overcoming objections, and closing. You should always encourage your prospect to move toward that ultimate gift decision. But your closing will seek to involve the prospect rather than to elicit a gift. For example, you might conclude a cultivation call with one of the following requests:

- "We would like you to give us your comments about the plans for our proposed new library."
- "We hope you will accept this invitation to visit the campus and talk with members of our Chemistry Department about the plans to improve laboratory facilities."
- "We would like you to give us your evaluation of our community service programs."

What does "no" mean?

When you were a very young child, your mother probably told you "no" if you pulled on the lamp cord or reached for the glass candy jar, but that "no" didn't necessarily mean "never." So it is with a prospect's "no." It may very well mean "not now" or "not for this particular project." Carefully evaluate the prospect's potential and interest to determine whether he or she means "Absolutely never!" or "Try me again later."

Setting goals to overcome call reluctance

Development officers who spend all of their time in their offices are not really fund raisers. Some say that only volunteers should make gift requests and that their job is only to educate and motivate volunteers. Nonsense! If you have armed yourself with the knowledge described earlier in this chapter, no volunteer is better prepared to make a case for your institution or has a better understanding of your institution's role in society than you do. That doesn't mean you don't need volunteers or that volunteers shouldn't make some calls by themselves. However, setting an example for them to follow helps establish your credibility.

In the solicitation of major gifts, volunteer help is critical. Involving a volunteer to whom the prospect has great difficulty saying "no" is often crucial to success. And when you ask for a major gift, you may well be at the same time finding and training a new volunteer. One of the best methods of cultivation is to ask a donor to ask another prospect to match his or her level of support.

The most successful programs require a minimum of five gift/cultivation calls per week per development officer. Anyone who has been in this business for even a few years can identify institutions that are falling well short of their potential because they don't visit their gift prospects regularly. One way to avoid this under-achievement syndrome is to set goals for the number and types of calls to be made by each development officer at your institution.

The president of your institution should contact major gift prospects at least twice each year and some as often as monthly depending on the relationship with your institution. Every major gift prospect should be assigned to a staff member whose job it is to ensure that the prospect is contacted by the appropriate person at the times and for the purposes agreed upon by the president and other development colleagues.

Follow-up is also important. Write a file report on every call, write a letter to the prospect immediately after every visit, and set a time (not an appointment) for the next staff contact with your prospect.

Practice making calls in role-playing sessions with colleagues. Be constructive in your criticism and realize the objective is to strengthen everyone's skills. Use video if available.

Gifts from Carl Gustav Jung [2]

Carl Jung, the great student of Sigmund Freud, developed a system for the classification of personality types. Today, this system is commonly used as the basis of presentation skill instructional programs for professionals.

While Jung's system may help you identify ways in which you might better relate to your prospects, it's not foolproof; in other words, don't take it too seriously and don't expect your prospects to conform invariably to "their" personality types as described here.[3]

Jung identified two rational personality types (thinking and feeling) and two irrational types (sensing and intuiting). Thinking and feeling are rational functions because they require judgment, whereas sensing and intuiting do not. According to Jung, the personality is made up primarily of one rational and one irrational characteristic—one of which will dominate. Other characteristics may be present but not dominant enough to control personality. This means your prospect may be one of eight types:

- Thinker/Sensor or Thinker/Intuitor (Thinker is dominant);
- Feeler/Sensor or Feeler/Intuitor (Feeler is dominant);
- Sensor/Thinker or Sensor/Feeler (Sensor is dominant); or
- Intuitor/Thinker or Intuitor/Feeler (Intuitor is dominant).

To further complicate the situation, your prospect may be either an introvert or an extrovert.

The Thinker (rational). The Thinker connects ideas in order to arrive at a general concept or solution to a problem.

What to look for in the Thinker's office: stacks of reports. Many reference books or papers relating to his or her profession. Magazines like *Popular Mechanics* or *Scientific American.* Office is arranged in a logical manner and furnishings are functional rather than decorative—may be cluttered with papers and books. Thinkers may be accountants, lawyers, engineers, scientists, financial planners, systems analysts, and so on.

What to expect: The Thinker wants to know *why* (proof) a project or program is being done and expects to see the documentation. He or she would like architectural drawings, reports on who benefits from a scholarship program, information as to how many from a department go on to graduate and professional programs and what the chemistry majors from the Class of '70 are doing today. If you have done your homework and can provide information, you're much more likely to succeed with this person.

Thinkers are uncomfortable in unfamiliar surroundings. If you're going to take a Thinker to a restaurant or out for a drink, ask him or her where to go.

Follow up your visit with a letter recapping your presentation—state all of the things you agreed to. Send timetable for the completion of projects or programs. Ask for evaluation of developing programs or projects.

The Feeler (rational). The Feeler is evaluative; he or she accepts or rejects an idea on the basis of whether or not it arouses pleasant or unpleasant feelings.

What to look for in the Feeler's office: photographs of family, friends, and favorite places. Furniture tends toward ornamental and may be antique or specially designed. Colors will be rich warm tones. May see poetry, novels, *People* magazine, etc. Feelers may be entertainers, fund raisers, salespersons, writers, teachers, psychologists, social workers, retailers, nurses, physicians, and so on.

What to expect: The Feeler wants to know how it will feel to be in the new library. "What color is the building?" "Will the users have a nice place to read magazines?" "Will this scholarship program help someone who really needs help?" Feelers need to be liked.

Take the Feeler to a busy and colorful restaurant.

Follow up the visit with personal interest stories on people who benefit from the work of your institution. Send the clipping on the students and professor who are doing "save the whales" research. Send birthday and special occasion cards. Make an occasional phone call to ask, "How are you getting along?"

The Sensor (irrational). The Sensor reacts primarily to immediate stimuli and is interested in the bottom line.

What to look for in the Sensor's office: This person will normally have a Spartan, functional office. Keeps a clean desk, may have little or no office equipment with the exception of telephone and personal computer. Sensors may be entrepreneurs, craftspersons, airline pilots, military strategists, models, athletes, physicians, and so on.

What to expect: The Sensor wants to know immediately what you're there for. Will ask how much the project costs and what you want him or her to do for you. Will look for a bottom-line benefit, i.e., this project will make our library operation more efficient; this scholarship program will bring more exceptional students into the mathematics department. Don't expect much time with the Sensor—15 minutes maximum. Get to the point of your presentation and close quickly. The Sensor may interrupt your visit by accepting phone calls or other visitors.

Unless you know this person as a friend, do not take the Sensor to a restaurant or out for a drink. The Sensor will be reacting to other stimuli in the environment, and you will not be able to hold his or her attention in busy surroundings. If a lunch meeting is in order, have food brought in.

Follow up with a short note, recapping the bottom line of your visit. Provide updates such as how far you are from your goal or specifics as to how the Sensor's participation will help accomplish an institutional objective.

The Intuitor (irrational). The Intuitor listens to a voice from within; he or she marches to a different drummer and is a visionary or an intellectual.

What to look for in the Intuitor's office: This person will have a hodgepodge of furniture types. May have color schemes that appear to clash—offbeat wall colors and abstract art. Magazines will include *Omni* and *Discover;* books are likely to be science fiction or dealing with theories as yet unproven. An Intuitor is likely to be an artist, scientist, professor, writer, or planner.

What to expect: Will ask questions like, "What is the next project after you complete the library?" "How will the chemistry department use computers to monitor laboratory experiments in the future?" Wants you to help him or her look into the crystal ball and see your institution 10 years down the road. You should have a grasp of your institution's five- and 10-year plans (hope your institution has these) and be able to articulate those plans. Ask the Intuitor for an evaluation of the concepts. Take the Intuitor to a "new" restaurant.

Follow up by asking advice on a "complex idea" such as the plan for the next physical plant expansion or the development of a research program to address a special problem in biochemistry. Invite this person to make presentations to appropriate audiences.

Conclusion

Although Jung's theories may give you some clues into the personality of your prospect, the successful call still requires:
- a strong commitment to your profession and your institution;
- a solid foundation of knowledge about your institution, its peer institutions, and the techniques of your profession;
- a continuing effort to enhance your skill; and
- practice, practice, practice in the four basic components of a call.

As an early proponent of education and public service said: *If we do not lay out ourselves in the service of mankind, whom should we serve?*—Abigail Adams

Notes

[1] William Strunk Jr. and E.B. White, *The Elements of Style* (New York: Macmillan, 1959), pp. 65-66.

[2] Calvin S. Hall and Vernon J. Nordby, *A Primer of Jungian Psychology* (New York: Signet, 1973), pp. 96-109.

[3] Personality type indicator tests based on Jung's theories are available. If your

institution offers testing services, the *Myers-Briggs Type Indicator* may be available at your workplace. Or you can order it from Consulting Psychologists Press. Call (800) 624-1765 for pricing information. Orders must be official college or university purchase orders and can be mailed to the press at 3803 East Bayshore Road, Palo Alto, California 94303, or faxed to (415) 969-8608.

Section 3

Special Programs
To Boost Success

Chapter 13

Using the Computer To Advantage

Mary Anna Dunn
Vice President
University of Colorado Foundation, Inc.
Boulder, Colorado

I once worked for a boss who swore by 3-by-5 cards. Don't fret about late computer reports, he'd say; go back to the cards! The old cards-in-the-shoebox method of fund raising does have its advantages: Cards are portable and always accessible, and if the electricity goes out, you can read them by flashlight. On the other hand, if you're dealing with an audience of 3,000—or 30,000 or even 300,000—those cards quickly lose their utility.

In truth, we live in a computerized age. The term "database" was not even mentioned in the last annual fund book; now, few of us could run an annual fund without one. The computer—whether a shared institutional mainframe or a PC in the development office (or both)—serves the annual fund both in management and in production.

The computer as a management tool: Audience management

Managing information about our audiences is the primary benefit of being computerized. As about one-fifth of the U.S. population moves every year (and nearly half of those in the recent graduate age range), just keeping up with address changes is a major challenge. Then, every address change may mean other information ("data") to capture: new phone number, new employer or retirement, new (or ex-) spouse, children, changed income level. Those old 3-by-5 cards would quickly be worn out.

If you are new to annual fund work or to your institution, set yourself an early goal of learning the capabilities of your database. What data can be stored? You may find as few items as degree information, address, phone number, and giving history. Or you may find those items plus family details, attitudinal information, student and alumni activities, and more.

You may find a big difference between capability and actuality: How many of the available blanks are filled in? I once planned to solicit an audience of 40,000 alumni by major area of study—until I discovered that 17,000 of them had no major on file in the alumni database.

Filling in the blanks and keeping data current are essential to annual fund work. Whether or not recordkeeping is handled by your office, you will need to work closely with records staff. Be sure to take advantage of the many audience contacts that you make. Use, selectively, "Address Correction Requested" in your mailings, and include record update requests in your phonathon scripts. Then, make sure the information you gather—whether from one-on-one contacts or from mass appeals—gets promptly into the computer. (Learn how that process works!)

Further, take advantage of computerized address and telephone number update services. The U.S. Postal Service certifies commercial firms that can provide new addresses for people who have recently moved (National Change of Address database or NCOA). Other firms specialize in matching the addresses in your list to national databases of phone numbers. These services cost money, but the budget commitments are well worthwhile.

Thus, managing your audiences by computer means that you must first take steps to stay in touch. Tracking down "lost" alumni is a subject beyond our scope here, but see Nancy Barr's article, "What's Lost Can Be Found," in the May 1989 CUR-RENTS and the 1981 book, *Finding Lost Alumni: Tracing Methods Used by 19 Institutions,* written by Brian Gorman and published by CASE.

Computerized management also means segmenting your audience so that you can appeal to alumni and others at their closest point of identification with your institution. These contacts may be by class year or by school, by residence hall or by department. The database allows you to select and sort records according to the information on file.

Computerized analysis: A key management resource

Tracking results is an essential function of the computer. Your database should have space to capture information on your donors' motivations. At the University of Colorado Foundation, our solicitation code system records which mailing, phonathon, or other appeal stimulated each gift. Summary reports show the number of gifts and dollar totals resulting from each appeal or project. By using computerized spreadsheets to keep cost records as well, we can calculate cost per dollar raised for each appeal. As a manager, I can then evaluate the effectiveness of various appeals, decide how much to invest in certain programs, compare to other years, and report to academic and development officers.

Maintaining results data on the computer is far more efficient than keeping manual records. Further, you can easily manipulate the data to answer such questions, among others, as:

- How does the new donor's average gift compare to that of the repeat donor?
- What proportion of gift income comes from phonathons?
- Do anniversary appeals pull better than school appeals?

You can also use the computer to analyze your audience. You need to know how many people there are in your chosen segments and in your total audience. In fact, looking at the numbers will probably help you identify your segments in the first place. For example, what is the proportion of new graduates in the alumni population? Should they be targeted as a separate group in order to appeal to their interests? Has your institution always been coed? Have there been academic or demographic changes in your institution's history? Study the numbers to identify segmenting criteria—by degrees, by geography, by age (or inferred age), by whatever traits you can sort and count.

After an extensive alumni census in 1986, the University of Michigan (UM) performed one of the most sophisticated audience analyses. Using biographic, demographic, and giving data, UM's institutional researchers created profiles of their audience, complete with predictors of gift potential. (See Gerlinda S. Melchiori, "Ranking Achievement: Use Your Alumni Data to Identify Your Best Prospects," CURRENTS, July/August 1988, and *Alumni Research: Methods and Applications,* edited by Melchiori and published by Jossey-Bass as part of the New Directions for Institutional Research series.)

The university not only gained an overall picture of its alumni (such as percentages of males and females), but also identified prospective individual donors. The analysis revealed, for example, that having children who also attended UM was one of the most significant predictors of alumni giving. Studies such as this may be the ultimate in management tools.

On a less sophisticated but still helpful level, annual fund officers can discover gift potentials by studying selected lists from the database. If you're just getting started, spend some time reviewing details about people who have given $100 or $1,000 to your institution. If you are considering a 25th reunion campaign, review that whole group, enlisting volunteer help if possible. Although the computer provides the report, you'll have to devote enough of your own time and attention to know your audience.

The computer as a production tool

Computer "output" lets you connect with your audience. In addition to lists such as those mentioned above, you'll need mailing labels, phonathon forms, leadership prospect forms, pledge reminders, and so on. If you have an established system, acquiring these necessities may be as easy as saying, "Please run labels for all engineering alumni since 1980." Or you may need to start from scratch in figuring out how to format the information into mailing labels or how to design a functional phonathon form.

While the computer will handle the bulk of the work (selection, sorting, printing), someone must tend to the details that can make or break your appeals. If a mailing goes to the wrong people, or if phone calls can't be made on time, the annual fund suffers.

Here's a glimpse of the types of decisions you'll need to make:

• Does the mailroom need Cheshire or pressure-sensitive labels?

• Is phonathon output printed on continuous forms, and if so, who "bursts" them?

• Can pledge reminders be run so that people who have just paid their pledges are excluded?

• Are people who have already given this year routinely excluded from subsequent appeals?

• What if the library wants to mail to *everybody*?

A relatively recent computer boon for annual fund production is the ability to download to the word-processor. You can define the types of records you want to select (such as members of the class of 1935) and have the information transmitted electronically to your word-processing system. For us, that means we get a disk containing names and addresses that we load into our operator's PC. We do some editing, create a merge document, and run personalized letters—without having to retype the information.

Computerized signature machines take these miracles to yet another level of sophistication. Special components let you write a signature on a pad, record it on a disk, and repeat it almost endlessly with a "real" pen.

Whether or not your office has the need or the resources for such advanced equipment, let the computer do as much of the work as you can. In particular, let the machine handle repetitive tasks. For example, if you're doing a phonathon, you'll want the forms sorted by time zone and possibly by past giving or class year. Rather than doing those sorts manually, specify them for the computer output. When you're ordering labels for a bulk mailing, remember to specify ZIP code order. If you've ever forgotten this detail, you know the misery of handling that sort on the coffee table after hours. Similarly, ask for counts with each run of labels or forms. Computers are much better—and faster—than people at sorts and counts.

Boon or bane?

One universal feature of development work is that we know that much more *could* be done than *can* be done. Annual fund staff have to learn to balance ambitions with resources. The computer resource is nearly always limited, and so you need to learn to work smart and often to compromise.

Here are a few nuggets of basic advice:

• Do use the output that comes to you, both standard recurring reports and custom items that you have requested. Don't let reports accumulate unexamined in some corner—and then ask for data that you may already have at hand. In other words, *don't waste the resource.*

• Learn to read the reports. If possible, have the data presented in English rather than in code. If that isn't an option, refer to your database dictionary and learn what the codes mean. Make a crib sheet of frequently used codes.

• Plan ahead. Submit requests for output well in advance so that systems people have time to ask questions, prioritize, schedule. In general, everyone's busy season comes at the same time. Your urgent need may not outrank everyone else's.

• Invest effort in working effectively with information services staff. Development officers and systems people each have their own languages. (LYBUNTs? Data elements? Pagebreaks?) Since development types are supposed to be master communicators, assume that it is your responsibility to connect well. Shed development jargon and convey your needs in plain old English; over time, learn to use computer terms accurately.

• Check your output. Errors can occur, and it's counterproductive to send the "Please make your first gift" letter to long-term donors. Further, even when you get exactly what you asked for, you may be in for a surprise. Computers (and programmers) are very literal. Did you really mean *all* past donors to the library or just *people* donors?

• Don't stress the system and system staff needlessly. If a project turns out to be unrealistic or if it creates unnecessary emergencies, modify your plans. Use existing report formats as much as you can rather than asking for new layouts. Or wait for a relatively slow season to request creation of new reports.

• If you find yourself devising ways to *avoid* using the computer, such as typing labels rather than requesting computer output, beware. Step back and evaluate. If output is chronically late or inaccurate, if stress levels between development and systems staff members are running high, it may seem expedient to type the senior class address labels from the campus phonebook. Wait! The problem here is not the labels, but an overall situation where ambitions and resources are out of balance. It may be that the development office does not have sufficient access to a shared computer. You may need a new machine ("hardware") or a new database system ("software"). You may need more "personpower." Or you and your colleagues may need to take a hard look at program expectations and timing.

Computers are definitely the boon of the annual fund. They extend our reach, accelerate our ability to contact our audiences, and allow us to be more "personal." If you are new to this work, however, you'll have lots to learn in order to use the resource well. You'll probably find that your life is full of struggles and compromises. If you are lucky, some day you'll be able to take this resource for granted. Whatever your situation, forget about those 3-by-5 cards.

Chapter 14

Matching Gifts

John M. Womble
Development Management Consultant
Macon, Georgia
(Formerly Senior Vice President for University Relations and Development,
Mercer University, Macon, Georgia)

S ince its inception in 1954 by the General Electric Foundation, the concept of combining corporate philanthropy and individual employee contributions has provided more than $1 billion to educational institutions nationwide. By 1989, more than 1,000 companies were matching their employees' gifts to education, as well as to some other charitable causes.

The Council for Aid to Education defines gift matching as "an arrangement through which an eligible employee makes an eligible gift to an eligible institution, and that contribution is matched in cash by a gift from the employer." Some companies now match employee contributions at a 2-1 or 3-1 ratio. Because of the widespread acceptance and adoption of the program by corporate entities, at least some alumni or other supporters at most educational institutions work for a matching gift company.

Matching gift programs benefit a company's philanthropic policy by relieving management of the sometimes sticky decision regarding which institutions to support. Nevertheless, the institutional fund-raising officer should not rely on the corporate entity to promote the program. It's up to the institution to actively promote participation, and the key to encouraging participation is communication.

Here are some techniques you can use to encourage your donors to take advantage of their employers' matching gift programs:

1. *matching gift reminders:* Utilizing computerized alumni database information, you can send promotional material to alumni who work for matching gift companies. Contact the company personnel office to find out the proper procedure for each company.

By careful use of database information, you can also track contributions from matching company employees that arrive without matching gift forms. You can then send the donors a reminder to mail in the proper forms. Always include a return envelope to make it as easy as possible for donors to respond.

2. *volunteer organizations or in-company "mini-campaigns":* If you determine that a significant number of alumni work for a certain company, you can enlist volunteers to contact fellow alumni employees and urge them to participate. You might recruit a chair or form a steering committee to contact alumni employees through correspondence or personal contact or both.

If the firm is large enough and employee placement is widespread, consider setting up volunteer contact programs in divisions, departments, or plant locations. Competition between groups or locations can be stimulating. If numbers or salary levels are diverse, you might set percentage participation goals, which would enable all groups to reach "victory."

3. *following up:* Before the end of the institution's fiscal year, check to see if all eligible alumni employees have participated, especially those who have given before but not yet this year. You can use reminder vehicles (cards, letters, phone calls) to encourage them to give before the end of the fiscal or calendar year.

Follow-up should also include careful monitoring to assure that the corporate match is received in due course. When the match comes, you should notify the participating employee (post cards or short word-processed letters work nicely) and remind him or her of the total impact of the gift.

4. *addendums to other mailing pieces:* The development office would do well to add a note to all alumni correspondence calling attention to the matching gift program. Include a reminder in alumni publications as well. Plan a marketing effort; advertise in publications.

5. *retired employees:* Most matching gift companies continue to match gifts after employees retire. Don't overlook this important segment of your older alumni. Participation by this group can be especially important for 40-year, 50-year, or older class reunion fund-raising efforts. Some institutions encourage reunion classes to consider class gifts of scholarships, chairs, or support for special programs. Matching of their gifts can be very encouraging to alumni as they work toward a special goal.

The institution's responsibilities

If you are developing your institution's matching gift program, consider the following hierarchy of responsibilities:

1. *board responsibility:* The governing board of the institution should direct by policy that adequate internal controls are in place to protect the donors as well as the assets and reputation of the institution.

2. *the chief executive:* The institutional president or CEO should establish the general administrative structure to assure appropriate procedures. Generally, this is delegated to the chief development officer and/or the chief financial officer.

3. *the development office:* Usually one development officer is responsible for

administering donor and company matching gifts. This includes verification of eligibility, records, reports, and correspondence with participating companies.

4. *related foundations, funds, or associations:* Some institutions may designate a separate, incorporated foundation or association to administer the matching gift program. For example, in a large state university, the alumni association may be responsible for the program. This arrangement should include continued clear communication with the parent institution.

5. *reports to corporations:* Although many corporate participants do not require audits or detailed reports, they do appreciate a response or acknowledgment when gifts are received. The donor recognition program of any institution should include a mechanism for thanking matching gift companies and informing them of the status of their gifts and the impact on the institution.

Conclusion

A successful matching gift program benefits the institution, the eligible alumni donors, and the participating corporate entities. Careful planning and aggressive implementation by the development office can unlock a significant source of funds.

For further information

For further detail on matching gift programs, consult the following resources:

• *Case Studies in Matching Gift Administration: A Workbook.* Joint Task Force on Matching Gifts. Washington, DC: Council for Advancement and Support of Education, 1988.

• *Guidelines for the Administration of Matching Gift Programs.* Joint Task Force on Matching Gifts. Washington, DC: Council for Advancement and Support of Education, 1990.

• *Matching Gift Details: The Guidebook to Corporate Matching Gift Programs.* Washington, DC: Council for Advancement and Support of Education, updated each January.

• *Matching Gift Notes* (quarterly newsletter that updates *Matching Gift Details*). Council for Advancement and Support of Education.

• *Matching Gifts; Patterns and Practices in Corporate Matching Gift Programs.* New York: Council for Aid to Education, 1986.

• *Research Report* (periodic reports of recent statistics and tables). New York: Council for Aid to Education.

Chapter 15

Alumni Directories

William R. Lowery
Vice President for Development and Public Affairs
Lake Forest College
Lake Forest, Illinois

Not all universities will be able to report, as the University of Missouri is said to have done, that an alumni directory linked two former sweethearts and made their marriage possible. But any school, college, or university that produces an alumni directory will find *some* positive impact on its programs and will usually raise more money for operating support.

We all know that alumni directories provide subscribers with lists of names and addresses, usually telephone numbers, and often employment information, addresses, and phone listings. As advancement professionals, we should also consider the benefits to the institution of producing and disseminating a directory.

Benefits to alumni

An alumni directory has several advantages in addition to the obvious one—alumni who receive a benefit from the institution are more likely to give to that particular institution.

First, the alumni directory lets the reader confirm that his or her own record is correct. Isn't it human nature to look yourself up first just to make sure "they've got it right"?

Second, and only slightly less important, alumni directories enable your alumni to find out what happened to their college friends and acquaintances. Everyone is curious about the fate of former lover John or best friend Suzie, and the directory has the answer.

Third, the directory can be a useful guide for an alumnus relocating to a new area: The newcomer can find a doctor, dentist, broker, or even a former classmate when he or she is surrounded by strangers.

Fourth, the directory may provide the alumnus with useful business information. We may discourage such use; in fact, we may go so far as to include a warning that the lists are not to be used for business purposes, but this remains a powerful attraction for a very small number of alumni: The directory may contain names of many potential clients.

Finally, most elusive but perhaps most important, the alumni directory reaffirms the valued connection between the alumnus and the alma mater and reminds him or her that the bond is still there.

Benefits to the institution

These are all wonderful benefits, and we as advancement professionals are happy to convey them. But without more tangible benefits to the institution, most of us would not go to the bother of publishing a book. So let us look at the advantages that accrue to your school, college, or university.

First, you may find that there's increased alumni interaction. If alumni can find each other more easily, they may get together more often.

Second, there are likely to be better relations with your alumni public, although these will be hard to measure. Alumni who are reminded of the vitality of their institution through handling a well-produced book that contains their names are likely to feel more positively about the institution. And they will feel even better if they don't have to buy the book, but receive it as a gift.

Third—and here the benefits become tangible—your directory information will improve. Even if you use only a questionnaire to obtain corrected information, you'll find that you have better addresses, telephone numbers, business information, and perhaps information on children and spouses—all information that the alumnus provides so that it will be accurate in the directory.

Some publishers will return your electronic data with new ZIP-plus-four information, addresses provided by the National Change of Address service, and formerly missing telephone numbers and social security numbers. And depending on the services offered by your publisher, you may find that inconsistencies in your existing records are eliminated. You may never have realized how many different ways "IBM" appears, for instance, or that towns beginning with "Saint" may appear in your computerized lists in three or four different versions, thus forcing them to appear three or four different times in an alphabetical list.

As a fourth, related benefit, depending on how you design your questionnaire, you may derive a substantial amount of good nondirectory information. For instance, you may now be able to sort your alumni according to graduate degrees, personal interests, clubs, affiliations, religion, political party, or income level; you may be able to track their career histories more easily.

Fifth, some publishers will compile from your data a list of employees who work for matching gift companies so that you can tailor solicitations to those alumni whose gifts can trigger employers' matches.

A sixth benefit may be of great value if you have not already used an electronic prospect evaluation service. Several directory publishers use the corrected data the directory-publishing process provides for screening and evaluation. This process can give you ratings of great value; they let you know who is most likely to be able to respond to a request for a larger annual gift. Such services are valuable, if not foolproof, and to have such analyses provided at no cost beyond that associated with the directory can be a tempting carrot.

Finally, you may find that alumni give more when you publish a directory. When you *give* the directory to donors, or to donors above a certain level, gifts will increase. There is disagreement about whether giving increases when an institution charges for its directory, but anecdotal evidence seems to indicate that gifts and number of donors do increase—perhaps because those alumni who buy the directory have already crossed the psychological barrier against writing the first check.

A review of the three main methods of publishing a directory may help you decide which is best for your institution.

The no-cost directory

So labeled because it requires no outlay of funds on the part of the institution and very little staff time, the no-cost directory relies on a publisher who takes your electronic data, corrects and verifies them, produces a book, markets it, and delivers it to subscribers. When the process is finished, the institution receives a tape with the corrected data so they may be merged with what is already on the institutional computer.

The no-cost directory publisher mails (and usually designs) the questionnaire, keyboards the corrections, analyzes data to identify matching gift employees, and screens and evaluates your alumni. In some cases, the publisher telephones all alumni—those who have mailed questionnaires, to *verify* the information, and those who have not, to *derive* information in the first place.

Publishers of no-cost directories take no money from your institution; instead, they provide data that might otherwise cost you substantially. They derive their income solely from the sale of directories, and therefore their books must be fairly expensive—far more than the cost of typesetting, printing, and binding. Some publishers rely only on questionnaires for the information that will be included in the directory, and they also use the questionnaires to solicit orders. Others use telephone follow-up to solicit orders, placing no order information on the questionnaire itself. Books that use telephone verification (and sales) generally cost more than those that rely only on mail questionnaires.

Perhaps alumni understand that these techniques are necessary; in any case, publishers of no-cost directories sell substantial numbers of books, and institutions that have used this method seem to be pleased with the results.

What are the benefits of no-cost directory publishing? Data files are corrected effortlessly. A substantial (but unknown) number of alumni buy directories and therefore have current information about their peers. Alumni who have purchased the book may feel an increased connection with the institution. And usually the institution receives analyses that will make fund raising more successful.

What are the drawbacks? The book costs more than when the institution plays a larger role in production, and some alumni may not order it at the higher price. There is no guarantee that alumni leaders—who may be donors but may not wish to buy a book—will have copies. Some alumni may be riled by a telephone call that combines data verification with a sales pitch. And some alumni may feel that they can't give to the alumni fund and buy an expensive directory in the same year. They may resent having to make the choice.

The low-cost directory

This method of publishing a directory eliminates some of the problems of the no-cost directory. The publisher of the low-cost directory does not keyboard the new or corrected data, and the institution may assume responsibility for marketing the book, billing, and providing a list of subscribers—thus reducing the price charged by the publisher. The institution may even subsidize the book, further reducing the cost to the subscriber. Usually no telephone verification or sales are connected with the low-cost directory.

Thus, the low-cost directory may arrive in more alumni hands; more alumni interaction may result; more may feel closer to the institution; fewer may encounter price resistance; alumni giving may increase.

There are also benefits of a technical nature, having to do with the way data arrive. Since the institution is responsible for keyboarding corrections, alumni files are corrected in-house immediately; with a no-cost directory, the corrected data arrive only when the process is complete and the book is in production. And the institution may easily request data it plans to use later—data useful in a future campaign, for instance, or data the use of which relies on restructuring a computer program at some future date.

The low-cost directory, however, provides fewer good data than the no-cost directory, especially the no-cost directory that includes telephone verification. Ordinarily, no data analysis—either matching gift list or screening/evaluation—goes to the institution. And even the low-cost directory goes to fewer alumni than the next method—the premium directory.

The premium directory

This directory goes to alumni in certain categories. In the case of a large university or a large alumni club, it may go to all members of record (those who have paid their current dues). Or it may go to all donors of $100. Or it may go to all donors, regardless of the size of their gift.

The premium directory has some of the shortcomings of the low-cost directory: Data verification will not be optimally thorough; there will be no record analysis.

And although IRS rulings have not yet spoken specifically to this issue, most books cost more than the IRS usually allows for a tax-free premium, and you are well advised to warn your donors not to claim the value of the book as a gift when they are listing charitable contributions.

But this kind of book has advantages. The institution has more freedom to design a book to its unique needs and specifications. The premium directory will increase alumni giving, both in dollars and in number of donors, more than the other kinds of directories. It will go to the largest number of recipients, and it will be in the hands of those alumni the institution is likely to value most: its donors. And alumni who feel, as so many do, that every mailing from the institution asks for something, will be gratified to receive a gift instead of a request.

The premium directory has the same technical advantages as the low-cost directory—alumni files can be corrected immediately, the corrected data are readily accessible, and so on.

Choosing your publishing method

You can summarize the advantages and disadvantages of the three publishing methods as follows: The no-cost directory is easiest on staff and costs the least. Moreover, it provides analyses not usually available in other modes. The low-cost directory, however, may reach more alumni, encounter less price resistance, and provide data to the institution earlier and in a more controllable form. It, too, may cost the institution little or no money, but it will demand greater staff involvement. While the premium directory will demand the greatest amount of staff time and will cost the greatest amount of money, it has the greatest potential for public relations benefits, widespread distribution, and immediate alumni fund increases.

If institutional cost (both in funds and in staff time) is a factor at your institution, then the no-cost directory is probably your best bet. It will be relatively hassle-free, it will provide good information and some special bonuses, and the product will please purchasers.

If institutional funds are scarce, but your staff can give time to a demanding project, a low-cost directory is a good option. Subscribers will bear the cost of type-setting and printing, the institution will control updating data, and the product will please purchasers.

If your institution has fences to mend with alumni—or if you wish to maintain superior relations—and cost is not a factor, then the premium directory may satisfy. The cost to the institution in staff time may be more than the low-cost directory, if you hire out keyboarding and proofing as well as typesetting and printing; if you perform these tasks in-house, the cost in staff time may be the same as the low-cost directory. Whichever mode is chosen, the dollar cost will be highest, because you pay for publishing.

Whatever form of directory you select, publishing it will improve your database, make it possible to raise money more effectively, and improve your relations with current and potential donors.

Chapter 16

Challenge Gifts

Gordon L. Decker
Consultant
Mountain View, California
(Formerly Director of Development, Union College)

Paul J. Adamo
Director of the Annual Fund
Union College
Schenectady, New York

I n the early 1780s, a group of Schenectady citizens petitioned the State of New York to charter a college. They pledged just over $35,000 in cash and gifts-in-kind, ranging from lumber to cattle. Local leaders made the case to the state government to provide goods and services to accomplish their goal—the birth of a new college. In a real sense, this was Union College's first challenge fund. Indeed, many colleges can trace their roots to similar visions and challenges.

There is something very appealing about the concept that if you take an action, others will follow suit. As children we "dared" each other; as adults we respond to the "dare" of a challenge fund, and in doing so we combine our efforts and create something wonderful in which the whole is larger than the sum of the parts.

Challenge funds inspire both the prospective donor and the challenger, as both are encouraged to join together and philanthropically do their very best for the institution or organization. The challenge fund focuses attention on involving worthwhile people in a worthwhile cause.

Accelerating the giving spiral

There are four states in a donor's giving cycle:
   • *awareness:* An individual has to be aware of your cause before he or she can

117

give support to your institution;

• *interest:* An individual has to be interested in your cause before your institution receives support above others;

• *involvement:* An individual has to be involved before your institution receives significant support; and

• *commitment:* An individual has to be committed before your institution becomes a high priority for major support.

At Union, we prefer to think of this process as an upward spiral. The cycle that a recent graduate follows bears great similarity to that of a member of the 50th reunion class. In fact, most of our major donors and top leadership volunteers have completed several cycles, moving to higher levels of support with each one.

A challenge gift can speed a donor's passage along the spiral or even encourage him or her to jump to a higher level. A challenge can turn a token donor into a committed supporter and a closet volunteer into a dynamic leader.

Attracting the challengers

How do you identify the challenger? At Union College we do it, as the Beatles' song goes, "With a little help from our friends." We use prospect screening, peer identification, and research.

Whether the challenger will be an individual or a consortium of donors depends on two factors: the potential in the group to be challenged and how much money is needed for the challenge. In addition, you must determine whether the challenge will be more effectively promoted with one, two, or more key individuals. This also depends on the potential of the group being challenged and the size of the challenge fund.

Experience indicates that it's best to involve the challenge donors as promoters and solicitors to contribute to the challenge fund or to serve on the challenge fund committee. As membership on the committee requires at least a minimum leadership gift, these volunteers often commit a gift far larger than their previous levels of giving. The "bandwagon" principle is at work—if others are participating, it must be worthwhile.

Presenting the challenge concept to potential challengers involves many standard fund-raising techniques. In addition to asking the questions of "Why?" "Why now?" and "Why me?" the donor also wants to know, "Why a challenge fund?" He or she needs assurance that the challenge fund technique is genuine and will indeed produce the desired results.

To demonstrate proof of how effective a challenge can be, review the performance of past challenge funds at your institution or at others. "Before" and "after" tables of gifts will show the overall improvement in giving that resulted from a challenge fund. Such a table of gifts also helps to raise the giving sights of prospective challengers as 80 to 90 percent of the new "stretch" dollar goal will still have to come from relatively few donors.

Choosing the type of challenge fund

There are many types of challenge funds, and yours should be tailored to the group you are challenging and the amount you hope to raise. The challengers, who are often peers of the prospective donors, can help you determine the most effective type of challenge fund.

Individual or group challenge funds

Although you can offer a challenge that is based on group performance, one that is based on the actions of the individual is likely to be more successful. When the people being challenged can see what their own gifts will mean, they are likely to respond more enthusiastically than if the challenge requires action on the part of the whole group—for example, the class must reach 70 percent participation in order to secure a $10,000 gift for the institution.

The most popular match for individual giving is one that matches on a dollar-for-dollar basis, with each donor required to increase his or her gift level by a minimum amount. It is important that minimum increases stretch donors and encourage them to step up to the challenge. For example, the donor might have to qualify for the next highest gift club in order to meet the challenge. Or he or she might have to make a minimum increase over last year's gift or the last gift or the largest gift. As you decide what qualifies for the challenge, try to keep it simple: Remember that procedures must not be too complicated to explain to donors and to volunteers.

You also need to establish the maximum that will be matched. You could state a maximum total for the entire fund or a maximum match per individual.

You can use bonuses to stimulate specific giving. For example, a bonus for first-time donors or a bonus for those who qualify for a specific gift club may be just the incentive to achieve large increases.

You can also offer a bonus to match the gifts from a group. A bonus of $10,000 could reward the class when it reaches 70 percent participation or when it passes its previous giving record.

Whatever the type of challenge fund you use, it should be tailored to the targeted group and large enough to gain attention and to provide motivation. Once you have created the perfect challenge, you must properly market it.

Marketing challenge funds to constituencies

Marketing a challenge fund is often the most difficult step. Marketing or "packaging" the challenge *precedes* any form of solicitation. In this stage, it is vital that you design the challenge fund to answer the questions that prospects will ask: "Why?" "Why now?" "Why me?" and "Why should I make *such a large gift now?*"

Effective marketing presents the case for support, underscores the seriousness of the goals, and describes the terms of the challenge. The marketing plan must inform donors and prospects of the existence of the fund, capture their interest through an effectively communicated message, and motivate them to action.

Unless publicity by newspaper, radio, and television is a viable option, direct mail is often the quickest way to reach a large constituency with news about a challenge. Newsletters can also be an efficient means of publicizing the challenge and providing updated progress reports. You can use other publications such as the college magazine, brochures, leaflets, and even post cards as alert announcements, solicitation pieces, or status reports. Speeches, individual visits, or phoning sessions provide a more personal approach to communicating the challenge, especially to donors of leadership gifts.

Once you have established the marketing foundation, it is time to put the plan to work and to *ask, ask, ask* for gifts.

Personal solicitation

Personal, face-to-face solicitation is the best method of raising gifts, especially major gifts, during a challenge fund campaign.

Let your volunteers choose the prospects most likely to respond to their appeals. Most volunteers will probably be willing to contact five to 10 prospects, with an option for more or fewer if they wish. Volunteers need an explanation of the challenge fund, a timetable, instructions, solicitation materials, prospect information (including biographical and giving information), suggested gift goals, progress reports, and insider memos.

Before the volunteers begin their solicitations, they should be asked to make their own gifts. They will find it far more credible and easier to ask a prospect to do what they have already done—make a gift to meet the terms of the challenge. Rather than saying, "I plan to give *something* in the near future," the volunteers can announce, "I am asking you to *join* me by making a gift of $1,000 or more, which will mean an additional $1,900 from the challenge fund." These committed volunteers can then explain the challenge and why they are supporting it with both their money and their time.

Personal contact communicates a sense of importance and urgency. It provides a captive audience and a direct focus of attention. In addition, personal solicitation enables the volunteer to answer questions about the challenge, to negotiate the commitment, and to call for action.

Personal contact solicitation, when properly used with identified major donor prospects, is the most successful means for raising gifts of $1,000, $5,000, and $10,000 or more.

Time and resources normally dictate that only a relatively small number of personal asks can be made by volunteers, professional staff, or both in tandem. When face-to-face solicitation is not possible, telephone solicitations can provide some of the same benefits.

Telephone contact

The second best method of solicitation is the telephone. The volunteer can focus attention on the challenge, explain why it is important, extend an invitation to participate, negotiate a commitment, and call for action.

Phonathons provide the opportunity to reach out to a larger number of prospects. They generate excitement, ensure that calls are made, and produce measurable results.

Phonathon "challenge" workers should also make their own gifts first; then they should call those individuals most likely to be receptive to their appeal; and finally they should contact remaining prospects. Provide callers with regular phonathon materials, copies of the challenge description, a suggested gift goal, and a sample approach to use. After an initial pep talk, you or your staff can provide one-on-one training whenever it is needed, as well as feedback and encouragement to the phonathon challenge workers.

For those prospects your phonathon callers cannot reach, mail contact can produce significant results.

Mail contact

Direct mail is the third most effective form of solicitation. While you cannot answer questions or negotiate with the prospect by mail, a well-composed letter can reach those who otherwise might not be notified of the challenge, and the results can be encouraging.

To increase the chances that the envelope will be opened, mark it "personal," use a handwritten or typed address, a first-class stamp, and a volunteer's return address (not the institution's). The letter should be signed and, if possible, composed by a volunteer and handwritten or typed on his or her stationery, and it should contain the proper personal salutation and a personalized message. The letter should explain the challenge or refer the reader to an enclosure, extend an invitation to join the volunteer at a certain level, and call for action. Include a return envelope, marked to the attention of the challenge fund.

If you cannot afford the time and/or the money to do a personal letter for all prospects, you can send a form letter, but do use a special envelope and stationery to help increase readership. In addition to the "personalized" form letter from a volunteer, enclose a brochure or flier describing the challenge fund and explaining how gifts are matched.

The marketing of the challenge fund and the methods for solicitation are interrelated. Be sure to design every challenge to be successful whether the solicitation is in person, by telephone, or by mail. Each challenge fund will have its own identity and purpose, and the audiences challenge funds are created for can differ in ages, giving potentials, and present relationships with your institution.

The payoff to the donor

Whether the donor has created the challenge or responded to it, he or she should receive several benefits from participation in the challenge:

Satisfaction. The creator of a challenge fund has the satisfaction of knowing that he or she has helped the institution through this leadership gift, motivating others either to increase their gifts or, in many cases, to make their largest gifts. Some challengers prefer anonymity, but many enjoy the publicity and attention the challenge focuses on them.

Donors responding to a challenge fund feel good about providing a gift that is increased by the challenge. They experience a greater sense of ownership in the institution. For most of these donors, this marks the largest gift they have ever made. And it feels good! Often, they will continue to give at the increased level in future years, even without the existence of a challenge, because they have understood the value of their gifts.

Recognition. Recognition for the donors who created the challenge and for those responding to it is critical to ensure that both groups feel adequately appreciated. Recognition can be a part of ongoing programs or a new special form of public thanks. Techniques include thank-you letters, donor reports, photographs taken at key events, insider progress reports or publications, stories in the alumni magazine, and announcements at reunion and homecoming weekends. You can provide special recognition for leadership donors by inviting them to dinners with the president, trustees, and peer donors. Along with asking for the gift, *saying thank you* is the most important action you can take.

Premiums. Many public television stations use premiums as an incentive to give. Although premiums are popular with many contributors, they can be costly and are subject to IRS regulations with regard to gift value. If you select your premium carefully, you can give your donors a small but meaningful token, such as a book written by an alumnus or a faculty member or another item specifically related to the institution that provides a tangible expression of gratitude.

Not all challenge donors like premiums, however. Some may object that their gifts are being used to buy recognition items rather than for the purpose they intended—to help their alma mater. To avoid this problem, you might consider asking a sponsor to cover the cost of the premiums. Then when you send the premium to a donor, you can include a letter explaining that the premium is provided through a gift by an individual who wanted to join the institution in saying thank you for responding to the challenge.

The value to the institution

In addition to the most obvious result, the support raised, a challenge benefits the institution in other ways:

- A challenge enables you to recruit and train new volunteers.
- Screening sessions for a challenge identify new major gift prospects.
- A challenge presents current donors with an even stronger case for support.
- A challenge gives every member of the target group an opportunity to participate.
- A challenge provides a new way to showcase the institution's present needs and future plans.

Short-term cost/benefit

The additional cost of a challenge fund is often minimal. Mailings, phone calls, and visits to secure gifts would probably have been made anyway as part of regular program activities. The immediate benefits or "profits," however, will often be many multiples above what they would have been without a challenge. For example, classes with reunion giving challenges commonly raise three or four times more than the amount raised in previous years.

Long-term continuing benefits

Don't overlook the long-term benefits of challenge funds even though these are sometimes hard to measure or, even, identify. Often the long-term benefits will be many times the immediate return. While a challenge usually produces greater short-term results from an older class than from a recently graduated class, a challenge fund for the younger class may actually have long-term results far beyond what the challenge itself brings in.

Here's why: Suppose that the fifth reunion class of a college has 500 members; of these, 200 (40 percent) would give an average gift of $25 for a total of $5,000. But if the class has a challenge fund, giving could increase to $8,750 (50 percent participation with an average gift of $35). If 80 percent of the increased giving is sustainable (that is, of the $3,750 increase, $3,000 is sustainable), by the time the class celebrates its 50th reunion, that modest increase would mean an additional $135,000 to the college ($3,000 every year for 45 years).

Challenge funds raise giving sights and promote annual gifts. Assume that a previous year's challenge fund helped to train volunteers to ask annually for increased gifts and classmates responded accordingly. Thus, to take the example above one step further, if the sustainable increase of $3,000 per year grows by only 5 percent annually, by their 50th reunion that same class would have contributed an additional *$503,056.*

Imagine how much money would be available to that college if every class had a challenge fund at least once every five years! In addition to the increase in annual giving, many more alumni could move along the giving spiral to the point where they considered the college to be one of their top priorities for capital and estate gifts.

Challenge funds at Union College

Union's annual fund, begun in 1912, is considered by many to be the oldest continuous modern-day annual fund in the country. Union used challenge funds periodically in its early days, but its first broad-based challenge funds did not occur until the 1970s. Then, a series of four all-alumni challenge funds ranging from $50,000 to $100,000 were established by two alumni, by the chair of the board, and by the board of trustees. While more than 50 percent of Union's alumni were supporting the annual fund, many were in the habit of giving the same amount they had contributed for years. The challenge funds were designed to encourage alumni to increase their gifts by $25 or more over the previous year.

The result: quantum jumps in giving. Overall gifts increased by 43 percent in one year. The following year, over 80 percent of those who increased their giving continued to sustain that new level of support. The creators of the challenges also sustained their increased giving. The trustees, for example, more than tripled their annual support to the college as a result of being asked to provide a leadership challenge for the annual fund. In addition, class agents, leadership agents, and phonathon workers benefited from four years of training in asking alumni for increased gifts.

Recent challenge funds

Most of Union's challenge funds in the 1980s were targeted toward classes, often in conjunction with a reunion. These challenges emphasized *increased gifts* at annual fund major gift club levels ($1,000, $3,000, $5,000, and $10,000 categories). We worded the challenges to encourage donors to think about larger increases and to maximize their gifts by earning new challenge money for the college.

We had eight challenges to reunion classes during the last four years, and all of them inspired donors to make significantly increased gifts, especially at the $1,000 level and higher. As a direct result of meeting the terms of the challenge, all eight reunion classes established new giving records for their class, often more than doubling their previous high. In addition, seven of these classes also established new Union College reunion giving records. Publicizing these records has helped us raise the giving sights of other classes even higher.

The class of 1949 40th Reunion Challenge

In 1988-89, the class of 1949 established a $30,000 challenge to all members of the class. Crafted by the Reunion Leadership Gifts Committee and more complicated than most of our other challenges, the 1949 40th Reunion Challenge stated:

> 1. Increases from $100 to $1,000 over last year will be matched dollar for dollar.
>
> 2. New contributors or those who have not given in the last five years will have gifts from $50 to $250 matched two for one. Over $250 will be matched one for one.
>
> 3. A $1,000 bonus to our class will be awarded for first-time Terrace Council ($1,000 to $4,999), Inner Circle ($5,000 to $9,999) or Garnet Society ($10,000 or more) members.
>
> 4. A $1,000 bonus will be given to our class for each percentage point over 61%—our record level of class participation.
>
> 5. As an added bonus, the challenge will match every dollar raised above $85,540—the all-time record of giving set by the Class of 1943.

After screening the members of the class of 1949, the Reunion Leadership Gifts Committee identified more than half of the class as potential donors of $1,000 and up. Each of the eight committee members selected 10 to 15 classmates to whom they promoted the challenge through personal and telephone contact. They met to discuss strategies on prospects. And several classmates who initially said "maybe" or "no" were reassigned to other committee members who were able to solicit a positive response.

Stressing increased giving paid off. The class achieved a new dollar record of $87,431 from 164 donors. Forty-eight donors joined new giving clubs, and the class reached 67 percent participation. In addition, the class of 1949 set a new college record for unrestricted annual fund giving by a class in one year.

The year before the challenge, the class raised only $36,873 from 133 donors. The challenge fund was the key to a *137 percent increase in gifts.* The success the class achieved helped to make the class reunion celebration on campus even more spirited. It was a proud moment for the class of 1949 when the results were announced to all classes during Reunion Weekend.

Other challenge funds

Challenge funds have stimulated the annual giving of other constituencies at Union College. A parents fund challenge resulted in a 45 percent improvement in giving. The parents fund committee increased gifts to help meet the terms of a challenge from a foundation designed to create a Presidential Discretionary Fund. (Unrestricted gifts to the annual fund provide the trustees flexibility in budgeting and planning.) The parents fund also responded to a challenge from the National Endowment for the Humanities to increase giving to support the humanities.

We've used challenges to encourage cumulative gift giving. One example is our promotion of Distinguished Membership in the Terrace Council (Union's major gift clubs, which in 1989-90 were separated into $1,000, $3,000, $5,000, and $10,000 levels), awarded to alumni, parents, and friends who have been Terrace Council members for 10 or more years. This challenge, to sustain a decade or more of membership, has helped create the habit of leadership annual giving. Eighty percent of the members of the Terrace Council renew their membership each year. And most members can tell you exactly how many years are left until they qualify for Distinguished Membership. As an extra form of recognition, an alumnus provided an endowed fund to pay for Distinguished Membership rings, which he and his wife helped design. Many Distinguished Members proudly wear their rings at Terrace Council and other college social functions.

Recently three volunteer leaders in the class of 1966 challenged their classmates to give at least $1,000 to the annual fund to qualify for a homecoming weekend drawing for a Union College captain's chair. The volunteers also paid for four of these chairs in a special challenge to young alumni.

The Class of 1966 Challenge to the Ten Most Recent Classes required these classes to achieve large jumps in their percent participation. For those classes that achieved their goals, donors' names were placed in a hat. Class members could put their names in the hat every time they sent in an increased gift, made a gift of $100 or more, served as class agent, or attended a phonathon. The drawing took place in front of several hundred volunteers during our Homecoming Appreciation Dinner. We awarded a chair to a member of each of the three classes that met the terms of the challenge. We also drew a name to award a "consolation chair" to an alumnus from one of the six other classes that did not meet the challenge goal but did establish a new class record.

Union attempts to educate students about challenge funds as well. For the past several years, an alumnus has offered a challenge to seniors. The alumnus has paid the cost of class T-shirts, which are designed by a member of the senior class. We give the T-shirts to seniors who contribute $10 or more to the senior gift drive. This challenge helps seniors achieve class identity and a high percentage participation. For the past several years, the senior class has achieved a percentage participation that rivals many of the young alumni classes. Most important, these students are learning the giving habit *before* graduation.

A challenge to reach

Challenge funds provide volunteers and donors with an opportunity to help raise additional funding for the institution. Challenges develop ownership by donors and extend recognition to volunteers.

Challenge funds work. They provide vital support for the institution. They serve to stimulate both the challengers and those who are challenged. The cost to the institution is minimal, and the benefits are sizable and far-reaching.

Challenge funds are also fun. Be creative when you design the terms of a challenge. Stretch the imagination of your donors and their charitable resources, and your institution will reap the rewards.

Chapter 17

A Strategy for Planning Successful Events in Support Of the Annual Fund

Diana J. Martin
Consultant
(Formerly Director of Development, Trinity University, San Antonio, Texas)

A rt shows, auctions, dinners, galas, walkathons, phonathons, telethons, raffles .... Although the final result may take many forms, the orchestration of one or more events in support of the annual fund always represents a significant investment of time and talent. There are two primary reasons such activities have become an integral part of institutional fund-raising efforts. First, they serve as one of the most effective methods for fund raisers to meet and communicate with donors and potential donors. Second, well-organized events foster greater involvement—involvement that can engender commitment.

Yet despite the sound reasoning behind the growth in the number of annual fund events, there is always the danger that these events may become ineffective, directionless traditions that drain staff energy and skills from more focused fund-raising efforts. The challenge lies in creating and conducting events in which imagination, ingenuity, and intellect shape an activity that produces the desired, measurable results for the institution.

Systematically planning a successful event involves five steps:
- clarification of goal;
- determination and allocation of available resources;
- delineation of processes;
- determination of event structures; and
- evaluation.

Goal clarification: What should the event *do?*

Your first step is to define, simply and clearly, what you wish the event to accomplish. You will need to review what may seem to be a multitude of objectives in order to clarify a focus for the activity. For example, you may wish to raise a specific number of dollars *and* to thank current donors, but only one of these goals should be the basis of the event. Don't try to design an event that accomplishes both. Although the event may serve several purposes, it should have one focus.

You can develop a sharply focused goal by using diagnostic data (such as written reports, staff and donor interviews, informal and formal goals) to determine which of the following will be your primary objective:

• *a dollar goal:* When you choose a dollar goal, your emphasis will be on the total amount of money raised. You'll need to concentrate on securing a relatively small number of large gifts. Research can identify current donors and new prospects who are willing and able to make immediate and significant donations.

• *participation goal:* In direct contrast, a participation goal requires an increase in the overall donor base and, by definition, targets a larger "audience" of donors who will be making smaller average gifts. Phonathons and faculty/staff drives, for example, usually have participation goals—that is, the number and/or percentage of donors becomes the measure of success.

• *recognition and retention of donors:* Designed to acknowledge contributions and encourage continued participation, these events may take the form of luncheons, receptions, or dinners for members of major gift clubs.

• *enhancing the visibility of the institution:* For example, you might hold a reception for parents and/or alumni to meet the university president, or you might sponsor a lecture series featuring presentations by outstanding faculty or distinguished alumni.

Determining which of these four objectives best meets *your* specific annual fund needs will streamline efforts to design an event. Although a successful event will actually achieve several goals—and may, in fact, achieve all four types of goals—it will best attain the single purpose on which the planning processes focused.

Determination and allocation of available resources

Once you have charted the direction of the event, you need to determine what resources are available to bring about its accomplishment. Mobilizing all available energies to transform ideas into actions requires careful planning including consideration of the following questions:

• What human resources (staff, volunteers) are available for this project?

• How much capital (money, gifts-in-kind, donated services) is available?

• What talents (intellect, knowledge, ingenuity, creativity, skills) may be drawn upon?

• What information (research records, historical data) might be utilized?

Equally significant is the allocation of resources according to the relative importance of the specific event within the overall fund-raising program.

It is imperative that you review your resources early in the planning process. A small college embarking on its first national phonathon might, for example, explore the available information, learn that its database is incomplete, and determine that comprehensive research of "lost" alumni must take place before telefundraising can succeed.

Delineating processes: A plan of action

Once you have analyzed your resources, you can develop a plan of action. It's easiest to begin with the processes that must take place to reach the targeted goal of your event. Any activity in support of the annual fund should create what author James Gregory Lord has termed "authentic involvement" for its audience.[1] People who are knowledgeable about an institution, who feel they have an insider's view of it, will develop a genuine sense of commitment that results in continuing philanthropic support. To foster this type of relationship, which is at the heart of institutional advancement, events should:

• *"show off" those institutional characteristics and qualities that donors will be proud to support.* Include in your event true representatives of your school, college, or university. Enabling participants to interact with the faculty and students is one way to develop pride in the institution; showcasing institutional facilities and resources is another.

• *demonstrate that the institution is a wise and prudent fiduciary of gifts.* Events should educate donors about the reasons gifts are an intrinsic part of the institution's growth and development. To communicate this message, your event should be thoughtful and creative without giving an impression of extravagance.

• *focus on the charitable concept—the relationship between the event and the cause must be easily discernible.* A nationally known performer may ensure a huge turnout for your gala, but if he or she is all that your guests remember, the event has not fulfilled its mission.

• *underscore institutional quality, strength, and purpose.* A master of communication, Winston Churchill once gave the young Prince of Wales the following advice, "If you have an important point to make, don't try to be subtle or clever. Use a pile driver. Hit the point once. Then come back and hit it a second time—a tremendous whack."[2] You cannot overstate your case. An event should provide the setting and opportunity to demonstrate clearly the vitality and worthiness of your cause.

• *communicate to participants their individual and collective importance.* It's a maxim in fund raising: You cannot thank donors too often. This means you will need both direct and symbolic expressions of gratitude. In *A Passion for Excellence,* Peters and Austin describe their research regarding the importance of this strategy: "Attention *is* symbolic behavior . . . . It all adds up to this: *Every* system, *every* seating arrangement, *every* visit is symbolic behavior."[3] You communicate your concern for participants through your attention—through, for example, a carefully and thoughtfully planned event that your guests enjoy. The attention you pay to their needs and interests will encourage donors to see themselves as an integral part of your institution.

• *include a strong dose of fun and excitement.* An event or activity is a powerful form of communication. The greatest impact is produced by messages of energy, ebullience, and optimism. Those events that are most effective are memorable because they sparkle with charges of imagination, insight, and originality.

Event structures: Putting it all together

Planning now moves from "*What* will happen?" to "*How* will it happen?" Using the information you gathered when you defined your goal, surveyed your resources, and developed your plan of action, you must now determine the specific details—theme, staging, staffing, and facilities—that will shape your event. Although putting together a "walk-a-thon" differs significantly from organizing a black-tie gala, whatever the kind of event, you will have to consider the following details:

• participation: Whom will you include in the audience? How many people will participate? What types of facilities are available to meet participation requirements?

• program: What messages will your event convey and how? Who will communicate them? How will setting, staging, theme, menu, recognition, and other methods also convey your messages?

• communications: What is the plan for publicity, invitations, scripts, press releases, follow-up, and printed materials?

• budget and staffing: Approximately how much will it cost? What timetables and schedules will you need? What human resources are available? How will they be used?

Evaluation

Effective event planning begins when you define the goals of a proposed activity and ends when you assess the outcomes. Comparing what you hoped to achieve with the actual results can reveal new insights for future planning and provide powerful information for use in defining decision alternatives. Your event evaluation will be most effective when you base your assessment on at least three sources of information:

• data analysis: quantitative information describing actual gifts, contacts, or other measurable results;

• evaluation by staff: assessment based on direct observation by the people who were responsible for conducting the annual fund activity. Following the event, you and your staff should examine what happened, how it happened, and how procedures might be improved;

• feedback from event participants: obtained through informal interviews or structured questionnaires. This type of information provides an important "reality check" through which you can accurately monitor the impact of your efforts on your audience.

Conclusion

Special events in support of the annual fund promise significant benefits. However, unless your resources are unlimited, you will need to do careful and systematic planning to be sure that you are providing meaningful involvement of donors and prospective donors. You will build a measurable record of success if you tailor both the details and the critical components of your event to fit your specific goal and if you examine outcomes to facilitate future decision making. Such a results-oriented approach will generate a synergism that positively impacts not only on the annual fund, but on all aspects of institutional advancement.

Notes

[1] James Gregory Lord, *The Raising of Money* (Cleveland: Third Sector Press, 1988), p. 29.

[2] Winston Churchill, advice to the young Prince of Wales on speechmaking, cited by Herbert V. Prochnow and Herbert V. Prochnow Jr. in *The Toastmaster's Treasure Chest* (New York: Harper and Row, 1979), p. 113.

[3] Thomas Peters and Nancy Austin, *A Passion for Excellence* (New York: Warner Books, 1986), pp. 318-20.

Section 4

Reaching Your Constituencies

Chapter 18

A Philosophy of Fund Raising At the Thacher School

Frederick C. Twichell
Director of Development
The Thacher School
Ojai, California

Willard G. Wyman III
Director of Development
St. Mary's School
Medford, Oregon
(Formerly Director of Annual Giving and Alumni Affairs, The Thacher School)

"Education is not merely the making of scholars," wrote Sherman Day Thacher, who founded a school on his Ojai, California, ranch in 1889. "It is the making of men and women. It is the training of the younger generation in the art of living for their own greatest good and the greatest good of their fellow citizens."

That training has, by our reckoning, been extraordinarily successful. The Thacher School begins its second century secure in the knowledge that there is a deep well of affection and appreciation for the school among alumni new and old and among other people who have had a stake in the school, particularly parents and past parents.

Our philosophy of fund raising is simple: We seek to tap—and replenish—that reservoir of good will by keeping alumni and other friends involved in, or at least aware of, the life of the school. Our methods range from the ordinary (writing letters) to the exotic (sponsoring a three-week retreat for alumni and other friends at the school's Golden Trout Camp in the High Sierra).

The results have been gratifying. Our recently completed centennial capital campaign raised more than $18 million over six years. Our annual fund grew every year but one in the '80s. In fiscal 1989 the annual fund results were $555,000 with 57 percent participation from alumni and 83 percent participation from parents. This from a school with an enrollment of 225 and just over 2,100 living alumni! In 1989, alumni contributions accounted for about 55 percent of the annual fund total, which reached a record level of $586,529 by June 30, 1990.

The big three: Alumni, parents, and friends

We divide the annual fund into three main categories: the Alumni Fund, the Parents Fund, and the Thacher Committee Fund (past parents and other friends). Each is a separate organization with its own volunteers and schedule of events, although many events, programs, and mailings embrace all three constituencies. Each of our five gift clubs, for instance, includes alumni, parents, past parents, and other friends. These people meet at the annual club dinner in their region.

In addition to the "big three," we identify two other constituencies in our fundraising efforts: One includes corporations and foundations, and the other, alumni of the Thacher School Summer Science Program, a rigorous six-week course for high school juniors that has been held on the Thacher campus for 30 years. Together these two constituencies provided about 13 percent of the annual fund total in 1989.

Our approach to soliciting funds from alumni, parents, and friends is based on our confidence that these people found their association with the school rewarding and meaningful and that they have an interest in providing that same experience to future generations. Our job, as we see it, is to keep them abreast of campus life, to give them opportunities to be involved in that life, and, when the school has specific financial needs, to communicate those needs to them. To that end everyone receives *The Thacher News* three times a year. This magazine contains news about the school; profiles of students, alumni, and friends; historical articles; plenty of photographs; and an extensive "class notes" section devoted to alumni news. It does *not* contain appeals for money.

We rely on a network of volunteers to do most of the actual solicitation of the big three. The role of the alumni and development office staff is to give these volunteers information, technical assistance (computer help), and encouragement. The alumni and development office organizes events, on campus and off, for each constituent group and sends publications and other mailings at regular intervals. In each case, we try to emphasize keeping people informed about and involved with the school; we keep solicitations to a minimum.

While all Thacher constituents receive some common mail and attention from the alumni and development office, there is a good deal that is different about the three main groups and how we work with them.

Alumni. All schools worth their salt believe their alumni are a unique and extraordinary group. We are no exception. The loyalty and generosity of Thacher alumni are legend, at least in our small corner of the universe.

Like many independent schools, Thacher can boast a long history of great teaching and sterling academic programs, but that alone does not explain the grip the school maintains on those who have passed through here. For 100 years the school has been distinguished by its adherence to the values of ranch life—self-reliance, resourcefulness, and plain dealings with people.

While in many ways Thacher is a vastly different place today than it was when Sherman Thacher tutored his first student in the original rough stone school building, at heart it is very much the same kind of place. Every freshman, regardless of background and experience, must care for a horse and learn to ride it. Every student spends at least two weeks a year camping in the mountains. The school's honor code, which undergirds every aspect of campus life, reflects Thacher's devotion to "honor and fairness and kindness and truth."

This continuity and the loyalty it has engendered in students through the years make it relatively easy for Thacher to raise money from alumni. All of us who work in development understand and appreciate the school's ideals and history, and that enables us to pursue our fund-raising goals wholeheartedly.

Among the activities we sponsor are fall, winter, spring, and summer alumni weekends. The fall and winter weekends include athletic contests between alumni and varsity teams. The spring weekend celebrates horseback riding and derring-do at the gymkhana, a rodeo-like competition. The summer weekend centers around reunion celebrations. In addition, alumni are invited to local receptions, dinner meetings of our gift clubs, and other campus events. The annual alumni retreat in the High Sierra occurs in July.

Our alumni solicitations aren't nearly as extensive as our alumni programs. In fact, each year the alumni office sends no more than three direct mail appeals signed by the president of the Alumni Association. We rely on our loyal class representatives to make at least two personal contacts with their classmates each year, either by phone or by mail. Our class reps usually serve three to five years and sometimes work in pairs. The younger classes, which are larger, have more reps. Toward the end of the fiscal year (June 30), we do a bit of nudging by organizing phonathons in Ventura, San Francisco, and Los Angeles.

Parents. The director of alumni affairs and annual giving organizes the Parents Committee, a group of about 35 parents who hold an annual business meeting in October during Parents Weekend. Parents Committee members solicit a maximum of seven prospective donors, and we give them a schedule to coordinate their appeals with mailings from the school and letters signed by the president of the committee. Parents are solicited by fellow parents twice a year. Parents receive many of the same mailings as alumni, including invitations to gift club dinners, local receptions, and the spring gymkhana. They also receive the *Parents' Post,* a monthly publication prepared by the admissions office that highlights students' activities and accomplishments.

The Parents Committee runs a silent auction during gymkhana weekend each spring. The auction raises 10-15 percent of the Parents Fund total and is part of a day-long program that includes gymkhana events, a western barbecue, and a square dance for parents, students, and faculty.

Parents have a vital stake in the school, particularly in the annual fund that helps run the school while their children are here. Thacher parents understand this, as their 83 percent participation figure in 1989 suggests.

Friends. We take much the same approach in raising money from former parents and other friends of the school. The president of the Thacher Committee coordinates a cadre of volunteers. As with parents, the emphasis is on the richness of school life and the importance of the annual fund in maintaining and expanding classroom and extracurricular programs.

Special solicitations and participation

Broad-based participation gives strength to any campaign. To achieve such support, we try to convince young alumni, parents of scholarship students, and parents of alumni that their contributions, no matter how small, are important.

Alumni. Thacher seniors are introduced to the Alumni Association at the reception held in their honor about a month before they graduate. They meet with, and hear words of welcome from, class reps and other alumni, school staff, trustees, and volunteer leaders of the annual fund.

Our younger alumni are the ones most likely to return to campus to play in alumni games or participate in gymkhana events. We do our best to stay in touch with these young people. Although difficult, keeping track of ever-changing college addresses is worth the effort. We suggest sending the school newspaper to alumni for the first three years after they graduate.

Our initial goal with younger alumni is to get them in the habit of giving to Thacher or at least putting Thacher at the top of the list of institutions they *would* give to if they could. We find that alumni who do this become donors before long.

Once an alumnus is giving on a regular basis, we stress the importance of increasing the gift as he or she gets older. A good method of doing this is to have a series of gift clubs that offer donors special recognition for their contributions. We established a Century Club for young alumni donors (out for 10 years or less) to encourage a larger gift ($100-249). We also have an intermediate club (donors of $250 to $999), and leadership clubs at various levels—$1,000, $2,500, $5,000, and $10,000. Having several gift club levels gives our best supporters the incentive to move up the ladder.

Club membership pins and annual appreciation dinners have proven to be all the recognition our best donors need. (With recent IRS interest in these freebies, you should tell your donors to consult a tax adviser; premiums such as dinners and recognition items may affect the amount of their tax deduction.)

Finally, we cultivate leadership donors and keep them in touch with the school by inviting them to small breakfast meetings with our headmaster.

Parents and friends. Establishing a good Parents Committee to solicit parents has worked well at Thacher, particularly since the annual fund money is spent on programs that benefit current students. For past parents and other friends, we emphasize that the school needs their continuing support to maintain long-held standards of excellence—the very standards children of past parents enjoyed.

Organizing and motivating volunteers

A director of development's most important task may well be selecting and nurturing volunteers. The performance of your volunteers, from the board of trustees on down, determines whether your campaign will be a success. For key roles, look for people who have not only demonstrated a real commitment to your school, but have shown they can get a job done; avoid those who talk a better game than they play. Beware the volunteer with a hidden agenda; for example, "My daughter is about to apply for admission . . . " is a danger signal.

Volunteers have a right to expect specific assistance from the institution. You should explain as clearly as possible what is expected of a volunteer who is, after all, giving his or her time. Clear information and consistent support are essential.

Be sure you have realistic expectations. For instance, in a capital campaign, assign each solicitor no more than three or four prospects at a time; in an annual fund campaign, ask each class representative to contact no more than 15 classmates. Limiting the numbers makes it easier for the volunteer to complete his or her task, and you can adjust the workload as some people finish their assignments early and easily while others run into problems.

Developing and maintaining a high level of motivation requires three basics:
- frequent contact with volunteers—especially chairs and committee members;
- effective troubleshooting; and
- timely updating of information.

Simply stated, a volunteer's job is to cultivate and solicit assigned prospects and be accountable for the results. Although volunteers may contact prospects by letter or telephone, it is better to meet them face-to-face—for lunch or dinner or perhaps as part of a larger social gathering or outing.

During the actual solicitation, the volunteer may prefer the oblique approach, steering the conversation to memories of school and then to a discussion of the school's needs, while some older alumni get right to the point. But eventually the volunteer must ask the bottom-line question, "Would you be able to include the school in your charitable giving this year?" or "Do you think you could see your way clear to make a contribution of $____?" Never leave it to the volunteer to determine the size of the request. School staff should always provide a dollar amount or, preferably, a range.

The volunteer should be prompt in reporting the content and outcome of each contact as well as the result of each ask. With this information the school staff can provide better coaching and troubleshooting and prevent duplicate solicitations.

Conclusion

Establishing a personal relationship with every individual in every constituency group is the best way to raise interest in the school and its needs. At Thacher we keep it simple and personal; we want our constituents to know our needs, celebrate our successes, and continue their involvement with the school. While your school may be very different from the Thacher School, we believe these basics of fund raising will apply.

Best wishes to you as you build your school's advancement team and program.

Chapter 19

For Class and College:
The Class Agent Approach

Robert (Bob) V. Behr
Director of Alumni Relations
Williams College
Williamstown, Massachusetts

A t a dozen or so small (under 20,000 alumni) colleges in America, particularly in the Northeast, over 60 percent of the alumni respond to the annual appeal. The dollars follow the participation, exceeding or approaching $4 million at a few institutions. And yet many of these annual fund offices are small shops. How do they do it? By organizing a network of volunteers, alumni who pitch in and solicit for their college and their class.

This is the class agent approach, and here's how it works:

Let's imagine that Joe or Jane Alumnus receives a mass mailing, asking for a gift to the Siwash College Annual Fund. The nameless or unfamiliar voice making the appeal isn't very likely to alter Jane's or Joe's sales resistance, and the mailing will probably go to the bottom of the stack of bills—or perhaps into the circular file with the rest of the direct mail.

But what if the appeal is a personal letter, written by an old friend who is also a classmate? What if the letter is on class stationery? That check to the college is much more likely to be written, and that annual alumni fund is much more likely to prosper. Therein lies the secret of success: Use the class connection as the personalized hook to capture the heart (and the check) of your alumnus.

When a response to the annual appeal will benefit both class and college, there's a twofold reason for Joe or Jane to respond. And when the solicitor is an acquaintance, the personal tie is even more likely to produce results. But who *is* the person making the appeal?

He or she is *not* a professional development officer, but a class agent, a volunteer who has the responsibility for contacting a segment of the class. He or she is also a graduate of Siwash College; thus, for Joe and Jane the class agent is a friend and classmate, a fellow alumnus who is donating time and energy for the class and for the college. Potential donors already have a bond of sympathy with this solicitor and are therefore less likely to say "no."

At Williams College, two-thirds say "yes" every year. That's two-thirds of the *entire* locatable alumni population—everyone who ever earned a credit, except for those who have written formal letters of resignation from the Society of Alumni.

Organizing the class agent network

Class agents can be organized into a team for each class, with each agent contacting 50 of his or her college friends and acquaintances. There are 510 in a current Williams class; thus, each team has 10 agents, and each of these agents contacts about 51 people.

The class network is established and sustained as the agents make their appeals on special class stationery. There should be as many names as possible on the letterhead, reminding the volunteers of their responsibility and dignifying their efforts in the eyes of their classmates. The college supplies the volunteers with data (names, addresses, and gift history) and material, such as pre-addressed stamped envelopes, periodic reports, perhaps even a telephone calling card, and the special stationery. At Williams an artist or graphic designer from the class often designs the logo, typography, and layout for the stationery.

Some marvelously creative letterheads have emerged at Williams. One design has the names of all members of the class ghosted onto the stationery. The darker printing of the current message (offset, computer printed, or handwritten) is easily read, but each member of the class can find his or her name beneath the text. Another class letterhead logo employs the talents of a popular cartoonist, a classmate whose works were well-known in the college newsletter.

Home office support for the class agents must be personal and prompt. The director of annual giving and his secretary know each agent, field all agent phone calls, and respond quickly to all requests for assistance. Each agent receives individual treatment—it's taxing but it pays dividends.

During my 10 years as a volunteer agent for my Williams class, I had the pleasure of corresponding with my old classmates and friends, all 275 of them. (This was before we began using teams of agents.) With the college supplying pre-addressed and stamped envelopes and my personally crafted prose offset onto our class letterhead, I was in business. My "P.S.'s" carried a special hello or, when appropriate, a friendly jibe from our undergraduate days.

It was fun keeping up with my chums. Some would write back, and a truly valued form of reply was the copy of the gift receipt, sent to me from the alumni fund office. Then I'd write a quick note of thanks, often on a picture post card of the college. Another entertaining phase of the annual exercise was the mop-up phonathon. It was fun to chat with classmates at college expense—but never for too long, of course.

Class identity is the significant factor

A clear and positive class identity is central to this fund-raising method. Before you begin to work on the details, ask yourself this very important question: Does each alumnus have a sense of belonging to the very special class of 'XX? That critical class identity is first established during the undergraduate years and later built upon and nurtured during the alumni years by reunions, ample class notes in the alumni magazine, class newsletters, and any other means developed by the alumni relations office—not the least of which is sustained and vigorous class leadership through an officer structure for each class.

What happens during the undergraduate experience to create the bond of a class? Each college or university has its own class traditions and exercises. At Williams, freshmen live and dine together, and this creates a strong bond. The stronger the class bonding, the stronger the class, and strong classes will pull together to aid the college.

A smaller college the size of Williams (2,000) may have an advantage in the personal flavor of the undergraduate days. However, there are small groups even in a huge university: Find them and use personal solicitation from within.

Friendly competition helps

Friendly interclass competition can do wonders for the annual fund campaign. Interim reports of class standings will urge leading classes to hold their positions and will encourage lagging classes to catch up with the leaders. You can establish trophy races or competitions for various age groups: the youngest 10 classes, the reunion classes, the "old guard" classes (50 years out and over), the classes 25 to 50 years out, and so on. (Williams College awards 10 class trophies in each annual campaign.)

Class agents tend to be competitive people, and the lure of a trophy stimulates some heroic efforts. When the campaign is over, the winning classes are prominently rewarded—in print and in public presentations. The entire class can take pride in a victory, and the nonwinners can declare, "Wait 'til next year!"

Class volunteers can look for the class rankings published periodically in newsletters for annual fund workers. Does the class look good? Is it leading a trophy race? Setting a record for itself? Setting an all-time record in dollars or in participation for an age group? Class agents and other class officers can take special pride in the fund-raising accomplishments of their class. They can be the drum-beaters who urge their classmates onward to new records. Call it peer pressure if you will, but it works. And so does the bandwagon effect within a discrete class-size group. Even colleges as large as Dartmouth (some 50,000 alumni) can use the class as the basis for 60-percent participation.

The four charts in Figure 19-1 show various rankings and comparisons from Williams' 1988 alumni fund: a comparison of reunion class giving; reunion class records; the top 20 classes; and annual giving and participation for the total alumni body from 1964-1988.

These competitions all create wonderful leverage for the class agents as they make the "ask."

The hoopla surrounding trophy competitions can galvanize reunion groups. A less-than-stellar class can pull itself together for a grand effort in the name of its 20th, 30th, or 40th reunion. The reunion occasion also creates that special springboard for class agents, a good reason for asking for an increased gift. Reunions capture attention and create an emotional bond; even if you can't get there, you may feel an obligation to respond. Figure 19-2 shows some of the class agents who have helped achieve records for their classes.

When trophy races for dollars are close, decided by a few hundred dollars out of thousands, each class donor can feel a part of the effort. Indeed, the four- (or five-) digit donor can discern his or her gift in the published breakdown of class totals. That nice gift would be invisible in the grand total for the college, but in the class subtotal, the donor can see that his or her gift truly does make a difference.

With class trophy competitions also based upon participation, the small donor can note how his or her gift nudged the class percentages higher, perhaps to a trophy. The agent may use this facet of the competition to urge a former nondonor to make a modest gift "for the class." It works!

"For the class" adds another thematic dimension to annual giving. When "for the class" is combined with "for the college," you can expect new records for your annual campaign. The volunteers—the class agents—are the key to success in both the small shop and the large one.

Figure 19-1

RESULTS OF '88: Highlights of Past Performance

Annual Giving To The Alumni Fund (1964-1988)

Year	Amount	Participation
1964	422,652	56.95
1965	432,088	56.22
1966	521,984	57.02
1967	598,336	56.51
1968	648,901	56.17
1969	671,751	54.77
1970	732,164	53.01
1971	780,899	53.61
1972	921,717	52.40
1973	908,479	54.79
1974	923,143	53.18
1975	1,023,907	55.98
1976	1,111,897	58.50
1977	1,168,038	60.69
1978	1,373,021	62.16
1979	1,520,613	62.24
1980	1,594,016	62.50
1981	2,119,945	63.60
1982	2,349,536	65.44
1983	2,688,751	65.56
1984	2,860,533	66.28
1985	3,277,763	66.91
1986	3,909,119	68.94
1987	3,775,861	66.41
1988	4,023,966	65.41

The Reunion Classes — Comparative Performance

Reunion	Class	1988	1987	Increase
50th	*1939	$ 41,962	$ 28,731	+ $ 13,231
45th	1944	142,582	49,212	+ 93,370
40th	1949	68,832	56,824	+ 12,008
35th	1954	301,668	155,848	+ 145,820
30th	1959	84,018	58,187	+ 25,831
25th	*1964	58,086	51,467	+ 6,619
20th	1969	107,475	46,714	+ 60,761
15th	1974	55,713	31,776	+ 23,937
10th	1979	104,690	38,069	+ 66,621
5th	1984	15,146	9,054	+ 6,092

*The Classes of 1939 and 1964 were also engaged in capital fund raising for their 50th and 25th reunions respectively.

The Top Twenty Classes
Cumulative Giving Totals (through the 1988 Campaign)

	Class	Amount
1.	1954	$1,600,843
2.	1941	1,520,711
3.	1950	1,340,331
4.	1940	1,285,875
5.	1942	1,084,370
6.	1952	1,070,574
7.	1953	1,016,749
8.	1936	945,422
9.	1944	929,613
10.	1951	928,886
11.	1960	892,886
12.	1943	820,696
13.	1937	747,811
14.	1955	747,450
15.	1931	740,325
16.	1948	716,416
17.	1962	708,752
18.	1958	678,967
19.	1949	668,288
20.	1930	646,925

Reunion Class Records

Years After Graduation	Amount Contributed Class	Dollars	Percent of Participation Class	Percent
First	1988	$ 13,226	1961	65.88%
Second	1969	13,503	1976	67.71
Third	1980	11,225	1976	72.60
Fourth	1980	13,484	1958	70.63
Fifth	1982	19,489	1977	71.18
Sixth	1975	23,247	1976	70.52
Seventh	1979	32,796	1978	68.38
Eighth	1979	35,200	1977	71.77
Ninth	1975	50,460	1956	77.36
*Tenth	1979	104,690	1968	75.40
15th	1971	116,068	1965	75.54
*20th	1968	122,958	1965	87.31
25th	1962	84,253	1960	79.11
30th	1954	185,833	1959	77.65
*35th	1954	301,668	*1954	93.69
40th	1944	176,614	1925	98.48
45th	1944	142,581	1941	99.35
50th	1936	78,074	1925	96.87
55th	1931	72,594	1924	97.05
60th	1925	24,389	1924	100.00
65th	1921	17,682	Several	100.00

Figure 19-2

PREVIEW OF '89: Old Guard and Reunion Agents

OLD GUARD AGENTS

The 24 Old Guard Class Agents pictured below maintain excellence within the Alumni Fund year after year. In the 1988 Alumni Fund, no less than 4 Old Guard classes registered 100% participation. The average participation for all Old Guard classes was 78%. These 24 classes raised $393,097 of the $4M total.

Field '13   L. Hubbell '15   S. Hubbell '16   Powers '18   White '20   Schlesinger '21   Schenck '22   Lawder '23

Senter '24   Wilson '25   Riegel '26   Martin '27   Bisbee '28   Beavers '29   Corwin '30   Wineberg '31

Higinbotham '32   Babcock '33   Allen '34   Morrison '35   Strauss '36   Lowe '37   Blake '38   Cooper '39

REUNION AGENTS

In the 1989 Alumni Fund, the ten Reunion Class Agents will raise as much as 25% of the total goal. Reunions are a time for stepped-up giving. The Classes of 1940 and 1965 are having 50th and 25th capital campaigns this year.

Hoffman '40   Cholmelev-Jones '45   Prescott '50   Perrott '55   Bagnulo '60

Small '65   McCurdy '70   Bestebreurtje '75   Underhill '80   Martin '85

Chapter 20

Handbook for Volunteers

Peter V. Buttenheim
Director of Annual Giving
Williams College
Williamstown, Massachusetts

Most schools, colleges, and universities use alumni, parents, and friends as volunteers in annual giving programs. In some annual funds, the volunteers work directly with the staff at the institution, and most of the mailings and phonathons emanate from the campus. In other annual funds, the volunteers and staff segment the donors—most often by class (year of commencement)—and the vast majority of the volunteer effort takes place away from the campus.

Whether the volunteers assist staff on campus or work as class agents "off shore," the system of volunteer or class agent support should be spelled out clearly in a volunteer or class agent handbook. This handbook should be a ready reference book for volunteers that states exactly what the volunteers should do and how they should do it. It should be written and prepared by the staff of the office that runs the annual fund.

Developing the contents

The following is a list of the topics most useful to volunteers and class agents (the topics are given in the order in which they should appear):
- the purpose of the handbook;
- a brief history of the school, college, or university;
- campaign procedures;
- planning a successful campaign;
- tips for increasing participation;
- special appeals;

- writing a successful appeal letter;
- help available from the office;
- letterhead concerns;
- phonathons;
- special and memorial gifts;
- class competitions; and
- expenses and miscellaneous.

Purpose of the handbook. You should state the purpose of the class agents handbook at the beginning of the book. This opening paragraph is similar to a mission statement. In a few sentences, the nature of annual giving at the school, college, or university—and its importance—should be tied to the operation of the annual fund. In this way, the volunteers know exactly why they are giving their time and why they are asking others to give their money.

History of the institution. Include a brief history of your school, college, or university. Often a new volunteer has been out of touch with alma mater, and the section on the institution's history serves to rekindle old ties of loyalty and affection. On a more practical level, the background information contained in this section comes in handy when donors ask those tough questions of volunteers.

Campaign procedures. This is the real "meat and potatoes" part of the handbook. Typically, this chapter includes the following information as well as anything unique to the particular campaign:

- the kind of campaign;
- length of campaign;
- methods of solicitation to be used;
- office support;
- timetables and deadlines;
- materials to be supplied; and
- volunteer responsibilities.

This chapter should be exhaustive and written in a very clear, practical manner. Begin by assuming that the volunteers don't know *anything*. It is far better to explain too much than to explain too little. Volunteers want the specifics when it comes to campaign procedures.

Planning a successful campaign. This chapter addresses the methods for achieving the campaign's goals. Here, the professional staff members explain the campaign timetable in detail. Be sure that deadlines for office staff support and volunteer services are printed in large bold type. Include a description of special projects, campaign objectives, telethon schedules, the availability of support materials, and the like. If your campaign relies on telephone credit cards, fax equipment, or computer modems, include a list of the important telephone and fax numbers. The key to a successful campaign is excellent planning, and that planning must be conveyed clearly to the volunteers.

Tips for increasing participation. Most annual giving volunteers are hardworking, businesslike, and just a bit competitive. These volunteers always want to know how to increase participation. Since no two institutions run annual giving programs in exactly the same way, there is a great deal of room in institutional advancement circles for what at Williams we call "legal piracy." Encourage your staff to jot down any creative ideas regarding participation and pass them on to their volunteers. Even within one institution, ideas for increasing participation can be tried by different classes at various times within a campaign. This chapter of the handbook might be nothing more than a list of 20 or 30 tried-and-true ideas for improving participation. For the most eager volunteers, you might also include a short bibliography on books and articles about increasing participation.

Special appeals. Annual giving campaigns are often tied to a major event in the institution's history. Many colleges and universities link annual giving with special reunion programs. If your volunteers are involved with these special appeals, they need a full understanding of how these programs work within the overall context of the annual giving operation. Again, you need to provide these volunteers with as much detail as possible.

Writing a successful appeal letter. This will be the chapter of most interest to those volunteers who will be drafting their own letters to their classmates. If your staff writes generic appeal letters for the volunteers, you can omit this chapter.

New volunteers always like to know what has worked well in the past, and you can show them by including sample letters in the appendix. Volunteers also want practical information about the length and tone of the letters, letterhead, factual versus philosophical approaches, and so on. The handbook should address all of these topics in detail. However, staff must remember that volunteer-driven appeal letters are highly personal and idiosyncratic, and that what works well for one volunteer and his or her classmates may be unsuccessful for another.

Help available from the office. No volunteer-driven annual giving campaign can succeed without help from the office. Volunteers need to know who the professional and support staff people are and what they do. Volunteers need to know whom to call if they have questions about recording, acknowledging, and receipting gifts; availability of envelopes, post cards, and letterhead; and much more. Knowing what help is available from the office makes volunteers' jobs much easier and dramatically cuts turnaround time for requests. It's essential that the staff be responsive to the needs of the volunteers.

Letterhead concerns. If your institution uses individualized letterhead for each class, you need to tell volunteers how to order letterhead, which class officers to list, and what campus scene or institutional logo might be appropriate for the masthead. If a class is lucky, it may have an artist among its members who will offer to—or agree to—design a logo. This will make the letterhead even more significant to the members of the class.

Printing 60 or 70 different class letterheads is an ambitious job; be sure to include the various proofing deadlines for the volunteers. This will give you a better chance of keeping up with the printing schedule. Include in the appendix some samples of successful letterheads.

Phonathons. If your annual giving program relies on phonathons, you'll need to include a chapter highlighting some of the details, such as:

- dates, times, and locations of phonathons;
- availability of class directories or telephone numbers;

- hints for first-time callers; and
- general phonathon procedures for each class.

While finding the phonathon site, planning for food, and providing the printed materials are usually the responsibility of the annual giving staff, volunteers appreciate being informed. And this chapter should also promote the concept of phonathons as the ideal follow-up to letter-writing campaigns. "Classes that call—win it all" is an apt saying.

Special and memorial gifts. Each year, annual giving campaigns receive some gifts in honor or in memory of someone, and each institution has its own approach to receiving, recording, and acknowledging these gifts. Volunteers need to know these procedures as they deal with donors. It's also essential that volunteers know which sorts of special and memorial gifts can be credited to annual giving. This chapter should spell out these distinctions.

Class competitions. At many institutions, annual giving is fueled by class competition. The handbook should highlight these competitions and list the awards. At Williams we have 10 silver cups and bowls that are awarded at the annual meeting of the Society of Alumni in June and again at the Class Agents' Weekend each September. These awards recognize outstanding dollar and performance records among the young, middle, and older classes. Whatever form of class competition, volunteer recognition, or award system your institution has should be explained in this chapter as a vital part of volunteer incentive.

Expenses and miscellaneous. You can put this chapter at the end of the handbook and include in it everything not covered previously, as well as expenses. Make it clear to volunteers which expenses can be reimbursed and which cannot. You can also include those other items peculiar to your institution's annual giving program.

Handbook format

Once you and your staff have written or assembled all of the chapters and appendices for the handbook, you must determine its format. Some colleges and universities print a 40- or 50-page hardcover book. Others use a more informal softcover edition that is stapled rather than bound. At Williams, we printed our 1990 handbook on three-hole paper and put it in a loose-leaf notebook with the college seal on the cover. We'll be able to use this handbook for years by adding new materials and replacing out-of-date sections.

Whatever form you choose, if your handbook is well-written, accurate, and sufficiently detailed, it will keep your volunteers informed. And nothing is more important to an annual giving program than well-informed volunteers.

Chapter 21

Reunion Giving: A Plan that Works

Sherwood C. Haskins Jr.
Associate Director of Development
Phillips Exeter Academy
Exeter, New Hampshire

M ost development professionals agree on the tenet that individuals will more generously support projects or special campaigns that are of personal interest to them. As a result, we are constantly trying to personalize our approaches to potential donors, whether it be for annual giving, capital campaigns, or special needs projects.

We have designed a plan for reunion giving at Phillips Exeter Academy that is applicable to secondary schools and most colleges. With individual fine-tuning, your institution can enjoy similar successes with this approach.

The approach to reunion year giving

Reunion giving programs provide us with unique opportunities to match the special interest of donors or classes with an appropriate need of the institution.

Reunion giving programs are most often linked in some way to the annual giving program. While each year we look to non-reunion classes to increase their level of support according to a calculated formula, the net results are only marginal increases from year to year. On the other hand, a reunion giving program can provide a boost to annual funds each year as classes (and individuals) increase their levels of giving significantly. With greater demands on the annual fund each year, reunion giving can become the source of those critical additional funds required to meet operational and capital needs.

The monies generated from reunion programs may be used to support annual giving or operational needs, or they may be segmented out to support capital needs, endowed funds, or special projects. Whatever the case, the reunion campaign takes on a capital campaign mentality and requires a more thorough approach in organization and planning. This chapter focuses on a reunion fund designed to meet capital endowment needs.

At Exeter we decided to combine capital giving with the annual fund because we had just completed a major capital campaign. While we knew that our constituency, volunteers, and staff were not ready for another major effort immediately, we did have a clear perspective on the institution's needs for subsequent years. The challenge was to find a way to meet these capital needs outside of a major campaign structure.

By marketing the needs of the institution to the class gift committees, we enabled each one to adopt a project that was most meaningful and salable to that particular class. Whether it be scholarship assistance, faculty compensation, or physical plant needs, each class could select an attractive and attainable project.

The response to this program has been phenomenal. These mini-campaigns held on a five-year cycle have been extremely successful. We are now in our second cycle, and the enthusiasm is still high among the classes that launched the program five years ago.

An exciting new approach that has proven most effective is combining two class reunion giving programs over an eight-year period—that is, including the year prior to the 45th, the 45th, four non-reunion years, the 50th, and the year after the 50th. The 45th and 50th reunion combination provides an interesting case study. Although alumni nearing the 45th reunion have begun thinking about retirement and financial planning, generally they are still earning a maximal income. By enabling potential major gift donors to plan their leadership giving over an eight-year period, one class raised over half of the total amount raised in Exeter's previous major capital campaign.

Gift crediting with reunion year classes

The process of gift crediting in reunion giving campaigns can be confusing to the donor and complicated for the institution. It's an issue you and the class committee should deal with before solicitations for the reunion campaign begin. Generally, you can accept gifts made toward reunion pledges over several years. If your fiscal year is July 1-June 30, a donor would have six months of the first calendar year, 12 full months of the following year, and six additional months for the final year ending on June 30. In other words, a donor may spread the payment out over three tax years. In cases of extraordinarily large capital gifts, you may have to lengthen this payment period at the donor's request.

Flexibility should be a key component in the crediting process as gifts will probably include cash, securities, real estate, insurance, and planned gifts as well as gifts-in-kind. As donors become more sophisticated in their understanding of philanthropy, you need to be prepared to meet their needs graciously and efficiently. Here are some methods that may help:

- List individual goals for the annual giving and capital giving components;
- Allocate monies received first to annual giving to meet the operational needs of the budget;
- Credit gifts received later to the capital project and those that are strictly designated for a specific component;
- Split all gifts (or gifts over $10,000) on a percentage basis, reflecting the difference between the individual components of the total goal; or
- If you plan your operation budget accordingly, you can allocate all of the reunion gifts for one or two classes (e.g., the 25th and the 50th) to a special capital project. Of course, if a donor contributes to another area of need outside of the class project, the dollars should count toward the overall class gift.

The social program vs. the fund-raising plan

Let's look at the other enormously critical part of the reunion—the social side. Be sure class members are aware of the clear distinctions between the fund-raising plan and the social program. In most cases, alumni staff members manage the social side of a reunion, and the development staff manages the fund-raising effort.

It is advisable to keep the two areas separate—for the professional staff and for the volunteer committees. The alumni office provides direction to the social committee of a reunion, regarding program, attendance, and the class yearbook. The reunion gifts committee works directly with the development staff on its fund-raising plan. Making this distinction early in the organizational process prevents any confusion.

Successful reunion giving programs provide an ideal opportunity for staff members in all aspects of your program to work together. Annual giving, capital giving, and planned giving personnel all have an integral role to play in a comprehensive program. Communication and teamwork replace unnecessary competition between departments.

Competition between classes, however, works to your advantage in reunion fund raising. While competition exists in non-reunion years as well, reunions seem to bring out the highest levels of pride, and this leads to eager competition between reunion year classes. Each year there may be a new record to surpass for the 25th or 50th reunion, and this means increased support for your institution.

Finally, the timing of reunions at your institution is critical. You will need to carry on a continuous cultivation process for donors on a regular basis depending on the length of your reunion cycle. If you are focusing your capital fund-raising efforts around reunions, this schedule is ideal. You are reviewing class prospects 18 months before the reunion and probably have a follow-up procedure for those who did not meet your expectations in that specific year. Without conscious planning, you are directing a very successful donor tracking system.

The critical element: Volunteer leadership

How good is the class leadership, and how much early planning do you do? These are the two most critical factors in the success of reunion fund raising. Class leaders should include both new volunteers and veterans. While veterans provide continuity between reunions, new class leadership is essential for several reasons. Class officers can become ineffective after years of service, and the replacement process can be a healthy one. Newly appointed volunteers can inject fresh enthusiasm into the campaign.

When you are selecting a reunion committee, try to involve a broad representation of the class. Diversity of interests and level of visibility in the class are key elements. Class leadership can identify new volunteers and new sources of support as well. Geographical location can be a major factor in predicting the effectiveness of a volunteer. Class officers should be able to visit your institution or be easily seen by staff members.

Building class leadership with the right people makes all the difference. Here is one way to do it. The class president, who directs both the social and fund-raising sides of a reunion, is responsible for setting up and overseeing the volunteer structure. He or she selects a social chair and a reunion gifts chair to direct each effort. The reunion gifts chair works with two key individuals, the major gifts chair and the general gifts chair, and each of these chairs is assisted by a committee.

The major gifts chair and the major gifts committee are responsible for the solicitation of all major gift prospects. The chair should have a generous giving history or the potential to provide a key gift in the upcoming campaign.

The general gifts chair works with the general gifts committee to solicit the balance of the class. While the major gifts chair may be a newcomer, the general gifts chair may be the existing class agent. (If the class agent for annual giving is effective and fully involved in your fund-raising program, then appointing him or her to be general gifts chair makes sense. If, however, the agent is burned out or has not been effective recently, it may be the ideal time to suggest a change.)

In any case, the smaller the committee, the more effective it will be. For political reasons, you may have to include some people as figureheads, but if you possibly can, it's best to limit the committee membership to people who will accept responsibilities and be effective workers. You may follow the 5-percent rule— membership for each committee is no bigger than 5 percent of the total class. Geographical location and interest diversity are critical elements here as well.

Once the new team is in place, organization and planning begin.

The reunion timetable

Let's take a moment to highlight the critical stages in the schedule for a reunion planned for spring 1993:

Fall 1991. We begin the process of organizing at least 18 months prior to the reunion itself. Many institutions host a leadership weekend for volunteers each fall, and this provides the perfect opportunity to meet with class officers two and a half years ahead of the reunion.

October-November 1991. Class president recruits committee chairs.

Winter 1992. At Exeter we extend an invitation in the winter months to the new reunion team (social and fund raising) to return to campus for a leadership training session. At this program, volunteers hear from the head of the institution and other key administrators and meet with staff members and classmates to discuss the upcoming campaign, which will be launched officially in five months (July 1, 1992).

March-June 1992. The committees meet to finalize class goals, screen the class for gift levels, and develop the final fund-raising plan. At the same time, the staff is researching special prospects, coordinating cultivation and solicitation assignments with class officials and the major gifts committee, and assisting with volunteer recruitment.

Spring 1992. Class leadership together with staff representatives hold organizational meetings and class screenings to review class giving potential, discuss institutional needs, decide on the class project, and complete the volunteer structure.

Summer 1992. The final fund-raising plan should now be in place.

Spring-fall 1992. The initial leadership gifts must come from committee members themselves. The major gifts chair should solicit the committee members *after* he or she has committed to a leadership gift. A core leadership group should have provided a substantial amount toward the total goal before the second round of major gift solicitations begins.

July-December 31, 1992. Major gifts chair and major gifts committee are working on assignments of specific prospects in the class.

Fall 1992. We invite to campus all the volunteers who have worked on fund-raising programs. They receive recognition for the past year's campaign successes and are motivated for the upcoming campaign. The invitation includes all reunion volunteers. This occasion is an opportune time to review progress to date and to plan for the general appeal to the class.

Shortly after the fall volunteer weekend, the general gifts chair sends the first letter to members of the class who are not serving on a committee or are not major gift prospects. The contents of the letter may vary, but, in most instances, it includes a request for a specific dollar amount. The reunion gifts chair should continue to be involved and should be prepared to provide immediate support if any of the volunteers fall behind in the timetable.

December 1992-March 1993. The level of participation during a reunion year should increase. During the next few months, reunion classes may use phonathons to follow up on the first appeal and to reach as many classmates as possible. In early December, those who have not yet contributed receive a second general gift letter. The general gifts chair may write the letter, or it may be signed by the head of the institution.

Late winter 1993. The gift committees meet once more in late winter to follow up on prior assignments and to review strategies for the final portion of the campaign. The reunion gifts chair sends a third-class letter announcing the final phase of the campaign.

Spring 1993. Spring phonathons are the last appeal before the reunion in the late spring. Before the conclusion of the fiscal year and after the reunion, a mail-gram solicitation provides a final wrap-up in an attempt to increase overall class participation in the campaign.

Conclusion

A successful reunion giving program can bring many benefits to your institution. Reunion giving can have a significant impact on your annual fund. As important, when classes support capital or special projects, they meet institutional needs that otherwise might not be met without a capital campaign.

Reunion giving most often means increased personal giving by classmates. This increased level of support can have a residual effect on individual giving patterns, resulting in increased support during non-reunion years. Class participation during a reunion year should increase as a direct result of the personalization of the solicitation, class competition, and support of a single class project. These new levels of participation are the source of great pride for many classes and continue through non-reunion years.

A reunion campaign identifies new volunteer leadership, which may continue to lead the class after the reunion. With increased cultivation, new leadership donors are brought into the class giving program. Finally, encouraging alumni to visit campus for the reunion is one of the most effective cultivation programs you can offer. Alumni see the institution again; meet faculty, students, and administrative officers; learn about institutional needs and goals; visit with classmates; and, most important, enjoy reliving memories that will last a lifetime. Isn't that what reunions are all about?

Chapter 22

Planning a Comprehensive Parents Program

Mona Wheatley
Director of Special Gifts
Middlebury College
Middlebury, Vermont

M ost of us no longer wonder *whether* we should involve parents in the life of our institution, but *how* we should do it. While institutions have traditionally solicited parent gifts for their annual funds, the '80s witnessed the establishment of full-fledged parents programs at increasing numbers of colleges and universities. And today, multifaceted parents programs are often the major responsibility of a particular development officer.

Despite soaring fees and cutbacks in federal funding, a significant number of parents continue to make unrestricted contributions to the institutions their children attend. While creative financial aid packages seek to ease some of that burden, parents still carry much of the responsibility for funding their children's education. And many obviously believe that education to be well worth whatever sacrifices they must make.

Parents who contribute to their child's institution understand that tuition and other student fees never cover the actual cost of a student's education. Gifts, grants, and the income from endowment must make up the difference. While tuition may cover a greater percentage of the cost at some institutions than at others, no institution can survive on tuition and fees alone.

Building your parents program

Developing or expanding parents programs can be challenging, exciting, and rewarding. Parents programs help forge a link between our institutions and the par-

have sent us their children. Students who are challenged and successful—or mainly so—in their educational pursuits generally have happy parents. We need to develop programs that will enable parents to share their children's successes without interfering with their children's newfound independence.

Whether you are starting or expanding a parents program, it's best to begin by asking yourself, "What kind of program is most appropriate for my institution?" The program must be compatible with the philosophies and traditions of your institution, and it should interface harmoniously with the other offices on your campus that are involved in parents programs.

If, at your institution, several different offices are responsible for activities such as freshmen welcoming parties, parents weekends, newsletters, handbooks, and fund raising, the biggest problem will be coordination. You are fortunate if you have a student affairs office or special functions office that works harmoniously with the development team, or if you have total control over the entire program.

Before you plan the scope of your program, consider how much support—staff and funding—the institution can commit. You will then need to recruit enthusiastic and reliable volunteers to serve as visible leaders of the activities. Choosing those leaders wisely is crucial to your success.

If you are starting a parents association, it's best to include all current and past parents as members. State the purpose of the organization in broad terms that include the expectations, responsibilities, and extent of the program. This statement of purpose should appear in appropriate institutional publications, such as welcoming material sent to freshmen families. Also include it when you are asking parents to serve as volunteers.

The parents association can be governed by a parents council or committee organized by class affiliation or by function or both. Making sure that all classes are represented equally will strengthen the organization and provide continuity and experience in the volunteer pool. Try for geographical balance as well, as this will be especially helpful in the areas of admissions and fund raising. You will need to develop written job descriptions that clearly state committee members' responsibilities. Include these when you invite parents to serve.

The association's program could include some or all of the following:

- assisting with newsletters, handbooks, and so on;
- welcoming freshmen;
- career advisement;
- establishing a job bank;
- coordinating a speakers bureau;
- recruiting students for admissions; and
- participating in fund-raising efforts.

The special character of your institution, as well as how much money and staff you have, should determine how you develop new programs or expand existing ones. A small, carefully crafted and manageable program that responds to the particular needs of your institution is preferable to a grandiose scheme that is programmed for failure.

Putting punch in your parents program

Maintaining high standards of communication should be your first priority. Keeping parents informed through newsletters, parent handbooks, and other campus publications strengthens their relationship with the institution.

Freshmen welcoming parties in late summer may be the first real link that new students and their parents make with your institution. Current parents and their sons and daughters are the perfect hosts for such affairs. They can answer many of those last-minute questions that make the departure for school so stressful for everyone involved.

Parents can be an important resource for your career counseling and placement offices. They can locate or provide opportunities for internships and externships, during academic breaks or as part of the curriculum. They can participate in panel discussions, either on or off campus, that deal with different job opportunities or focus on a particular profession. Parents are often willing to give students and alumni informational interviews about their particular careers.

Some institutions have job banks and/or speakers bureaus that are sponsored by alumni through the career counseling and placement offices. Parent involvement can significantly strenthen such programs.

Parents can serve your admissions office by identifying talented young people in their communities and referring them to your institution.

Whether it's for a weekend or a day, bringing parents to campus should be a highlight of your program. If you can, invite parents at a time when they can attend classes. Offer a wide variety of events—lectures, athletics, plays, musical performances, picnics, dinners, dances, and opportunities to meet with faculty.

The parents fund

Because of the special relationship that parents share with parents of other students while their children are at your institution, parents can be the most effective solicitors of this constituency. With help from your research department, regional screenings, and information from other parents and alumni, establish a pool of special gift prospects and arrange for parents committee members to personally solicit these people. As you assign solicitors to prospects, try to match as many of the following factors as you can:

- geographical location;
- profession;
- student's class; and
- student's independent or high school.

A combination of personal solicitation (face-to-face or by telephone) followed by a personalized letter containing a pledge card is effective.

Develop a tracking system to record the results of this special solicitation so that you can report them to the parent volunteers. A good computer system can produce a one-page list for each solicitor so that appropriate follow-up can be done either by the original solicitor or by the development office.

For the rest of the parent constituency, plan at least two general letters during the year. Segment the mailings as much as you can. If you write a letter specifically for parents of alumni, you can convey a different message than you would to parents of freshmen or parents of seniors. Consider sending nondonor parents of the graduating class a letter stressing the importance of participation. You might encourage a contest among parents of the four undergraduate classes or ask parents to give to a senior class fund in honor of the impending graduation.

Don't overlook the phonathon. Some institutions use students to call from campus. Others use regional phonathons in which parents committee members do the calling. These sessions enable parents to contribute their time, to meet and work with other parents, and to receive feedback from the parent prospects they call.

Don't forget "second parents." For those students whose parents have remarried, make sure you include both sets of parents on your mailing list.

Late in the fiscal year, develop a special letter to send to LYBUNT and SYBUNT parents (those who gave last year but unfortunately not this or gave some year but unfortunately not this). These parents often just need an extra reminder to renew their support.

Whatever you do to raise funds from the parents of your students, you should already have in place appropriate acknowledgment procedures. This might be a combination of thank-you letters from institutional personnel and the chair of your parents committee. When you thank parents committee members for their gifts, don't forget to thank them for their service to the institution too. You can also include parent donors in your institution's donor roll and/or annual report.

When the year is over, evaluate your program carefully. If necessary, revise the purpose of your parents association and redraft job descriptions. Count your successes and build on them. Don't be afraid to scrap projects that didn't work and plan new and better ones. By this time, you've probably discovered that some parents are willing and able to work as hard for the institution as your most loyal alumni. These people will often serve and support the institution for decades as long as you continue to cultivate them, communicate with them, and thank them.

Chapter 23

Organizing a Parents Council

Diane K. Brust
Director of the Annual Fund
Hollins College
Roanoke, Virginia

A parents council is a significant resource and can serve your institution in a variety of ways. It can function as a liaison and a conduit, speaking for the institution in the communities of the individual members and channeling back any information that might be beneficial to the mission of the institution. Parents council members frequently provide the most credible endorsements of your institution to secondary and preparatory counselors as well as to other parents.

The council can also serve in advisory capacities. Parents council members are undoubtedly one of the best resources for evaluating the effectiveness of your programs and for providing suggestions for improvement. However, by far the most important function of the council is the solicitation of other parent donors who are capable of making leadership gifts to the annual fund.

Parents usually support an institution because they perceive that it is or has been beneficial to their child. They may continue to support the institution after their son or daughter graduates because they hope to ensure the value of their student's degree. Also, in a broader context, they may choose to support the institution because it has demonstrated its leadership in certain academic areas. Finally, parents may be motivated by altruistic concerns because they realize that an uneducated and uninformed public would have long-range and very negative implications for both them and their children.

The parents council, then, is the means by which an institution can most effectively solicit and involve its significant parent donors. Parents council members set the standard for parent giving by contributing leadership gifts to the annual fund campaign and by helping the institution solicit other parent special gift prospects.

Forming a parents council

The first step in selecting a council is to determine how many of your parents are leadership gift prospects. Consult with your researcher, if your institution has one, or consult the admissions office. This office has financial information on each student that will help you determine whom to solicit for special gifts. You can then segment the prospect list geographically or according to the son's or daughter's designation (i.e., sophomore, senior, alumnus, and so on). If your council is sufficiently large and geographically diverse, you may choose to do both since the more you target your prospects, the greater the opportunity your council members will have for developing a rapport with their prospects.

Because parents council members usually serve in volunteer capacities with other organizations as well, it is wise to limit the number of parents you ask each council couple to call. Between 10 and 15 is a reasonable number. You can then determine the number of parent couples you will need on the council. If, for example, you decide each parent couple will solicit 10 prospects, and you have 150 to 200 sets of parents on your prospect list, your council should include at least 15 to 20 couples.

You can select some of the members of the council from a list of individual prospects who have already demonstrated either the potential or the commitment to make leadership gifts. But gift giving should not be the only criterion. You should also consider community involvement, geographical location, professional experience, and corporate and foundation connections. Once you have developed a list of prospects, show this list to senior administrators and other development staff and ask for their comments. They may have important information about some of the prospects. For example, a parent may be upset about poor grades his or her child received, another may be struggling with financial difficulties, a third may be overextended and unable to meet deadlines.

You might ask the president or chancellor of your institution to sign the invitation to participate in the parents council. You should also mention in the letter the names of the council leadership who will provide personal follow-up by calling or visiting. That phone call or visit confirms the request to serve, focuses on the function of the council, and describes the responsibilities of membership.

Enlisting leadership

The leadership position may be filled by one parent or a parent couple who serve as co-chairs. The primary task of the chair or co-chairs is recruiting and soliciting other members of the council. You might also ask the leadership to contact the most significant parent prospects. If possible, the chair should have served on the council for at least one year and should be a leadership donor. It is also helpful if the chair, or at least one of the co-chairs, has corporate connections and management experience. The chair or co-chairs will be more effective if they are recognized as leaders in their own communities.

Once your council is in place, you can begin the fund-raising work by assigning the calls to be made. One good way to organize the calling process is to invite members of the council to your campus. Having the council members on campus not only enables you to educate them about your institution and their responsibilities, but also allows them to develop a sense of community with one another and a commitment to the institution.

Parents weekend, if it falls early in the school year, is the perfect opportunity to conduct such a session. At Hollins College, we invite parents council members to a breakfast at the president's home and then introduce them at a mid-morning forum attended by all the parents. In the afternoon, council members attend a workshop and later serve as hosts at an evening reception at the president's home.

At the workshop, which is conducted by the council leadership with development staff in attendance, the staff explain the solicitation process and distribute volunteer manuals and solicitation packets to council members. The packets include the assignments as well as sufficient information to help council members develop a rapport, pledge cards, business-reply envelopes, and a record-report sheet to be returned to the annual fund office on completion of the calls. Council members have the opportunity to share concerns about the solicitations, ask questions, and make suggestions.

Before personal solicitation of leadership donors begins, these prospects should receive a letter that states the case for the parents fund and that informs them that they will be called by a council member. If you send these letters, as well as those to the other parents, as soon as possible after parents weekend, you can capitalize on the positive feelings generated by the weekend.

The letters will meet with a more favorable reception if they are written—or at least signed—by volunteer leadership. But remember to coordinate this solicitation with the other offices on campus. If your letter immediately follows an announcement of a tuition increase, not only will the results be diminished, but your letter may generate a negative image.

The solicitation

Each parents council member is responsible for the following four steps in the solicitation process:
- personally contacting the prospects;
- sending out the pledge cards with business-reply envelopes;
- reporting all pledges and gifts to the institution; and
- providing a report describing the status of the calls.

Always provide council members with a timeline of due dates. Should members not return reports on their activities by the specified due date, ask the volunteer leadership to call them to discover if there are problems and to encourage them to complete their calls. It is also the responsibility of the chairs to call those members who have not made their own gifts and urge them to do so.

Council members should receive regular reports containing an update on the parents campaign as well as individual status reports on those prospects for whom each parent solicitor is responsible. A parents newsletter, if your institution has one, provides a wonderful opportunity to keep all parents aware of the campaign and the institution's need for their support.

You should always notify council members when you receive gifts from "their" prospects. In turn, council members are responsible for writing acknowledgment notes to the donors. All gifts are also acknowledged by the institution, and significant gifts, of course, should be acknowledged by the president.

To keep enthusiasm high, consider holding a second parents council meeting in the spring. This provides an opportunity to evaluate the progress of your campaign and to redefine or restructure the program if necessary. In addition, it is an important occasion on which council members can compare notes about their efforts on behalf of the institution, and staff can get a firsthand look at the excitement and motivation of the volunteers.

A parents council can also serve your institution by functioning in a wider role than just annual fund solicitors. Council members who have appropriate connections can advise the staff member who is responsible for corporate and foundation solicitation. They can provide information about potential gifts and grants, assist in contacting officers of corporations and foundations, and make introductions. One of the best ways for council members to assist staff is by accompanying them on calls or by hosting sessions at which staff and grant makers can get acquainted.

The parents council can also assist your institution by working with the offices of admissions and career counseling. A designated parent leader can serve as a coordinator and work with the staff of those offices to organize other parents to assist in these two areas.

The admissions coordinator may organize parents in different areas of the country to host admissions events or may form calling teams to contact parents of prospective students. Parents can be organized to help in career counseling by:
- assisting in obtaining internships;
- finding living accommodations for student interns;
- making presentations to students about their respective career fields; and
- providing your institution with information concerning specific career opportunities.

Parents are the second largest natural constituency of an institution, and they usually take great pride in the institution their children attend. They are an important resource for financial support and service. A parents council can impact significantly on the success of your institution and your annual fund programs by providing a means to identify parent leadership, cultivating interest in the mission of your institution, and creating lasting relationships between parents and your institution.

Chapter 24

Charity Begins at Home: The Faculty/Staff Campaign

Lilya Wagner
Vice President for Institutional Advancement
Union College
Lincoln, Nebraska

The "I-gave-at-the-office" syndrome often characterizes faculty and staff attitudes toward appeals for fund. "Why should I give money to the institution when I've already given so much else—time, energy, attention, effort, devotion? And besides, salaries are notoriously inadequate here." Faculty and staff may well ask this question—and many do—but often the answer is a persuasive one: Charity begins at home, and those closest to the institution know it best and have the most invested in its welfare.

As a result, successful faculty/staff campaigns dot the educational landscape and stand as monuments to emulate. For example, consider the case of Ball State University's Campus Campaign. Focused on the campus community, it was managed by professional staff, was goal- and information-oriented, involved lay leadership and volunteers, and reached all campus employees. Professionals at Ball State recognized that a once-a-year memo was not sufficient to inspire faculty and staff to give. They also realized that an institution's employees probably know little about the needs, goals, and dreams of departments and areas outside of their own, so information sharing played a vital part in the on-campus campaign.

When Ball State's campaign ended, giving had increased from less than $1,000 in the early years to more than $166,000 in 1988.[1]

The Ohio State University launched a five-year, $350 million capital campaign in 1985. One of the campaign's goals was to raise $12 million from faculty and staff. A volunteer committee representing faculty and staff across campus set the policies, while professional development staff provided the support and guidance for this segment of the overall campaign. By December 1986, $11.6 million had been raised. The number of faculty and staff making gifts increased from 1,905 in 1984-85 to 6,655 in 1985-86. In addition, a greater awareness and support of the entire campaign by faculty and staff certainly contributed to its eventual success. By the end of the campaign (June 30, 1990), the Campus Campaign total was $15.7 million, and it was moving into an annual mode.[2]

At Northeastern University in Boston, the on-campus campaign exceeded the $1 million goal, which was part of a $175 million capital campaign. Faculty and staff tripled the amount they had been giving prior to this campaign. As in other cases, awareness and understanding of the needs of the campus and the overall campaign were increased.[3]

Successful faculty/staff campaigns are not limited to large institutions. A small, private college in Lincoln, Nebraska, began its capital campaign by publicizing lead gifts from its board and faculty and staff. The on-campus campaign at Union College had to be handled carefully because some negative perceptions lingered; faculty had felt pressured to give during an earlier campaign, and there was still some resentment.

Union's President-emeritus David Bieber, highly respected by faculty and staff, met with campus divisions and departments. We did not use much publicity, held no big kickoff, but depended on small group and one-on-one discussion about giving. We tried to explain the possibilities for giving and to show what a difference a gift could make to the college. This low-key approach to the on-campus campaign resulted in 74 percent faculty/staff participation for a total of $78,500 of the overall goal of $4.7 million. This was the highest amount Union College had ever raised on campus.[4]

Why you should begin "at home"

It's logical to expect a faculty/staff campaign to be successful. After all, charity begins at home. This adage, first expressed by the Roman author Terence two centuries before Christ, is as true today as it was then. Consider these significant reasons for beginning your campaign "at home":

1. Faculty/staff giving will motivate others to participate in a campaign. If those most affected by campaign income do not give, why should others?

2. A campaign goal reached by faculty/staff giving can serve as a significant kickoff gift for a campaign and provide excellent publicity.

3. A faculty/staff campaign can establish unity on campus. If an information campaign precedes the "ask," if faculty and staff understand the need for a campaign, if they can visualize their role as key players in a successful program, and if they realize how a successful program affects and benefits them, then they will be unified in their support of the campaign.

4. A "development-wise" faculty and staff not only will promote the on-campus campaign, but can also be a valuable resource for aiding the success of the over-

all campaign. You need to educate your faculty about this particular campaign as well as about fund-raising principles and programs in general. Educated faculty and staff can assist the development effort in many ways—from providing a good public relations influence on off-campus groups to serving as active solicitors.

5. An involved faculty and staff can serve as a valuable source for ideas on how to promote an institution and a campaign. Is there a program on campus about which they are enthusiastic? They can share this enthusiasm with others during campaign promotion. Faculty and staff, who are at the heart of the institution's raison d'etre, have insights that others may miss.

These are some of the most significant reasons for conducting a faculty/staff campaign; no doubt you will have others that are pertinent to your own institution.

Starting your campaign

If you are about to begin a faculty/staff campaign, here are five essential steps:

1. *Get faculty and staff involved in the campaign.* There are several strategies you can use to do this:

• You can establish an advisory council of representative faculty and staff who can speak for and influence the campus and the campaign. Use this group to determine the "pulse" of the campus—that is, what institutional needs do faculty and staff perceive?

• You can train selected individuals who are willing to cultivate prospects, both on campus and elsewhere, and to serve as volunteer solicitors. Faculty and staff can function in nonthreatening roles, create a warm and friendly climate between the prospect and the institution, share a sincere interest with the prospect, and build an enthusiasm for the institution they represent.

2. *Show targeted results of the campaign.* Be clear on how the campaign will benefit the campus in general and faculty and staff in particular. Include members of the faculty and staff when you are planning their participation in the celebration once the campaign is finished. Give them a voice in deciding how faculty and staff should be recognized and honored for their participation.

3. *Make sure that faculty and staff do not feel the campaign is imposed upon them by the administration.* Faculty and staff should play a significant role in implementing a campaign—it should not be "owned" by the administration. Faculty and staff can determine who should solicit and when, what kinds of materials will appeal to their peers, and what kinds of information and publicity are needed. In most campaigns, a respected on-campus peer is a suitable campaign chair; allow the faculty and staff to have a voice in the selection of this person. If a peer is not the most desirable chair, then request faculty and staff suggestions for a respected outsider to fill this role (such as a professor emeritus).

4. *Provide timely updates once the campaign is under way.* Use reports, newsletters, and regular verbal announcements to indicate progress and provide appreciation. If you have already established a positive communication climate on campus, information will flow readily and through the right channels.

5. *Provide a nonthreatening environment for an on-campus campaign.* Create a climate in which giving is a privilege. Show faculty and staff how their giving program ranks with those of other campuses; let them know how their gifts are spent; and ensure confidentiality.

The details of a faculty/staff campaign are similar to those of other giving programs, but keep in mind these aspects:

• Use appropriate materials. A brochure or pledge card that was designed for alumni will not have the same effect as one prepared especially for faculty and staff. Beyond these two basic items, each development professional can utilize on-campus resources as they are available. For example, some campuses develop a video that can be shown either at the campaign kickoff or during the solicitation. Other institutions find a direct mail approach to be more useful.

• Consult key personnel. Seek advice from faculty and staff in selecting the campaign chair and steering committee members. Personally encourage selected faculty and staff to be solicitors. (And use these capable volunteers after the conclusion of the on-campus campaign.)

• Offer several options for giving. These options may include payroll deductions, outright cash gifts, planned gifts, in-kind gifts, or volunteer service.

• Develop appropriate recognition procedures. Publish articles featuring faculty/staff giving, achievements related to campus programs, and involvement in the overall campaign. Seek testimonials from faculty and staff for dinners and other special events. Make faculty and staff feel significant to the success of the campaign and include them as members of your team whenever possible.

• Prevent multiple requests for faculty/staff donations. Attempt to channel all solicitations through the development office so that faculty/staff giving potential is not overburdened and unfocused.

Maintaining success

Once your faculty/staff campaign is established and functioning, don't think your role is over. You can maintain the continuing success of the campaign by taking the following steps:

1. Institute a checklist for new faculty and staff that includes a stop at the development office where information on giving options will be shared. Arrange to have a respected faculty or staff member visit the newcomer and talk about giving to the institution.

2. Give faculty and staff periodic reports on all aspects of the campaign. Focusing on results and successes will keep enthusiasm alive.

3. Continue recognition procedures and involve faculty and staff in plans for a celebration at the close of the campaign.

4. Network with other fund-raising professionals for new ideas on how to make your on-campus program work.

The late John Herrick, one of the co-chairs of Ohio State's campaign, said in his letter to faculty and staff, "The commitment of all of us who are closest to Ohio

State and know it best will motivate and inspire donors as they consider their commitments." Indeed, charity *does* begin at home.

Notes

[1] Ball State won the U.S. Steel award for fund raising in 1972, 1976, 1977, 1979, and 1982. The Campus Campaign was included in 1982, the year the university won on the basis of sustained excellence.

[2] Ohio State's Campus Campaign won a grand gold medal for Special Constituency Giving Programs in the 1987 CASE Recognition Program.

[3] Northeastern's Campus Campaign won a gold medal for Special Constituency Giving Programs in the 1988 CASE Recognition Program.

[4] In 1990 Union College won a CASE/USX AIMS (Achievement in Mobilizing Support) Award for Best Total Development Effort.

Chapter 25

Student Involvement

Frederick C. Nahm
Vice President for Development and University Relations
University of Pennsylvania
Philadelphia, Pennsylvania

I nvolving students in the annual fund has two goals: to take advantage of their effectiveness as fund raisers; and to involve them in the fund-raising process while they are still in school so that when they graduate, they will become active alumni, eager—and now able—to support their alma mater. Success in the short run will lead to success in years to come.

Although students are as multifaceted as other annual fund constituencies, they are distinctive—and especially challenging—for being a "fast-moving target" both in their relationship to the institution and in their giving capacity. In four short years, a confused, enthusiastic freshman becomes an experienced and even cynical senior. If you add another few years, that student becomes an alumnus with mostly fond memories of his or her alma mater and, you hope, a discretionary income with which to demonstrate that fondness.

Segmenting the population

Within this fast-moving target, there are several identifiable segments. The way you respond to each of these segments will not only determine how successful you are in involving students in the annual fund, but will also have a substantial impact on how involved these students will be when they are alumni.

You can segment the student body in many different ways. As in all market segmentation, it is essential to match the segmentation to the product being marketed. If your "product" is special-interest fund raising, then you should segment the market according to those special interests. For example, if you're beginning a fund-raising campaign for athletic projects, you would segment the student population according to athletes vs. nonathletes, football players vs. tennis players, and so forth. If the product is a campaign for scholarships in the sciences, then your segments should include science majors and students who have received financial aid.

Let's say that the product is the annual fund, and the goal is to identify those segments of the student body who demonstrate both positive feelings about the institution and a willingness to help it. Although every institution has its own distinctive groups, a typical four-year residential college might have the following four categories for annual fund segmentation purposes:

• **Segment A.** This group is made up of highly motivated and directed students who selected the institution because they believe it will help them achieve a specific professional goal, acceptance into medical school, for example. These students are usually too single-minded in pursuit of their goal to be willing donors or fund raisers while they are in school, but you might be able to "showcase" them in publications or at events. Members of this group usually become good donors if their goals are realized.

• **Segment B.** This segment consists of bright and gregarious students who selected the institution because of the perceived quality of the academic and social experience it offers. These students are ideally suited as donors and fund raisers if their college experience matches their expectations. This is the first group to consider for student volunteer leadership.

• **Segment C.** These students are usually full-paying students who did not achieve their academic potential in high school. They chose the institution as an alternative to their more selective first-choice schools, and they often find it difficult to have a sense of pride in or loyalty to a place they consider "second-best." Generally speaking, this group is not helpful either as volunteers or, later, as donors.

• **Segment D.** These students are serious workers who ranked lower in their high school classes than members of the other groups. Unlike the previous segment, however, they have the potential to mature academically in the proper college environment. This group usually is not effective initially as volunteers; however, if they have a good college experience, by the time they are seniors and beyond, they are often the most enthusiastic volunteers and donors. (The student who has struggled academically may become the alumnus who recognizes the important role that challenge played in his or her life.)

Again, it is important to recognize that each institution has its own characteristics for segmentation. In addition, there are subsegments within each major category that occasionally may be useful. For example, alumni children, fraternity/sorority affiliations, or hometowns may be important when you are matching phonathon callers with alumni to be called.

Once you have identified segments within the student body, remember that they will change as the students change during their years at the institution. Students' responses to the institution will be affected both by where students come from in selecting the institution and where they are in the progression from freshman to senior. When you consider that the enthusiastic freshman hasn't had time to get to know and appreciate the institution, and the experienced, knowledgeable senior may be focusing on finding a job, it may seem that the target is moving extraordinarily fast. You may feel that the "window of opportunity" is only about six months long.

Nevertheless, timing can have a positive effect on student involvement in fund raising. Freshmen often get involved in activities because they want to meet other students or because they are afraid to say no to anyone in the administration. By the time they are seniors, they are beginning to develop the characteristics that cause alumni to get involved—loyalty, the wish to pay the institution back for value received, and the desire to be a volunteer for a good cause.

When you have segmented the student body by characteristics and by year and have recognized that there will be a constant interplay between the two, you are ready to examine the ways in which students can get involved with the annual fund. There are three general categories of involvement:

- students as donors;
- students as solicitors; and
- students in cultivation and stewardship activities.

Students as donors

It is never too early to begin educating students about the need for annual giving—voluntary support on an annual basis for the current operating needs of the institution. Students have a better understanding of current operating costs than they do of endowment and long-term funding; for them, this kind of giving makes sense. Those who have participated in campus activities (a newspaper or film series, for example) can especially appreciate the need for ongoing funding. If you can get these students to give while they are in school, you can establish a pattern of giving that will lead to increased participation rates among young alumni and fewer "never-givers."

Class gifts and project gifts are effective vehicles for organizing students to solicit their peers. You should emphasize broad-based participation rather than the size of the gifts. "Stretch till it hurts" won't work with students who are probably already stretching. However, goals are important for students just as they are for your other constituencies.

As important as the giving process is the identification of students who are effective solicitors of their peers. Early in the junior year, you and your staff should begin the process of identifying, recruiting, and educating a key annual fund leadership group, and this should be accomplished before the beginning of the senior year. This group will not only serve as the committee for the senior class gift, but will also provide the volunteer foundation for class-oriented fund raising.

Planning for a senior gift should begin in the junior year with identification of the volunteer committee. The committee should discuss projects and goals and begin recruiting and cultivating student volunteers in the spring of the junior year. You should remind these committee members that they will have to repeat many of their efforts in the fall because of the break in momentum necessarily created by summer vacation.

By the fall of senior year, the class project should be ready for marketing by class volunteers, again with the understanding that breaks will make it difficult to sustain momentum. The "ask" should be scheduled for after the winter break so that the gift may be closed in time for spring graduation.

Throughout the senior year, student leaders should have opportunities to meet with both the institution's president and the administrators involved in fund raising. The president will reinforce the importance of the students' efforts, and the development staff will help them understand where they fit in the fund-raising picture. If possible, students should attend a meeting of the trustees' development committee to gain a truly comprehensive view of institutional advancement. (This also serves as a good cultivation activity for trustees.) The more the leaders understand, the more effective they will be in soliciting their classmates.

Students as solicitors

The most popular and perhaps the best way of involving students in the annual fund is as callers, volunteer or paid, for alumni phonathons. It is not important whether the students volunteer their services (with prizes and other incentives) or are paid to call alumni for the annual fund. What *is* important is that involving students in phonathons is the single best way to educate them about annual giving. (You should ask students for their own pledges just as you would ask any alumni callers.) In addition, most studies show that students are more effective callers than alumni, making more calls per session and producing better yields. Be sure to choose students who are knowledgeable and enthusiastic about the institution—remember the segments! (Choose your callers according to the specific audience.)

Strategies for maximizing student involvement in phonathons vary from institution to institution, and there is ample opportunity for creativity. You may choose to have the students compete as individuals or as groups (fraternities and sororities, for example), assigning points to new gifts, increased gifts, and so on. You can offer special prizes to the people or groups with the most points on a given day and over the course of the phonathon. Remember to supply good food so that the whole experience is positive and to give every student a gift or prize at the conclusion of the phonathon. Everyone should be a winner.

Some people like to use student callers in parent phonathons, but others believe that students should not see the giving records of other students' parents and that they shouldn't make calls that may result in conversations of a confidential nature. Those who continue to use student callers say that they are extremely effective and that there has been no negative reaction to the program. You'll have to consider your institution's circumstances and the makeup of its student body before you decide whether or not to use students for parent phonathons.

Many alumni are motivated to give by the belief that their alma mater is producing well-educated students. Sending alumni a well-written student letter is one of the best ways to confirm this belief, and it also provides a welcome change from letters from the president, the annual fund chair, the class agent, and so on.

When featuring students in direct mail solicitations, you should make sure that each written piece not only has the usual direct mail characteristics, but also reveals something of the student's personal experience. The objective is to encourage a sense of personal identification between students and alumni.

Students in cultivation and stewardship activities

Students can be the institution's best advocates. They represent its mission by demonstrating how well the mission is being fulfilled. The student who can talk about the curriculum or the athletic program or the importance of his or her own scholarship assistance will make new friends for the institution. No letter from the dean or the director of financial aid can make a better case than the student who tells an alumnus how much a scholarship has meant to his or her success at the institution. Likewise, a conversation with a student over dinner about a new course or program involves the donor as no article in a newsletter can. The more students talk to alumni and friends, the easier it becomes to raise money.

Involving students in cultivation and stewardship events requires careful selection and preparation. Here again, consider the segmentation of the student body. The enthusiastic freshman may be most effective at an informal gathering, while the mature senior may make a better impression at a formal dinner. You don't necessarily need to match specific interests—although you should do it when appropriate—but be sure to choose students who will be comfortable with those participating in the event.

Although it's standard practice to ask students to participate in cultivation and stewardship activities, many institutions do not prepare these students adequately for their assignments. When you bring annual fund donors and volunteers together for formal and informal interaction with students, it's important that you brief the students on the purposes of these events and the makeup of the groups. Consider giving students some basic information about their dinner partners that would help them with conversation. If alumni are interested in issues on campus, be sure that students know the administration's position—not because you expect them to spout the "party line," but so that they will understand the complexities of the issue. Students will be more effective representatives of the institution if they know their audience and why they are there.

Structure

If you have established a formal student organization for annual giving, this organization will be of great help in involving students in the annual fund. It can be structured in a variety of ways, but it must have the staff support necessary for creating a meaningful experience. This student annual fund organization can serve both as a means for involving students in annual giving programs and as a formal communications link to the student body. As noted earlier, it will also become the foundation for leadership in alumni annual giving programs.

Conclusion

There are three steps to effectively involve students in the annual fund. First, identify the major segments or categories of the student body, both by general types of students and by the length and quality of their relationship with the institution. Next, determine the areas within your annual fund program where student involvement can enhance results, both in the short- and in the long-term. Then overlay the student segments with the involvement opportunities, carefully tailoring each student's participation to his or her interests and abilities.

Once you have involved students in your program, you will find that they serve as a productive extension of your annual fund's capacity, both now, as volunteers, and in the future, as young alumni who understand the importance of annual giving to their alma mater.

Chapter 26

The Role of Trustees

C. Holger Hansen
Vice President for Institutional Advancement
Haverford College
Haverford, Pennsylvania

Trustees have many responsibilities. They are legally bound to hold, control, and manage the resources of the institution entrusted to them. They are responsible for selecting the president or chancellor who serves as their agent. They approve policies and establish institutional goals. They help clarify the mission of the institution.

Trustees are also essential players in every aspect of the development program. Robert L. Gale, president of the Association of Governing Boards of Universities and Colleges, writes in a recent AGB publication, *Fund-Raising Leadership: A Guide for College and University Boards:*

> Because higher education institutions today are locked in competition
> to attract students and financial resources, the need for governing boards
> and their individual members to participate directly and actively in fund-
> raising is unassailable.[1]

Leadership by example

Leadership in fund raising is a major responsibility of trusteeship. The board sets the example for all other donors to the institution. The board's leadership is exerted in several ways. As individuals, trustees and regents should be contributing money as well as time to the institution. Michael Radock, former vice president of university relations and development at the University of Michigan, says this of the board's fund-raising role: "First and foremost, trustees must set an example for others by making generous personal contributions within their means."[2]

As fund-raising volunteers, trustees should ask others for support. They should be recruited to work on the annual fund. As spokespersons for the institution and for higher education in general, trustees set the stage for fund raising by advocating the institution's mission and needs. (Advocacy usually comes naturally to trustees, many of whom are graduates of the institutions they serve.)

Finally, the board has an obligation to take an active role in establishing and overseeing policies related to the development program. It may delegate oversight to the president and the chief advancement officer, but it should not relinquish its role of approving and evaluating fund-raising plans. Trustees should know that strategies and policies are in place to assure adequate resources for current and future operating budgets. Policies regarding the annual fund are no exception.

Orientation

Every board member should be aware of the importance of the annual fund to the institution's financial equilibrium. The task of communicating this information is not as easy as it seems. Most boards, like annual giving offices, are subject to frequent changes in personnel.

Some board members were not contributors to the annual fund before they were appointed. Trustees are recruited for various reasons, and a history of giving to the institution is only one possibility. Even new alumni trustees may be only occasional donors to the annual fund, either because they support other institutional needs that they regard as having higher priority or because they have never developed the habit. Therefore, orientation on this aspect of trusteeship is necessary for every new trustee.

Annual giving officers and development staff must also take time to educate new trustees on how gifts and grants are raised and allocated in the operating budget. The Association of Governing Boards has a variety of publications and seminars that can be useful in orienting new board members in these matters.

In order for board members to understand the importance of annual giving in the operating budget, their orientation should include at least some general information about fund accounting. Trustees should understand the need for unrestricted as well as restricted current funds in the operating budget and the difference between capital giving and annual giving.

The development committee

The board's corporate role in fund raising is usually managed through a development committee that reports to it. The development committee should oversee the annual fund as well as other fund-raising programs. It should participate in establishing the goal for the annual fund and should monitor its performance at regular committee meetings.

J.W. Pocock, chairman emeritus of the board of the College of Wooster, suggests that the way to convince trustees of the importance of the annual fund is to involve them in the initiation and execution of fund-raising activities:

> Boards too often take the annual campaign for granted. It occurs year-
> ly and is often developed and executed by the professional staff with
> only token board participation. Yet the annual campaign is the foun-
> dation of the entire program.[3]

Several strategies can help board members better understand the annual fund:
- using trustees as solicitors;
- holding open meetings of the development committee so that members of other board committees can attend;
- providing the full board with regular reports on the annual fund;
- involving the development committee in the process of approving the annual fund goal and seeking members' advice on strategies for achieving the goal; and
- encouraging the chief financial officer and top annual fund volunteers to attend development committee meetings.

Soliciting the board

The annual fund director should schedule trustee solicitations during the advance gift phase of the annual fund. As with any leadership gift program, staff and key volunteers should establish potential gift ratings of board members, based upon past performance and increased goals. The annual fund director should then make solicitation assignments, using the president and trustees as solicitors. While some trustees can afford to give more than others, the level of support from each trustee should be visible and at the highest levels.

The names of several board members should appear in the top donor clubs, that is, at the $1,000 level and above. Although trustees have a deeper appreciation of their importance in the annual fund if they are solicited by their peers, in a few cases, it may be appropriate for a development staff member to make the ask.

Pocock reports that of the 344 private institutions responding to a 1987 AGB survey, 97.1 percent of the private institutions solicited board members. The chief executive, the board chair, and other trustees were most frequently cited as solicitors of board members, followed by advancement officers. Trustees at these institutions contributed approximately 12 percent of the total funds received in the 1985-86 fiscal year.[4]

Pocock rightly suggests that while many tasks conducted by trustees are important, the trustee's act of contributing funds is paramount. All trustees should be expected to contribute personal gifts. We all pay lip service to the objective of 100 percent participation from our board members. But that worthy goal appears to be the exception rather than the rule among boards of private as well as public institutions. The AGB survey states that among the responding private institutions, 83.3 percent of trustees and 45 percent of emeritus trustees contributed to their institutions in 1985-86. The most successful private institutions had trustee participation rates of 90.4 percent in the annual fund that year.[5]

We all know the excuses for not contributing, and trustees have the same reasons as other constituents. They may miss a year through oversight. Some donors still have difficulty in distinguishing between the fiscal year and the calendar year. Several may contribute only to another institutional objective. Or, heaven forbid, they simply were never asked to make the gift.

Whatever the reason, the board's leadership is so significant in the minds of our publics, both on campus and off, that we must continue to emphasize the centrality of the board's full participation.

One effective way to communicate the board's leadership role to both the board itself as well as to other constituencies is to seek from board members special challenge gifts to increase support for the annual fund. Challenges can focus on donor clubs, nondonor groups, young alumni, or parents. Institutions have used board challenges to raise new dollars from the corporate community, local businesses, and religious constituencies.

What trustees expect

While the institution should expect generous support from each board member, trustees also have high expectations of the annual giving staff. They expect professionalism in their personal contacts, in the appearance of printed solicitations, and in the performance of staff and volunteers. When they take on assignments, they expect guidance on the ask amount, on the story to tell, and on follow-up to solicitations. They expect to be asked to sing from the same songbook as other volunteers.

Trustees also expect careful and thoughtful coordination with other fund-raising activities. They ask questions. In his essays on trusteeship, Robert K. Greenleaf suggests that effective trustee leadership involves asking questions and persuading others, with the ultimate goal of achieving unity and clarity of purpose. Trustee leadership, says Greenleaf, is "the art of persuasion."[6] Trustees enjoy questioning and will probably ask some or all of the following:

- How does annual giving relate to class reunion funds? Do the materials available for the volunteers in these programs clarify these relationships?
- What is the pledge reminder system?
- Is the annual fund a part of the capital campaign?
- When will the annual report on last year's donors be mailed?
- How do our results in dollars and participation last year compare with those of our peer institutions?
- Have we invested enough money in the development budget to staff annual giving and achieve its goals?

Trustees want to be in a position to share their own experience and expertise. They want to be involved in the process. They want assurance that they are carrying out their charge to maintain the institution's financial equilibrium.

Trustees expect the staff to recommend annual fund goals that stretch. The goal-setting process is usually initiated in coordination with the chief financial officer and the budget committee before the budget is presented to the board for approval. The board expects that the goal for the annual fund will increase over the prior year. It is not unusual for trustees to press for a goal that exceeds staff projections. At that time, an annual fund director may feel overwhelmed by the apparent lack of understanding among trustees of the budget limits or the variety of strategies required to meet expectations.

Board members are more likely to understand if they have been closely involved in a variety of cultivation and solicitation strategies. Trustees who have been brought into planning and solicitation will be allies of the annual fund director. They will appreciate the difficulties involved in achieving sharply increased goals.

The board also normally has a role in approving allocations of unrestricted bequests and capital gifts available for the operating budget. These allocations may or may not directly bear on the annual fund. In any case, they may make a real difference between a surplus or a deficit in the general budget. If the annual fund has been promoted as a key element in achieving a balanced budget, these allocations will have a significant impact on the perceptions of the board and of our volunteers on the value of the annual fund. Usually, the annual fund director has no control over these allocations. But it is important that the director be informed of the allocations and treat them separately when he or she is measuring the fund's performance.

The board also expects timely and frequent progress reports on the annual fund. This is usually done as a part of the regular reporting on all voluntary support received year to date. If the annual fund is running behind the prior year, the board wants to know why. Therefore, annual fund directors usually find it helpful to include trustee volunteers and development committee members in mailings of progress reports to alumni and parent volunteers. At the end of the fiscal year, the board should receive a final report on results that includes some comparative data from peer institutions.

As we recall the many trustees with whom we have worked over the years, it is satisfying to know that most of them have been leaders in the annual fund. They enthusiastically embraced leadership roles as volunteers. They were glad to give personally and to solicit others. Those who could not be financially generous particularly appreciated the opportunity of serving in the annual fund program. We are remiss if we fail to ask them to be leaders in the annual fund and to provide their ideas and advice. Trustee involvement in the annual fund is essential if we are to achieve the educational mission of our institutions.

Notes

[1] Robert L. Gale, in J.W. Pocock, *Fund-Raising Leadership: A Guide for College and University Boards* (Washington, DC: Association of Governing Boards of Universities and Colleges, 1989), p. xi.

[2] Michael Radock, *The Fund-Raising Role* (Washington, DC: Association of Governing Boards, Pocket Publication no. 3, 1977), p. 2.

[3] Pocock, *Fund-Raising Leadership,* pp. 27-28.

[4] Ibid., pp. 116-17.

[5] Ibid., pp. 117, 54.

[6] Robert K. Greenleaf, *Seminary as Servant: Essays on Trusteeship* (Peterborough, NH: Center for Applied Studies/Windy Row Press, 1980), p. 18.

Chapter 27

A Case Study in Trustee Participation

Barbara E. McGill
Assistant Director of Major Gifts
Allegheny College
Meadville, Pennsylvania

As fund raising for higher education becomes increasingly competitive and sophisticated, one area often neglected is the role of the board of trustees in the annual giving program. In many institutions, the annual fund has never been considered a place for trustee involvement in any way beyond the gift itself. The changing culture of fund raising, however, now gives us many reasons for re-thinking the role of trustees, particularly within the annual fund.

As the cost of education steadily rises, so too does the need to curb substantial tuition increases. This makes the case for increased operating revenue more compelling than ever. More and more institutions are launching "comprehensive" campaigns that include an annual component. By definition the annual fund then becomes a higher institutional priority. Gone are the days when the beginning of a capital campaign marked the suspension of the annual program. Each effort is equally important to the overall success of a fund-raising program and consequently to the financial vigor of the institution.

Finally, in today's campaign world, the size of "meaningful" capital gifts has grown to astronomical proportions. Fewer and fewer people are capable of providing "lead gifts," often of seven figures. Even at the trustee level, relatively few can give an endowed gift large enough to provide the immediate equivalent impact of a smaller outright gift. There are indeed many reasons for the trustees of an institution to welcome the opportunity to become more involved with its annual giving program.

In light of these emerging trends, Allegheny College, an undergraduate liberal arts institution, chose to redefine the role of our board in the annual fund. Within the past several years our trustees have become increasingly active and involved with the annual fund. They have taken on a highly public leadership role and, as a result, have spurred increased giving from other constituencies.

Involvement did not come naturally to all trustees, however. We had to provide the structure that made it possible. The following case study explains how we did it. Of course, ours is not the only way. Before you begin a similar project at your institution, you'll need to examine the fund-raising environment and the current perceptions of your trustees in order to determine your course. But our case study may help you develop general goals and give you ideas of specific strategies for achieving those goals.

Where we started

For many years, Allegheny trustees had supported our annual fund. They did so, however, without any formal program to guide their gifts. There was no goal for trustees. They were solicited randomly—sometimes by peers, sometimes by staff, sometimes not at all. And they didn't all participate. At board meetings, annual fund reports were brief if they were included at all. And most trustees believed that their gifts were more important to capital drives than to the annual fund.

Several factors led us to examine this situation with an eye toward change:

1. We were faced with a need for substantially increased operating revenue as we contemplated various program initiatives.

2. We were concerned about a lackluster annual fund performance over several years with static participation rates.

3. Finally, we were eager to better define trustee responsibilities and to showcase our trustees as the college's leadership.

One solution that seemed to speak to all of these needs was the creation of an organized trustee campaign within our annual fund.

We began by suggesting to the board that all trustee solicitations be the responsibility of the development committee of the board. This first step, we felt, would centralize the responsibility for all fund raising and allow staff one group with which to work as we developed the campaign.

Next we developed a "case" that supported our reasons for increased trustee giving to our annual fund. In addition to the need for increased support for program initiatives (the trustees were already well aware of this), we articulated, both in oral reports and in written correspondence, the need to position the annual fund as the top fund-raising priority of the college. With this as our goal, the involvement of trustees was essential. Their visible leadership, we pointed out, would not only raise the sights of the general constituency but also enable us to obtain substantial, long-term commitments from the institution's most generous donors—the trustees themselves.

How we started

The process of organizing such a campaign had to be carefully and sensitively executed. We began with the chairman of our development committee. Well versed in fund-raising issues, he was sympathetic to our efforts. In numerous conversations between the president, the vice president of development, the director of annual giving, and the chairman, we developed a consensus on fund-raising priorities and the need for trustee leadership in the annual fund.

With the help of the chairman, we then organized a core group within the development committee to assist staff in planning and presenting our ideas. We included the board's largest annual fund donor, but were careful to keep the group small enough that work could be done efficiently. The core group worked with the staff to determine a strategy and timeline.

When and what we did

Coordinating our efforts with the board meeting schedule (the board met in October, January, and May), we used the summer to prepare for an announcement at the fall meeting. In order to set an annual fund goal for the trustees, the core group assessed past overall performance (all gifts) of trustees, what we knew of individual capacities, and the expectations for the overall annual fund in the years to come. The result: a goal of $200,000 with 100 percent participation of our 50-member board. If achieved, this would represent a 40 percent increase in giving over the previous year and 15 percent of the total annual fund goal.

Next we determined individualized solicitation strategies for each trustee. This was by far the most time-consuming part of the entire process. We worked with the core group and our research department to determine appropriate asks and solicitors for each board member. We had no intention of simply asking each member to increase his or her giving by 40 percent. Instead we considered each trustee and his or her involvement, capacity, and other board relationships to determine the most effective approach, who should do it, and how much he or she should ask the board member to give.

We kept track of the individualized strategies by translating them to computer code for easier, more accurate processing. We also developed packages for each trustee solicitor that included:
- a donor information/profile on each assignment;
- the "case" for trustee giving;
- standard "how to solicit" information for volunteers; and
- pledge cards.

At the October meeting, we gave the packets to the development committee and explained all assignments. The chairman of the committee made a report to the board explicitly outlining the purpose, strategy, and timeline of the trustee campaign. Each board member knew exactly what to expect and why.

The chairman made it clear that solicitations would begin immediately and that gifts or pledges from the board were due before December 31. We encouraged trustee solicitors to make personal contacts whenever possible, using the telephone only as a last resort. We gave them two weeks to make an initial contact and asked them to mail an information return sheet back to the annual fund staff to report on the contact and the expected outcome.

Every two weeks, we sent all solicitors reports indicating whether or not their prospects had pledged. The director of annual giving was also in regular phone contact with most of the solicitors throughout the fall. In December a letter went out over the chairman's signature asking all trustees who had not yet made a commitment to do so before the end of the year. This concentrated solicitation period created both a sense of purpose and a sense of urgency, and it worked. We received all but four pledges before December 31.

This enabled us to give a positive report at the January board meeting where we announced progress to date and thanked everyone profusely for their commitments and timely response. The annual fund as a whole was also doing well, largely as a result of the trustee campaign.

Throughout the spring, trustee solicitors continued to receive progress reports, which now emphasized who had not paid their pledges. The director of annual giving met with all trustee solicitors to hear their critiques and their suggestions on adjustments of assignments or asks. The solicitors became an important resource in developing strategies not only for the next annual fund but, in many cases, for capital gifts as well.

Late in the year, we focused on those trustees who had not made gifts. They were all visited or phoned by the chair of the committee or by the annual giving staff. We mailed regular pledge reminders to those who had not completed their pledges. These efforts bore fruit. At the May board meeting, we were able to announce the successful completion of the trustee campaign.

What we accomplished

Numerous benefits resulted from our work with trustees. Not the least of these was our ability to highlight the board publicly as an example of leadership annual gift commitments. We lost no opportunity to announce trustee campaign results in college publications and news releases. During college events and personal calls, the staff praised trustee participation. This kind of recognition rewarded the trustees' efforts while raising the sights of other constituencies.

We also found that trustee involvement and interest in the college and in many of our activities increased immensely. The trustee campaign necessitated regular activity and contact not only between the college and the trustees, but also among the trustees themselves outside the board meeting arena. New alliances and friendships formed, and trustee involvement took on a new dimension.

Finally, the development office obtained new and enlightening information about several trustees. Forced regular review of individual financial capacity required timely research. And debriefing sessions with each trustee solicitor resulted in additional gift opportunities and revealed contacts and relationships between board members we had not previously known about.

Not to be overlooked: We increased our annual fund total by a full 13 percent over the previous year.

What we learned—some universal truths

While the above is a case study of how Allegheny College was successful with a trustee campaign, our techniques may or may not work at your institution. There are, however, some truths about trustee involvement that are widely applicable. As you review these, remember that, however you approach your trustees, you should do it with the utmost care. Trustees are your most important constituency and often the quickest to criticize.

1. *Educate your trustees.* Not only must you tell trustees the right things, but you must tell them in the right way.

• Understand and use the permissible lines of communication with trustees. Appropriate contact with the board varies widely from institution to institution. In many cases, annual giving directors do not have direct trustee contact. At some institutions you can pick up the phone and call the board chair directly, while at others you must deal with all board members through the vice president or president's office. The credibility of the trustee campaign depends heavily upon presenting it through the correct channels. Don't underestimate the importance of this.

• As with any volunteer group, never assume that trustees understand annual giving or their role in it. Education of our board was a major part of our overall strategy. Many trustees are accustomed to being approached only on a capital or endowment drive. Asking them for a substantial annual commitment may confuse them if they haven't been properly approached. Use staff and a core committee to talk through the new strategy with each member of the board *before* the goal is announced.

• Take the time to train the solicitors. Provide them with the same kind of how-to information that your other volunteer solicitors receive, but be sure to include specific information on the trustee "case."

2. *Personalize and proofread.* This takes time and thought, but it's worth it. Your trustees deserve the most individualized attention of any constituency.

• Be prepared to spend time discussing solicitation strategy for each and every trustee. A successful campaign depends upon each board member being approached by the right person at the right time with the right ask. You can never spend too much time on strategy.

• Emphasize the importance of this project with all computer and clerical support staff. People who handle information about trustees should be fully aware of its importance and its sensitive nature. A little mistake here can cause years of hard feelings; it can cost your institution thousands of dollars in lost gifts.

3. *Report regularly and accurately.* Like all volunteers, trustees want to know what their hard work is accomplishing.

• Effective follow-up depends upon the staff's ability to provide timely and accurate solicitation reports. Written or computer-generated reports may be sufficient for some volunteers but not for trustees. Frequent discussions are necessary in order to glean information and to make any strategy adjustments.

• When you see that trustee leadership is having an effect on other constituencies, be sure to report it to your trustees. Let them know that their own giving has leveraged the giving of other donors.

• Be consistent in highlighting the annual fund in development reports at board meetings whether or not you are at the height of board solicitations.

Each of these areas is essential to the success of a trustee campaign. Each takes thought, care, and time to accomplish correctly and with maximum results. Involving your trustees in annual giving is not an easy project and should not be approached unless you and your institution are committed to doing it right. The benefits, however, are untold.

Once trustees become involved in the annual giving campaign, other possibilities will present themselves. Perhaps the development committee could challenge the rest of the board, or the board could challenge alumni. Maybe trustees could host other major donors at an annual dinner, or trustee solicitors could become trainers for other volunteer solicitors.

Trustees have an enormous impact on the life of the institution. Their involvement in annual giving is critical, and the potential results are endless. It worked for us, and it can work for you.

Chapter 28

Community Campaigns

Susan Cranford Ross
Assistant Director of Development and Director of Annual Giving
Duke University
Durham, North Carolina

C onsider three scenarios: You're the primary educational institution in your metropolitan area. Everybody loves you, but cheering for your sports teams doesn't translate into tangible support.

You're one of several institutions, but you have a unique tie to the community that can be developed—you're its oldest, its biggest, educator of more of its citizens, trainer of its employees, and so on.

You're looking for a new constituency whose interests will be broad enough to provide the critical unrestricted support that your institution needs.

In all three situations, a well-planned community campaign is one of the possible answers.

A community campaign can do a lot of positive things for your institution. Unlike traditional annual giving programs, this audience includes nonalumni as well as alumni. It is oriented primarily to the business community, which will account for most of the dollars contributed. A community campaign is a great way to develop new contacts with individuals and corporate executives. And finally, a strong community campaign is a great public relations opportunity within your local area.

A community campaign is not the answer for all of your institution's needs. For one thing, it is not likely to be a budget balancer. You probably will not have that kind of success to start with. The potential is there for future years, but this is not an instant cash program.

Two other cautions about your community campaign: It should not be a form of blackmail for your vendors, although they certainly should be solicited. And it should not be a program that will overwhelm your staff, who are already busy with direct mail, phonathons, parent programs, and other essential annual giving activities. Strike a balance between the ideal program and the time your staff has to give until you are sure of the potential this campaign has for your institution.

Where to begin

Your first step is to look at town-gown relations. Are they strong? Can you jump right in and begin soliciting? If not, you should work with others on campus to build strong public relations first.

Second, assess your volunteer base. Look closely at the corporate community for leadership. The chair need not be an alumnus, but he or she should feel strongly about the contribution your institution makes to the local economy. What about other volunteers? Can you identify 50 to 100 prospects for the corporate solicitation effort? If you are thinking of sponsoring a benefit or other major project, do you have enough volunteers?

Then evaluate your staff commitment. Is there support at the very top—your president? Will the corporate relations office help? How about public relations? Placement? Purchasing? How much staff time is annual giving willing to commit? Programs can be effective whether they are large or small, but taking on too much will frustrate everyone, including your community volunteers.

Finally, look at the giving history for your community: the corporations, individuals (especially nonalumni), and local foundations. You know you will be competing with other causes, but are such efforts generally successful? Is there a commitment to your institution? Are there particular campus programs that have inspired community support? For example, at Duke our pediatrics program's "Children's Classic Golf/Tennis Tournament" has been very well received. How will you capitalize on the success of these programs without just moving the same dollars around the campus? Your goal is new money, so you must make the case for unrestricted support over and above other types of gifts.

Decide on the scope

Community campaigns run the gamut in the United States. Some institutions go all out with "Siwash U. Day" in town. They work with local restauranteurs to donate profits from every slice of pizza sold that day or every Siwash Special submarine sandwich. The movie theaters and retail stores get involved. Siwash colors are everywhere, and the local press extols the virtues of the institution. Community leaders gather early in the day for a corporate solicitation blitz, all of which ends at dusk with a reception for the volunteers and perhaps fireworks on the main quadrangle. What a day! What a splash! If you've got the staff time, this can be a very effective way to go.

Duke's community campaign focuses on corporations. Duke volunteers canvass medium and large companies in United Way style over a four- to six-week period. One effective approach is to team up a volunteer with a member of the university faculty or administration. The volunteers or volunteer teams call on about five firms, of their own choosing if possible, and ask for gifts in pre-established ranges.

A third approach combines some elements described above with standard annual giving programs like direct mail or phonathons. Corporate direct mail is usually not very effective, but if you are reaching out to the community at large, it can help. And student callers in a community phonathon can be great ambassadors for improved town-gown relations.

Decide on your goals

Here again you have more options than you may have realized. One approach is to count everything that comes into Siwash from the community, whether or not it is generated through this campaign. This is not as far-fetched an idea as it might appear. If you are recognizing your community's gifts to the institution, why limit it to new gifts or to gifts pledged during a certain period?

If you want a separate program focused on just unrestricted gifts, you can do it. Just be realistic. If your institution has historically received a lot of research funding from a corporation, it is unlikely that the announcement of Siwash Day is going to alter the pattern dramatically. Probably your best approach there is to create a Business Association program with $1,000, $5,000, or $10,000 unrestricted support membership levels that will attract even these major funders. Think of some tangible benefits you can offer to the companies that join. Preferred placement interviews? Attendance at special lectures? Campus parking passes? Consulting?

An important step is to prepare a size-of-gifts chart that creates a role for smaller firms that give $100 to $500. Many of your institution's vendors will gladly give at this level if asked. Get your purchasing office to provide a list of vendors, then *judiciously* share this background information with the assigned volunteers. Ask them to keep it confidential and emphasize that they must never imply that giving a gift might affect purchasing decisions.

If a large-scale event or gala benefit is in your plans, carefully research costs and anticipated profit to be sure you can justify the extensive time and upfront expense such a program will involve. Dinners, dances, shows, and other benefit-type events can be disasters if they are not well run, and that takes time and money. A rule of thumb is that you should be as interested in the public relations value as you are in the immediate dollar return. Many now-successful benefits began with only minimal profits.

Part of your solicitation may have participation as its primary goal. Reaching out to a mass audience for small gifts has advantages, but go in with your eyes open. Assume that mass mailings, newspaper ads, coupons, and merchandising gimmicks will be good for community relations but will have little effect on your goal. They may, however, create a good mailing list of local "friends" that could be used to promote campus art programs, special campaigns, and so on.

Organize the campaign

We attribute the 40-year success of our Durham-Duke Campaign primarily to one factor: Our volunteers know they will be part of an organized, well-managed program so they agree to help year after year. If you set up your program correctly from the start, you will be charting a course that will serve your institution well.

Start with a complete schedule. This allows you, your staff, and everyone else involved to plan with your deadlines in mind. The first thing on your schedule should be recruiting a community campaign chair. He or she should be a prominent individual who is closely identified with your institution. The chair should have the reputation and stature to represent your institution publicly, attract other top volunteers, and deal on a peer level with your president and the business leaders in your community.

A good organizational technique, we have found, is to help your chair select a campaign cabinet of vice chairs charged with such tasks as prospect identification, volunteer recruitment, leadership gifts, and special events. You can use these leaders to recruit enough additional volunteers to adequately handle all the tasks or calls you have in mind. Aim for top community leaders—you will find you can get them if your campaign is perceived to be important and well run.

Prepare background materials for your volunteers that will enable them to feel comfortable and confident in their work. This might include:

• a brochure describing your institution's impact on the community—salaries paid, arts/sports programming, goods and services purchased, indirect value of hotel/restaurant/retail sales to students and parents, and so on;

• a cover letter from your president that can be mailed to prospective donors to introduce the campaign and say that the assigned volunteer will be calling on the institution's behalf;

• pledge cards to be hand-delivered and returned by volunteers to your office; and

• volunteer packets that include schedules, tips, and assignment sheets with accurate and complete background information on prospects.

Now you're ready to begin. Hold a kickoff event that will both train and inspire your volunteers. Try to involve your president or other top brass; their participation shows others how important the campaign is. If adequate parking can be arranged, hold the kickoff on campus so your volunteers feel totally immersed in the cause.

Whether your campaign is scheduled to run for one day or one month, your volunteers will need some help. Follow-up is especially important with longer campaigns and can be done by volunteer team captains or by staff members. Interim report sessions can help because they serve as additional deadlines for volunteers, but they are usually not very well attended. And, as in any effort, you need to be prepared to take over for delinquent volunteers when necessary.

Finally, hold a campaign celebration. This can be the closing event of "Siwash U. Day," or it can be a planned reception about three weeks after your campaign ends. This gives a sense of closure to the campaign, brings your volunteers and donors together, offers publicity opportunities, and sets the stage for next year.

An area hotel or group of caterers who do business with you may be willing to sponsor a first-class event in exchange for the publicity and the chance to impress a prestigious audience. It could also be their contribution or part of their contribution to your campaign.

This celebration should make all participants—contributors and volunteers—feel proud of their role in supporting your institution.

Conclusion

A community campaign can be a great way to raise important money with a bang. If you keep the drive short and simple, it can be a positive experience for both staff and volunteers. In the end, both your institution and the community will come away feeling successful and enthusiastic about their renewed commitment to one another.

Section 5

Recognition and Evaluation

Chapter 29

The Philosophy Of Recognition

Jake B. Schrum
Vice President for Development and Planning
Emory University
Atlanta, Georgia

T his chapter is dedicated to J. Pollard Turman, former chair of the J.M. Tull Foundation, who understood the importance of recognition but sought none for himself.

How do you feel when someone you have recently met sees you on the street and addresses you by your first name? My reaction is always the same. I am thrilled that that person thought enough of me to remember my name and to recognize me in that manner.

When you've worked long hours on your civic club's annual outing, do you get a sense of satisfaction when your club's president recognizes your efforts? Of course you do. Most people do. In fact, most people enjoy being recognized for any gesture they make on behalf of the common good.

The importance of recognition

In the advancement field all of us need to be aware of the important role recognition plays in our fund-raising success. Through four decades, the legendary chairman of the Coca-Cola Company, the late Robert W. Woodruff, insisted that his philanthropy be anonymous. Only in his later years, did he finally allow his friends in his beloved Atlanta to recognize and honor his exemplary generosity.

Robert Woodruff was the exception. Many well-meaning and generous donors and philanthropists would attest to the importance of recognition. It provides much of the motivation for philanthropy.

Who hasn't seen a Carnegie Library building at some time in their life? These libraries were the focal point of intellectual life for many of the small towns dotting the American landscape. Certainly Andrew Carnegie enjoyed this recognition of his generosity.

In designing our institutions' recognition programs, we should remember that there are more Carnegies than Woodruffs in our world of philanthropy. Why is this so? Why do people want recognition for their gifts?

At the basic level, I believe recognition is inextricably tied to acceptance. We need others to accept us, to like us, to appreciate what we do, to value what we have contributed to society. When our institution finds ways to recognize a donor, we are showcasing that donor's contribution to the common good. We are telling people that this donor should be accepted as a person who cares about others, as a person who has a love of humankind.

When I send $100 to my alma mater for the annual fund, I want the people there to know that I care about someone other than myself. I want people to say, "He's willing to part with $100, so he can't be all bad." Or "Count him in, he's one of the good guys."

Acceptance is extremely important to most of us. Our recognition programs make both small donors and major benefactors feel that they are accepted, that they are important because they have done something for the common good.

If you are designing or revising your recognition program, keep in mind not only "**i**mportance" but four other "i" factors as well:

- the **i**nvolvement factor;
- the **i**nfluence factor;
- the **i**ncrease factor, and
- the **i**deal factor.

The involvement factor in recognition

People enjoy recognition, and they appreciate the acceptance that accompanies recognition. This atmosphere of acceptance helps them to feel comfortable and often leads the way to greater involvement. In many cases, donors *need* to become involved, and their initial philanthropy is their way of checking to see if you will recognize that need and provide a means by which they can satisfy it.

While working at a liberal arts college in the Southwest, I received a telephone call from an elderly woman who lived across the street from the college. She was housebound, and she asked me to come to see her.

That afternoon I spent more than two hours with her, and I discovered a warm and caring person who wanted to be recognized by our college. She offered to give us her house to be used for an alumni center. It was a lovely home, and the college certainly needed a more inviting place than it then had to welcome its alumni.

Within a few months we had gratefully accepted her gift and begun work to restore her beautiful home. In the process, I discovered that she, probably without realizing it, was making this gift so that she could be more involved with people from the college. As we made plans for the restoration of the house, as we negotiated a life-use arrangement for the gift, as we talked about how we would use the house, she got to know many people from the college. Our public relations staff, our alumni staff, our fund-raising staff, our president—all became her friends. We loved her and she loved us.

She died very soon after making her gift, and this wonderful person, whom I had not known only 18 months before, left instructions that I officiate at her funeral.

She wanted to be recognized for her philanthropy, but even more, she wanted her philanthropy to pave the way for her involvement with the college and with those who worked there.

As you design your recognition program, keep in mind the very real possibility that people give not only to be recognized, but also so that they can become involved with your institution.

The influence factor

When I lived in New England, the autumn leaves would turn the landscape into a breathtaking collage of colors. In most parts of our country, however, you don't have to experience the beauty of autumn leaves to know that it's fall. In many cases, you only have to look at a woman's blouse or man's lapel for a tiny pin that, year after year, no matter what the design, carries the same message: "I gave to the United Way." That little pin is part of a recognition program that influences countless other people to give.

Is it a pressure factor? Maybe some people give only because they don't want their colleagues to know that they haven't given. When others see that they have a pin, they are recognized as people who care. But for the many who genuinely *want* to give, the pin serves as a reminder that it's time to make a contribution to the United Way.

Over the years I've noticed a characteristic shared by many major donors: They appear to be at peace with themselves. I believe it's because they have come to the point in their lives when they sincerely believe, "It is more blessed to give than to receive." This state of mind and heart frees them from the emphasis on materialism that characterizes much of our society. These people exude an aura of joy, and this aura often influences others to seek that same peace and joy.

Recently, friends of a local university who had never given a dollar to that institution decided that they wanted to establish a charitable remainder trust. After completing the very delicate and sophisticated arrangements for the gift, the family established a major endowment of several million dollars. The university then published several feature articles, citing the donors' remarkable generosity as well as the financial benefits to the donors of a charitable remainder trust agreement.

By and by, after several weeks had passed, good friends of these donors—who are also wealthy—asked them about the gift and contacted the university to discuss ways in which they, too, might make a major contribution. At least one other couple had been influenced to consider a gift of great magnitude.

I am convinced that recognition of the gifts of your donors can significantly influence the gifts of others.

The increase factor

In 1986, at the start of a capital campaign, a major research university in the Southeast had only four alumni donors who were giving at the $100,000 level. In the past, the institution had made no major effort to acquire gifts of this magnitude from alumni and had no program to pay special recognition to donors at this exemplary level of generosity.

Today this institution has well over 100 alumni whose names are on the honor roll in the $100,000-plus category. Most of these new major donors had given their alma mater something in the past. What influenced them to increase their gifts to such a significant level? I believe the increase was due, at least in part, to the university's recognition program.

When the campaign started, the advancement staff knew that many more alumni would have to give major gifts than in previous years, so they created a new recognition club. Its creation was well publicized, and those alumni who gave at this level not only received recognition in the alumni donor honor roll, but they also received a lovely sculpture. More important, their names were inscribed on a plaque that now hangs in the entrance to the university's administration building.

It is true, I suppose, that these alumni would not have given if they had not wanted to (and I'm sure each was individually cultivated and solicited). However, I believe that such a large increase in the numbers and in the amounts given was due to such a well-conceived and carefully implemented recognition program.

The story is told that Henry Ford III was in Bethlehem, Pennsylvania, on the occasion of the 75th birthday of Lee Iacocca's mother. At that time Iacocca, the Chrysler magnate, was still employed by Ford.

At the party, which was attended by several hundred people from the Lehigh Valley, a young development officer from a local university was so entranced by the solicitation opportunity presented by Ford's attendance that he seized the occasion. Cornering Ford, the development officer told him about a new building needed at the local university, and he solicited Ford for a gift. Mostly in an attempt to rid himself of this overly enthusiastic fund raiser, Ford agreed to give $5,000 and suggested that the young man come to his hotel the following morning to pick up Ford's check for this amount.

Early the next day, Ford read with dismay a front-page headline in the local paper, "FORD TO GIVE $50,000 TO LOCAL DRIVE."

When the young development officer arrived to receive Ford's donation, he confessed that he had shared the good news of the gift with the newspaper, but he swore that he had given the paper the correct amount. Obviously, the paper's editors couldn't believe that Ford would be giving so small a gift.

Finally, an exasperated Ford agreed to contribute $50,000 to the building project on the condition that the following inscription be carved in stone over the building's main entrance: "I was a stranger and ye took me in."

I believe recognition plays a key role in increased giving.

The ideal factor

Individuals and institutions enjoy being recognized as "the model" or "the ideal" for others to imitate. Most development professionals would agree that the Yale Alumni Fund, which celebrated its centennial in 1990, is the ideal. It began in the gay '90s with a handful of Yalies (then called "Elies" after Elihu Yale) attempting to raise less than $100,000 in unrestricted gifts to their alma mater. At its 100th birthday, the Yale Alumni Fund planned to reach a goal in academic year 1989-90 of $50 million. Has recognition played a key role in establishing this program as "the ideal"? I believe it has.

For many decades, Yale alumni have been recognized by their institution and around the world of higher education as some of the most generous and loyal to be found anywhere. This constant identification as "the best" or "the ideal" has caused many Yale classes to surpass the goals of previous classes so that Yale graduates and, indeed, Yale University will continue to be recognized as "the model" in alumni annual giving. I bet Yale reaches its centennial goal, and I believe Yale alumni will give, in part, so that Yale will continue to be recognized as "the ideal."

The ideal factor has also influenced America's corporate community. Over the last two decades, the twin cities of Minneapolis and St. Paul have set the pace for corporate giving. The majority of the large corporations in these two cities have followed the 5-percent rule, contributing at least 5 percent of their net pretax earnings to charitable causes. Their generosity has been recognized nationally, and that recognition has helped to establish them as "the ideal." Not wanting to descend from this pedestal as "the model" for corporate America, they have strived to maintain their percentage of giving even during lean years when earnings have fallen.

Individuals can also be influenced by the "ideal" factor in recognition. Several decades ago, during one of the "boom times" in Texas, a man named Jim West made a fortune in oil. He began to carry silver dollars in his pockets to hand out to the less fortunate on the streets of Houston. Within a few years, he became known as the "Silver Dollar King" and was considered by many of Houston's poor and downtrodden to be a model for philanthropy. They saw him as the ideal.

Legend has it that West never left his home without his pockets filled with silver dollars, and he was expected to give in order to maintain his image as a generous oil baron. The Silver Dollar King surely enjoyed being on that pedestal and probably vowed to himself that he would never lack for the silver dollars that had brought him so much recognition. When he died, his friends discovered that his basement floor was covered with silver dollars.

Conclusion

When designing your recognition program, keep the "i" factors in mind. Recognition is important to most donors. Well-conceived recognition programs usually cause donors to become more involved in your institution. Moreover, your recognition program might influence others to give, as well as cause others to increase their giving. And finally, if you can recognize someone as the ideal donor, then you and your institution have played a key role in developing generous and committed philanthropists.

A final note

Every day many of us begin a sentence with one of the following phrases: "I believe . . . ," "I feel . . . ," "I want . . . ," or "I give . . . ." We all want others to care about what we believe, feel, want, and to what worthwhile cause we give our resources. A development program that recognizes the importance of the needs of its individual donors will be a successful program for a long time.

Chapter 30

Techniques for Recognition

Cira P. Masse
Director of the Annual Fund
Hartwick College
Oneonta, New York

No matter how modestly people give a gift or perform a service, everyone enjoys being recognized. When you are planning your recognition techniques, you need to consider two constituencies that often overlap— donors and volunteers. Both groups may be recognized in much the same way with appropriate modifications.

Among the dictionary definitions of recognition are two that indicate the ways we use recognition most often:

• Recognition before a gift is made or a service is performed is cultivation, reflecting the dictionary definition of "a giving of attention or favorable notice";

• Recognition after a gift is made or a service is performed is appreciation or "an acknowledgment."

At some point in your fund-raising career, you probably learned the "Rule of Sevens"—find seven opportunities to say thank you to donors and volunteers.[1] This can refer not only to the number of *times* people are thanked, but also to the seven *methods* of recognition outlined here.

Consider the techniques below as a menu for donor/volunteer recognition. When you choose a dish from a restaurant menu, you consider how hungry you are, what you feel like eating, what your likes and dislikes are, and whether or not you plan to have dessert. Likewise, in choosing a method of recognition, consider which techniques are appropriate to the magnitude of the gift or service; the personality, likes, dislikes, and interests of the donor/volunteer; and whether or not (and when) you hope for more participation. Then add your own specialized creative ingredients that will make it just right for your institution.

No. 1: Oral ("Thanks so much . . . ")

Oral recognition is probably the easiest, least expensive, most efficient, and most timely way to recognize a contribution of time or money. It can vary in formality. A personal visit by the president, a faculty member, a staff person, a student, or another volunteer represents the most formal scenario of this oral tradition. However, a phone call by any of the above or even a casual "on the street" "By the way, thank you . . . " can serve well.

The greatest advantage of this technique is that it can be implemented promptly. You can say "Thanks for your help" to volunteers when they return their pledge forms; you can pick up the phone and say "Thanks for the gift" to a donor as soon as you have opened the envelope containing his or her check.

No. 2: Written ("On behalf of . . . ")

The written version of donor/volunteer recognition serves the purposes of both the person or institution doing the acknowledging and the person or organization being acknowledged. You can keep a written acknowledgment in your files to serve as a chronology of contact with your contributors. This is often necessary for auditing or historical purposes and provides a "paper trail." For the donor or volunteer, it can serve as a record of contribution for taxes and other purposes.

Written recognition can vary in formality too. A receipt with a preprinted thank-you card is a fast, easy way to acknowledge smaller contributions. A personal letter from the president, a staff or faculty member, a volunteer, or a student is appropriate for more substantial contributions or volunteer activities. The person who makes the contact should depend on the purpose and magnitude of the contribution, the way in which the contribution was solicited, and the familiarity of the donor or volunteer with your staff.

In many cases, it may be appropriate for more than one of the institution's representatives to write a thank-you note or letter. For example, a large contribution to a department may warrant an acknowledgment from the president of the institution as well as from a member of that department's faculty. A gift earmarked for scholarships may be appropriately acknowledged by a student who is receiving assistance from that source.

Donors and volunteers appreciate a personal handwritten note as a supplement to or a substitute for a more formal typed acknowledgment. Don't forget to keep copies of handwritten communications for your files, particularly if that is your primary method of acknowledgment.

Written materials that provide a donor or volunteer with up-to-date information are important ways of recognizing the individual's relationship to your institution. Newsletters, memos, progress reports, and printouts keep donors and volunteers abreast of activities and progress at the institution and make them feel part of daily operations.

Holiday and special occasion cards and notes tell donors and volunteers that you remember and wish to be part of their personal celebrations too.

No. 3: Publication ("For posterity . . . ")

Publication—the communication of information to the public—is the most formal form of written recognition; it also serves to communicate an institution's activities to its constituencies as well as recording them for posterity.

Annual donor lists are probably the most common form of publication in which to recognize the contributions of donors. You can include donor lists in the annual report of your institution or publish them separately. Either way, donor lists are an efficient method of publicly recognizing a large number of individuals. You can use donor club categories, boldface type, and various symbols to indicate special groups such as first-time donors, increased donors, and loyalty donors.

If the size of your annual report permits, you might include photographs of key volunteers (class agents, parent committee members, and so on). If you publish a directory for general or constituency use (alumni, parents, etc.), you can design it so that the contributions of individuals are indicated through a system of symbols. For example, asterisks might indicate the names of alumni board members or those who have performed other volunteer services. You can include a smaller version of the donor list in other specialized material such as programs for cultural and athletic events.

The computer has made the compilation of donor lists and directories infinitely easier. However, careful human monitoring of data is still essential. In some special cases, hand manipulation of data will be necessary.

Whenever donor lists are published, thousands of people are pleased to see their contributions recognized. However, more than likely, you won't hear from the thousands but from the few whose names have been misspelled, omitted, or put in the wrong category. The best you can do is to make the necessary correction and put your gracious letter of apology in the next mail.

Many of your donors and volunteers, either as individuals or as groups, have special characteristics or have made special contributions that are noteworthy. Feature articles in newspapers, college publications, and other forms of media recognize these unique contributions and activities. Such articles not only recognize the donor or volunteer, but draw positive attention to the institution and encourage giving and involvement by others.

Recognition and thank-you messages can have a wide public audience when they appear as boxed advertisements in college publications or area newspapers or as announcements on radio.

Perhaps the ultimate in recognition is the naming opportunity in which a donor's or volunteer's name appears on something tangible. Not every donor/volunteer will make a contribution great enough to see his or her name on a building or to endow a scholarship or an academic chair. However, many donors give enough to merit putting their names on bookplates in library books. This can be an effective cultivation for an individual who can only give a small gift now but may be in a position to make a larger contribution later.

Every institution has a "wish list" describing potential gifts at various levels. Your wish list can provide creative approaches to recognition that appeal to an individual donor's special interests. Just remember, a brass plaque can be affixed to almost anything. A study carrel in the library may be only the beginning of a donor's interest in your institution. He or she may decide to name the whole library with his or her next gift.

No. 4: Tokens ("Remember us . . . ")

Although your office may soon resemble a warehouse if you adopt this method, tangible items serve as effective reminders of the institution as well as tokens of appreciation for donors and volunteers. The item should be appropriate to the contribution, related in some way to the institution, and used judiciously.

Bookmarks, key rings, holiday ornaments, bumper stickers, paperweights, and bibs (for future alumni) are just a few of the many inexpensive items that can be stamped with your institution's logo and sent even before a gift is made.

You can use more substantial tokens—pewter plates, silver bowls, and brass clocks—to recognize leadership contributions, confirmed bequests, planned giving arrangements, and so on. Promoting your institution's faculty by presenting signed copies of their books can be especially meaningful to donors and volunteers who may know the authors personally. Audio and videocassettes of special presentations, concerts, lectures, or institutional events can bring the campus to distant supporters and can create a special link with the institution.

The possibilities are as numerous as the catalogs that appear regularly on your desk. Just be sure the token fits the occasion, the donor or volunteer, the contribution, the institution—and a standard mailing envelope (or your briefcase).

The Internal Revenue Service has recently issued new guidelines about the deductibility of charitable contributions that are attached to a premium or quantifiable privilege. Since IRS regulations are not easily interpreted to include every scenario, if you are giving donors or volunteers any kind of premium or benefit, you will need to consult your institution's legal or tax counsel. You should encourage your donors to do so also.

No. 5: Privileges ("Be part of us . . . ")

Inviting individuals to join a special volunteer group is a privilege that recognizes their unique relationship to your institution and their contributions—either the ones they have already made or the ones you hope they will make. The members of your alumni board, parent council, and advisory committees should have some identifying mark during homecoming, parents weekend, and similar events so that others will know who they are and will also wish to participate. Ribbons, buttons, and distinctive nametags are inexpensive yet effective ways to identify leaders and active volunteers.

For other donors and volunteers, particularly local ones, the privilege of using institutional facilities—the library, athletic areas and equipment, and public rooms—is appropriate. Pre-sale and complimentary tickets to cultural and athletic events; invitations to preview art shows or attend lectures, theater productions, and building openings; and the privilege of auditing classes and participating in campus projects—all make donors and volunteers feel that they are "insiders." (Again, these may constitute a quantifiable premium, so be sure to encourage donors to consult legal or tax counsel about the deductibility of their gifts.)

Additionally, donors and volunteers appreciate being consulted on substantive issues regarding college policies, community relations, and other decision-making processes. You can recognize or cultivate an important donor, volunteer, or prospect by asking him or her to represent the institution at an official gathering such as an institutional conference or the inauguration of a college president in another state.

Donor clubs encourage donors to increase their gifts. Membership in a donor club may be attached to some or all of the privileges and premiums mentioned here and in the section on tokens (and subject to IRS regulations). Often, however, the peer identification in a donor club is a strong incentive in itself. For this reason, make sure that donor club listings in your institution's publications are clearly marked and accurate. You can also use donor clubs to target an "ask" and to serve as criteria for challenge programs.

Privileges such as these develop a sense of ownership in your institution. And when volunteers and donors feel a sense of ownership, they will work for the welfare of your institution, contributing financially and through their service.

No. 6: Special events ("Share something special . . . ")

Special events can serve as cultivation or as appreciation. They can be small, intimate occasions or large, gala events. Once again, your constituency and purpose (and perhaps your budget as well) should dictate what form the events take.

Meals—luncheons, brunches, dinners—are popular forms of special events. They may precede other functions such as athletic events, theatrical performances, or lectures; they may be a focal point in a larger program of activities such as reunion weekend, homecoming, parents weekend or workshops; they may stand alone as a way to cultivate, appreciate, and inform your supporters; and they may incorporate award ceremonies, keynote speakers, and informative presentations about the institution. (Invitations to special events may also constitute a quantifiable benefit in the eyes of the IRS.)

Large-scale events for limited constituencies (parents weekend, reunions, and so on) offer a variety of activities. These events require careful planning and coordination by a team of cooperative individuals. This team should evaluate each activity as to purpose and appropriateness, design it to "show off" the institution to best advantage, and staff it well enough to provide a personal dimension for every person who attends.

Events that mix constituencies are often desirable. Inviting parents and alumni to participate in a career forum, for example, gives parents the opportunity to meet successful graduates and recognizes the expertise of both groups. Invite the community and faculty to selected parent and alumni events; parents and alumni enjoy meeting local supporters of the institution. Get-togethers such as these recognize the fact that all constituencies are involved in a common effort.

Lest we forget the purpose of our institutions, students should be included whenever feasible. Hosting guests, conducting tours, and assisting in planning are only a few of the ways in which students can be useful. Parents and faculty feel recognized and validated when they see their students actively participating in special events. Becoming acquainted with your institution's most promising students can provide the greatest incentive for donors as it shows them tangible proof of the institution's achievement of its goals.

Whether large or small, formal or informal, connected to specific interests or general in nature, your special event should be constructed so that it recognizes the interrelation of your donor and volunteer constituencies and the individuals who make up your institution.

No. 7: Challenges ("If you do this, we'll do that . . . ")

Challenge grants provide a unique opportunity to recognize both those who offer the challenge and those who participate in it. Challenges can bear the name of the institution, organization, or individual providing the challenge gift. Donors, in turn, can be recognized as participants in the special challenge group.

Challenges can be set up with a wide variety of criteria depending on their purpose. They nearly always urge individuals and groups (such as graduating seniors, reunion classes, and young alumni) on to new heights of fund-raising achievement.

Conclusion

An institution that has been in existence for even a short period of time is certain to have many stratifications of constituent interests, particularly among alumni. When you are selecting recognition techniques, the "old guard," the "baby boomers," the young alumni, and the athletes may each present their own set of challenges. It is your task to select either specialized or generic recognition techniques depending on the segmentation of each group.

The way you recognize the support of your donors and volunteers can make or break your fund-raising efforts. Recognition specific to the donor's or volunteer's interest and appropriate to the amount of his or her gift or degree of volunteer commitment is crucial to the progress of your programs.

The seven techniques outlined here provide a basis for implementing the "Rule of Sevens" with your constituencies. Your own imagination, your knowledge of your constituencies, your institutional profile—and your budget—will all determine the final form of your recognition efforts.

Note

[1] On page 57 in *Mega Gifts: Who Gives Them, Who Gets Them* (Chicago: Pluribus Press, 1984), author Jerold Panas attributes the "Rule of Sevens" to Mary G. Roebling, one of the leading bankers in the country:

> She was on the board of our college... and was heading a special campaign. We were talking about strategy and the mechanics of the campaign and she said: "Now, Jerry, one thing you must remember. People like to be thanked, they want to know that what they have done is appreciated, really appreciated. When we get a gift that we think is special, let's find a way to thank the person at least seven times before we ever ask them again for another gift." Seven times! It seemed an almost impossible task. But if you plan for it, it can be done. The dividends are extraordinary.

Chapter 31

Supporting Volunteers Who Support the Annual Fund

Pamela Hillman
Director of Annual Giving
California Institute of Technology
Pasadena, California

Christine Kozojet
Associate Director of Annual Giving
California Institute of Technology

S upporting the volunteers who support the annual fund is key to the success of your program. You need to establish a solid volunteer pyramid with strong leadership and provide excellent training and materials and accurate, timely reporting of results. In addition, you need a staff that is committed to consistent, personal involvement with volunteers at all levels.

Effective, excited volunteers may sometimes be born that way, but more often they are created through staff support and thorough training. Therefore, before you begin recruiting volunteers, you must commit the time and money needed to support volunteer efforts.

Building a volunteer structure

Creating your volunteer structure is perhaps the most important single aspect of alumni fund raising. Begin by working with your staff to select key volunteers who have already demonstrated their commitment and their ability through previous volunteer work.

Look at the people who have volunteered in the past. Be sure to consider all types of volunteer activity. For example, a good admissions volunteer is already sold on your institution and only needs to learn new techniques to become an effective annual fund volunteer. Look also for regular, significant giving history. An alumnus who gives generously and regularly is also sold on your institution; often, all you need to do is ask this donor to contribute his or her time. Don't forget former campus leaders. Alumni who had high visibility when they were on campus are usually good at rallying their former classmates to support their alma mater.

Once you have selected and recruited your key volunteers, supply them with the same information on prospects in their constituency that you used to recruit them. Educate them to the key things to look for when they are recruiting the next tier of volunteers, and provide them with all the materials they will need to contact these people. Key volunteers have an advantage in that they are often asking personal friends to join them in their efforts.

Key volunteers can provide support and motivation to other volunteers. They can set an example by making their own gift first. They can lead training sessions on how to recruit other volunteers and how to solicit for gifts. They can react to the ongoing needs of other volunteers by providing them with the information and materials that are needed to do their jobs.

Key volunteers can help the volunteers who work for them by functioning as liaison to the administration, reporting on the needs and concerns of their volunteers to the powers that be and conveying the priorities of the administration back to the volunteers. Finally, and of perhaps greatest importance, the key volunteers can offer personal, peer recognition for a job well done.

Motivate through training

Motivation is a key ingredient of a successful volunteer fund-raising effort. Motivate your volunteers by providing them with training and materials and by following through to award appropriate recognition for their efforts at the conclusion of your annual fund cycle.

Once your core group of volunteers is in place, you should schedule an annual on-campus training program. To ensure attendance, your institution should pay the transportation and room and board costs for each volunteer. Remember that it's important to recruit volunteers nationwide. Alumni who live far away from campus should be contacted by individuals in their area. This will cost a little more, but will make the volunteers' job easier.

As your program grows, you may decide to reimburse only first-time and fifth-year returning volunteers for the full cost of getting to and from the campus. Others would receive only room and board expenses. A surprising number of volunteers will attend the training program while serving their second, third, and fourth years as volunteers. The success of your campaign rides on your ability to motivate these volunteers, so it is extremely important that you show your level of commitment to the program by enabling these key people to return to campus from time to time.

Take advantage of the fact that you have a number of interested alumni returning to campus. Make the training session an event. You want these people to leave with a renewed sense of pride and an enthusiasm that they will pass on to the alumni whom they ask for gifts. Give these important institutional advocates a reason to spend a weekend with you.

Invite your institution's president to attend part or all of the day's activities and give him or her the opportunity to make a state-of-the-institution address. Schedule your event at a time when students are on campus, and invite scholarship recipients to attend lunch or dinner so that volunteers will get to know the kind of students currently at your institution. Or you might invite faculty to serve as hosts for your volunteer dinner.

Your training program should not be all business. Set aside time for a faculty member and a member of the administration or admissions office to speak to the group. This is an occasion to discuss campus activities and individual faculty research or projects and to bring volunteers up-to-date on current events at your institution. A video highlighting your campus and any media attention you garnered in the last year is a helpful tool. Make copies available to your volunteers to use in recruiting the next level of volunteers.

Just as with solicitations, face-to-face contact is the best way to train and motivate volunteers. Not everyone will be able to come to campus for training. It often becomes necessary to take your show on the road. One or two satellite training sessions in key cities will enable you to reach many volunteers who can't make it to campus. Again, you should cover the cost of volunteers' transportation and room and board.

Although you will not be able to create the same atmosphere as you can on campus, you can make satellite training a shot in the arm nonetheless. You can provide all the same materials and a good nuts-and-bolts training session on their use. You can bring publications from your campus and share anecdotal information about what has been going on. And, most important, you can set the tone of the event by conveying your enthusiasm to participants.

Materials to educate volunteers

Once you have scheduled the training sessions, you must assemble the materials needed to educate your volunteers. Materials should be both complete and specific. A manual explaining reunion class solicitation strategy should differ from one that covers the general campaign.

Handbooks for each level of volunteer are a good way to inform your volunteers about everything from how to make the ask to how to fill out the report forms. The handbooks should explain what you expect from your volunteers as well as what they can expect from you and your staff.

At the training program, you should distribute other supplies needed to complete the job: pledge envelopes, matching gift brochures, and pledge cards with biographical and giving information on each volunteer assignment. You should also include institutional publications with statistical information and a mission statement to bring the volunteers up-to-date on the institution and enable them to answer questions that arise during solicitations. Hand out a goal sheet that lists annual fund goals for both percentages of participation and dollar amounts. Break down goals into as small increments as is feasible for your operation.

The volunteer should have all the materials he or she needs to make the job as easy as possible.

Keeping in touch

Accurate and timely reporting of results to your volunteers is essential. Your reporting system should provide volunteers with information that enables them to see the fruits of their efforts and to judge how those they have recruited are doing. Provide reports that are custom-tailored to your program.

The reports should be constituency-specific, that is, you should have separate reports for reunion classes, regions of the country, class years, and so on. Reports should be detailed enough so that each volunteer can see his or her individual results, and they should show campaign progress throughout the fund year. Give volunteers a historical perspective by including figures for the previous year so that they can be compared to this year's results in dollar amounts and percent of participation. The handbooks should explain how to analyze and interpret the reports.

Possibly the most important aspect of reporting is to remain flexible. Try to adjust to the changing needs and desires of your volunteers, and, if possible, provide special reports when they need them, i.e., by major or student activities.

Working with volunteers can be a rewarding experience, but it can also be a great deal of work. You must be available for your volunteers. You must be able to answer their questions or get the answers for them. Each volunteer should receive as much individual training and attention as you and your staff can afford to give. In particular, provide support to volunteers who are feeling uncomfortable about contacting prospects.

You will need to draft recruitment and special request letters for volunteers or to help them if they wish to write the letters themselves. Always keep your volunteers informed on the results of their efforts and be open to their suggestions. Follow up on their ideas and when their suggestions are implemented, give them plenty of recognition.

Above all, respond promptly to all of their requests and maintain as much personal contact with them as you can. Make a point to visit them when you are traveling in their area, and contact them by phone often. Be aware of their personal needs and serve as their advocate to the administration. Recognize important events or tragedies in their lives.

If you are able to select good volunteers, train them well, report to them accurately, and staff them with the real consideration they deserve, their efforts on behalf of your institution will make your annual fund a success.

Chapter 32

Evaluating Success

Marjorie E. Millar
Vice President, External
The University of Western Ontario
London, Ontario, Canada

E valuating the annual fund is an ongoing process that looks at subjective as well as statistical reports for each facet of the annual program. Evaluation is as important as planning, managing, and doing. It completes the cycle and assists with decision making when planning begins again.

An overall evaluation of your institutional advancement program will provide credibility within the university community and with your various external publics. Integration of a successful annual fund program strengthens the overall advancement program by providing annual financial support to the institution as well as creating an essential donor base. Your donor population is interested in fund-raising costs; again, a well-managed program provides credibility.

There are several basic methods to evaluate fund-raising programs. In recent literature, cost/revenue ratios seem to receive the most attention. Although they are an important management tool, they are only part of the process. There are several steps along the way to the "bottom line" that merit evaluation.

Evaluating goals and strategies

Many institutions set annual fund financial targets without determining specific goals for donor acquisition, donor renewal, donor cultivation, and volunteer participation levels. The best way to progress each and every year is by increasing, renewing, and cultivating your donors and volunteers.

Donor acquisition, renewal, and cultivation. Does your research give you a large enough donor base to ensure new donors? Do you communicate the purpose and goals of each annual fund clearly and specifically to your donors? Is your campaign communication effort supported by your institution's newsletters, alumni magazine, media releases, public events, and volunteer meetings? How do your audiences receive these efforts at communicating the annual fund message? Do you set a "new donor" target each year?

Do you communicate results of last year's efforts to your former donors? Do you thank them again when you ask for this year's gift, or are they treated the same as a new prospect? When donors do not renew, do you attempt to find out why?

You can quantify and measure results to see if you have reached your goals for donor acquisition and renewal, but donor cultivation goals are more difficult to evaluate. With your top donors, you might already be planning and tracking a certain number of contacts with each prospect annually. Evaluation of the overall quality of those contacts is important. Is there a right mix of personal contacts, telephone contacts, and written communication of various forms? Are your donor recognition clubs effective? Are your club members progressing through the levels to major donor status?

Volunteer participation. It is just as important to acquire, renew, and cultivate your volunteers as it is to acquire, renew, and cultivate your donors. The same criteria apply to annual fund volunteers as to all others; volunteers want to be informed, challenged, supported, and successful. Their personal motives for becoming involved are many and varied, but once they begin to participate, you should measure your effectiveness in motivating, informing, challenging, and supporting them. While volunteer questionnaires may be helpful, a one-on-one evaluation interview with your key volunteers at the end of the annual fund cycle will provide the best data.

Evaluating performance

In order to achieve success in any development program, you need to be adequately staffed in the annual fund office. What abilities and experience do you look for when hiring new annual fund professionals? Do you look for the person who will complement your existing annual fund team?

Evaluating the annual fund includes evaluating the performance of your staff. Do your annual fund professionals really know the institution? Are they team players in the entire development process? Do they know, understand, and effectively present the "case" to new donor prospects? Do they participate in establishing challenging goals and work productively to meet them?

You can do a meaningful evaluation if your staff has estimated in advance both the gift potential and the expected level of gift results. Do you include in your yearly plan a formal performance evaluation for each staff member?

Do you plan for experimentation? Do you make an effort each year to improve the way you do your annual fund program solicitation? What happens to new ideas? Do you use different criteria to evaluate an experimental program than to evaluate an ongoing effort?

Evaluating the bottom line

For most institutions, the ultimate test of performance by the annual fund staff is the amount of funds raised and the cost of raising them. Income totals are the easiest to chart and should show a steady progression over the life of the annual fund. We assume the gift income totals will improve every year, but this may not necessarily be so during the start of a capital campaign or when there is a public relations crisis.

Factors affecting fund-raising costs. As important as the total gift income level is, it is equally important to consider the fund-raising costs of raising that gift income and the many factors affecting those costs. Questions to consider include, among others: Is it a new program? Are the records adequate? Is the volunteer leadership adequate?

You can use several quantitative measures to gauge the effect of your annual fund program. At our institution, we use a list of criteria, which was presented at a CASE Fund-raising Institute at Dartmouth College.

1. *Dollars of gift income* received per year.

2. *Dollars raised for each dollar expended* for institutional advancement (development and public relations).

3. Dollars raised *per staff* development officer.

4. Institutional advancement *costs* as a portion of your *institution's budget.*

5. *Dollars raised* as a portion of the *institution's budget.*

6. Total *number of donors* for each of the past five years and percentage of alumni participation.

7. The *average size of gifts* received over the past five years.

8. Number of *volunteers* working in your program each year.

9. Number of *prospects visited.*

10. Number of *decisions made* ("yes" or "no") about a gift; percentage saying "yes."

11. Independent appraisal of the *quality of your supporting materials*—both those prepared for workers and those for prospects.

12. Analysis of gifts by *type of donor*—both in terms of total dollars and quantity. You need to know how you are doing with each constituency.

13. Analysis of *gifts by purpose.* Is unrestricted giving increasing or decreasing? Are endowment gifts up or down? You should watch this in terms of institutional priorities.

How to use comparative data. There are many data available comparing institutional results. These data can be helpful if you refer to them occasionally to establish ranges or if you use them as general guidelines. Data for organizations that are comparable in size, number of alumni, age, institutional budgets, endowments, etc., can be useful every few years to assist with long-range planning. The Council for Aid to Education (CFAE) publishes the most commonly used data in its annual report, *Voluntary Support of Education.* Because of the many variables affecting outcomes, comparative data are helpful only in the most general way.

The role of consultants in the evaluation process. If you want a fresh and objective look at your entire annual fund, you might consider hiring outside consultants. Their experience with many other organizations and their accumulated data might be useful in evaluating your total program. A consultant may be particularly helpful when you are expanding your program, justifying an increased budget, or changing staff. Consultants have credibility with senior administration and your board; their reports could provide valuable support for your program with those two groups. In addition to private fund-raising consulting companies, CASE offers an on-site consulting service.

Whenever you are using a management consultant, he or she will be most effective if you follow these three guidelines:

1. Have a careful definition of your project.

2. Think through your current annual fund situation with sufficient thoroughness to define problem areas.

3. Estimate the potential value to be achieved by solving current problems. Consultants can waste time and money defining and planning your project if you are not prepared to tell them about potential problems and what end results you hope to achieve.

The Council of Consulting Organizations, Inc., publishes a booklet, "How to Select and Use Management Consultants," that offers the following suggestions for using consultants:

• *Careful selection of the consultant.* A consultant should not be retained unless you are convinced of his or her objectivity and integrity, and unless the consultant is well qualified to meet the requirements of your project in terms of experience, organization, and resources.

• *Agreement with the consultant on mutual obligations.* It is general practice for you to share responsibility with the consultants for the definition of the purpose, scope, and general time and cost of the study. Follow-through is equally important. Findings and conclusions developed during the study have practical applications only to the extent that you review them, understand them, challenge them, and accept those suited to your requirements.

• *Proper supervision of the consultant's work.* It is important to set a clear and firm course and maintain an active interest in the progress made during an annual fund audit. You should have periodic meetings to explore progress, evaluate the direction of the study, and make certain the anticipated results appear reasonable and attainable. Interim progress reports help the consultant crystallize thoughts and conclusions during the process.

• *Follow-up recommendations.* It is important to implement changes recommended by the consultant as soon as possible. Internal reviews of progress should be made at the end of one, three, six, and nine months to measure the results. When the consulting relationship is completed, you should be able to evaluate your choice of consultant, your role in making the project a success, and the performance of annual fund staff. If the audit was carried out with a minimum of disruption, the cost and estimate times were realistic, and you have accepted the recommendations, then you have benefited enormously from the use of a consultant.[1]

Data analysis. You should analyze the evaluation data before you begin planning the next annual fund. If some of your objectives were exceeded or were not met, explore the reasons before setting new targets.

Longitudinal data are extremely helpful in identifying trends. You should also analyze the relationship of the annual fund to the entire advancement program and identify trends. Is the annual fund providing an increasing or a decreasing share of total support?

Rigor and realism

Evaluation takes time. Annual fund professionals are so involved in managing and doing that they often ignore formal planning and evaluation. Once you are convinced that evaluation is an essential part of effective decision making, it is easier to formalize the process and schedule it. The more established your program, the more rigorous and realistic your evaluation mechanisms should become.

Without evaluation your annual fund program can be successful, but with it, the sky's the limit.

Note

[1] "How to Select and Use Management Consultants" can be ordered from the Council of Consulting Organizations, Inc., 230 Park Ave., Suite 554, New York, NY 10169. Copies cost $3 (New York residents must add sales tax).

Conclusion

Ann D. Gee
Associate Vice Chancellor for Development
Texas Christian University
Fort Worth, Texas

Fund-raising efforts for colleges and universities have never been more in vogue than today. Both from the point of view of recognition given to the development professional and publicity accorded our efforts, our work is considered important and necessary.

The annual fund is the most significantly crucial component of the development program. Not only does it comprise the first effort in reaching your entire constituency, it involves the most complicated and technical procedures. No wonder annual fund officers have to be magicians and wizards!

In this era, annual fund staff are also expected to be computer-literate, to be innovative in programming, to keep current with tax laws in understanding donor recognition issues, and to work within the larger framework of capital campaigns. That means the annual fund *cannot* be considered a "tub on its own bottom." Your obligation and charge is to work with the entire advancement team for the overall success of the institution.

Now that you have read this book, you will have many new ideas to implement on your campus. You'll be tempted to try them all—but be judicious. Each institution has different strengths on which to capitalize. Finding those strengths and marketing them to *your* constituencies is the best way for you to promote your annual fund.

Remember that raising dollars for the annual fund is only a means to an end. Raising the dollars is only the *mechanism* to provide support for your current operations. The programs that are to be funded by these annual fund gifts are the basis for your efforts, *not* the dollar goals or the number of volunteers. If you have successfully made the case for your institution's needs, you will be successful in reaching the first goal of annual fund work. And the dollars should follow.

Fund raising demands a high level of energy, boundless enthusiasm, a tireless spirit, and the ability to juggle hundreds of balls in the air. Raising dollars for the annual fund requires these and more.

You may not think so now, but the chapter authors and I promise: Burning the midnight oil in approving brochure copy, deciding on asks, matching volunteers with prospects, and counting phonathon pledges *does pay off!* You'll see the results in the number of dollars and, as important, in the number of friends and the visibility the annual fund brings to your institution.

Good luck and happy campaigning!

About the Editor

Ann D. Gee, a 1976 journalism/public relations graduate of Memphis State University (Tennessee), began her career as an alumni field services representative at her alma mater on the day of graduation. In 1978 she became assistant alumni director at Texas Christian University in Fort Worth.

While assuming responsibilities in five consecutively more demanding positions in alumni and development. Ann also earned a Master of Liberal Arts at TCU. As associate vice chancellor for development, her current work involves managing all the development and development information services operations at TCU.

As a frequent speaker at CASE workshops and conferences, Ann Gee is best known for her participation as a faculty member at the annual Summer Institute in Educational Fund Raising in Dartmouth. She also serves as the District IV representative to CASE's Commission on Educational Fund Raising.